THE COMMON LAW ZONE IN PANAMA

A Case Study in Reception

*with some observations on the relevancy
thereof to the Panama Canal Treaty
controversy*

by

WAYNE D. BRAY

Introduction by Gustavo A. Mellander
Prólogo by Alfonso L. García Martínez
with an English translation

INTER AMERICAN UNIVERSITY PRESS

For information write:
Inter American University Press
G.P.O. Box 3255, San Juan, Puerto Rico 00936

Library of Congress Catalog Card Number 76-23354
International Standard Book Number 0-913480-35-5 HC

Library of Congress Cataloging in Publication Data

Bray, Wayne D
    The common law zone in Panama.

    Bibliography: p.
    Includes index
    1. Common law—Canal Zone. 2. Civil law—
Canal Zone. I. Title.
Law   340′.0972875   76-23354
ISBN 0-913480-35-5

Cover design by Neil Román
Composed, printed, and bound by Port City Press, Inc., Baltimore, Md.
Manufactured in the United States of America

To my wife
Johanne
who shared the unforgettable
experiences of living in
Panama from 1966 to 1969
which provided the inspiration
and some of the background
knowledge for this book.

INTRODUCTION

In essence the following work is a history of the jurisprudential consequences over the past seventy years of the acquisition by the United States in 1903 of jurisdiction over the Canal Zone "as if it were the sovereign."

Wayne D. Bray has set out to trace and analyze the course of reception of and transition to U. S. Common Law (exemplified by law and courts functioning in the Canal Zone), thus vitiating a four-hundred-year tradition of Hispanic Civil Law in Panama. The unusual and unprecedented transformation is a story worth telling and Bray has told it in a superlative fashion.

Those who would hope to understand the strange and, at times, contorted relationships between the Colossus of the North and the tiny republic would do well to ponder their intertwined history. The very narrowness of the isthmus, less than forty miles in certain sections, together with the relative calmness of the two great masses of water which caress its shores, appear to have predestined Panama to become, as present-day Panamanians are proud to boast, the "Crossroads of the World." Panama has had, however, to pay a price. Whether it was a just or unreasonable price is still an open question.

A transisthmian passageway had been the dream of thousands ever since Balboa and his motley band of twenty-six men stormed across the land in 1513. Not only were they the first Europeans to gaze upon the Pacific Ocean—or, as Balboa called it, the South Sea—but they helped establish the isthmus as an important international passageway. The fabled riches of the Inca empire, soon to be transported across the isthmus, whetted the greedy appetites of several European crowns. Thus did that narrow and crooked piece of real estate begin its history as an all-important conduit connecting the old and new worlds.

No country has been more intimately involved with Panama than the United States. That was certainly the case long before the former's independence in 1903 from Colombia, and it most assuredly has been true since. American interest began for purely economic reasons, but as is all too often the case, it quickly extended to the political arena.

United States interest in Panama, although dating at least as far back as the late 1700s, gained considerable momentum after the 1848 California Gold Rush. A sea voyage from the eastern United States to Panama for a mule train ride (although many paid a handsome fee to walk) across the isthmus, and then another boat trip on to California, proved in most cases to be quicker and

cheaper than crossing the American mainland. Literally thousands crossed the
isthmus. The demand was such that in 1855
American business interests completed the
Panama Railroad, which soon proved to be
one of the most profitable enterprises of the
era.

Before such a sizable investment could be
made, it was obviously necessary to reach a
political accommodation. The Mallarino-
Bidlack Treaty (1846) saw the United States
guarantee Colombia (New Granada) hegemony over the isthmus in return for guaranteed transit across Panama. Long a rebellious portion of New Granada, her leaders
feeling she had associated herself freely as
an autonomous partner when independence
from Spain was declared in November, 1821,
Panama was dissatisfied with the treatment
received from Colombia. There had been
many attempts to declare her independence.
Under the protective responsibilities assumed in 1846, the United States found
itself in the unenviable position of actually
having to land troops to preserve the
peace—and, incidentally, dissuade those
Panamanians who wished to separate from
Colombia. It did not take independence-
minded Panamanians long to learn that
Washington's predilection and interest were
as important as Bogotá's, if not more so.
During the period between 1846 and 1903,
the year Panama finally succeeded in securing her independence from Colombia, there
were no fewer than fifty-seven independence
uprisings on the isthmus. The United States
played a decisive role in thwarting all of
them—all, that is, except the last. In that,
she played a decisive role in ensuring its
success.

It is perhaps ironic that a country which
had been so instrumental and acted with
such faith in guaranteeing Colombia's control over Panama would ultimately under-
write the latter's successful secession. On
second thought, maybe it's not a question of
irony after all. It really amounts to rather a
classical dilemma which all nations and in-
dividuals might well ponder before seeking a
"protector."

Suffice to say in this Introduction that
America's involvement in the birth of the
Republic of Panama proved a unique event
historically: one that has been written
about almost as much as the French Revolution. To capsulize, after the United States
assured the success of the November 3,

1903, uprising by a judicious dispatching of
two American cruisers and refusing to move
Colombian reinforcements on the Panama
Railroad, a French citizen, dripping wet
with self-interest, obligated the new republic by signing the well-known 1903
Canal Treaty. Let the record show once
again that not a single Panamanian was
present during the negotiations.

The treaty, whose duration was to be "in
perpetuity," granted the United States
". . . all the rights, power and authority
within the Zone . . . which the United
States would possess if it were the sovereign
of the territory . . . to the entire exclusion
of the exercise by the Republic of Panama
of any such sovereign rights, power or authority." That language and subsequent
interpretations led to the setting aside of
four hundred years of existing laws, precedents, and procedures to conform and adjust
to a new legal order. How was it done?
That is the "sleeper" issue profoundly important but seldom mentioned in United
States-Panamanian history, and never before
fully explored. This book subjects that issue
to a magnifying glass, as it were. And the
transition in the Panama Canal Zone from
a Civil Law to a Common Law jurisdiction
or, as the lawyer-author is wont to phrase
it, the "reception" of the Common Law, is
a fascinating study.

Here was a territory which had lived and
been governed under essentially Spanish law
since the days of the conquistadores. Now,
at the dawn of the twentieth century, in a
relatively short time and with little or no
premeditation, that ten-by-fifty-mile strip
would have to adjust to an entirely different
system.

The narrative makes a compelling case
study for international lawyers; yet, sur-
prisingly, its substance has been largely
overlooked until now. Luckily for the
reader, Bray refuses to fall into the all-too-
familiar pedantic style of global forensic.
The book comes alive and truly reflects
both the foolishness and the common sense
of the men and women whose lives carved
out these chapters of isthmian history. The
author shows, somewhat paradoxically, that
the "reception" came about accidentally but
at the same time inevitably; that American
policymakers did not consciously plan it;
and that the process was evolutionary rather
than revolutionary.

The plethora of sources involved and the

literally thousands of details to be studied and evaluated could have easily produced a characteristically arid legal textbook. Nevertheless, the reader is fortunate, for this is a most engaging study. Anyone who has ever heard of and wondered about Panama will find it entertaining and informative. Bray is most assuredly a serious scholar; but, thank God, he has a sense of humor and an eye to appreciating mankind's foibles. He remains an excellent storyteller with a succinct and pleasing style. In fact, the narrative holds one in its grip like a good action novel. The reason is apparent right from the beginning: the author knows his subject well. And Panama, the country, the people, and their politics are exciting and interesting.

Serious students of American involvement in the isthmus will find this book interesting and informative. Bray could hardly have picked a better time to write his book. United States-Panamanian relations have been bubbling for years; the existing treaty will undoubtedly be revised within a very short period of time. The work forms an extremely scholarly treatise of the past, and it provides a prescient picture of what may well lie ahead. Relations have reached the point of no return.

Bray therefore, albeit invariably buffeted with facts and logical suppositions, projects boldly into the future. When Civil Law reasserts itself in the Canal Zone, will it nudge Common Law aside? Can they be expected to coexist peaceably? Or will there be a clash injurious to person and property? The annals of jurisprudence do not disclose precedents in which the clock is turned back after seventy years. Still the issue must be anticipated and courses of action studied. Pragmatic solutions to jurisdictional problems will have to be found when Canal Zone courts give way to Panamanian courts. The effect and continuity of the Canal Zone Code presents a concomitant problem. Will civil-law courts in Panama apply a Civil Law interpretation to the long-implemented Common Law Canal Zone Civil Code? Will United States courts retain jurisdiction with respect to cases triable by them in the Canal Zone prior to the dissolution of that zone?

These are just some of the devilishly complicated questions identified in this book. Those who will be called upon by the always fickle and invariably unpredictable muse of history to grapple with these multifaceted problems will be advised to read and study Wayne D. Bray's work most assiduously.

GUSTAVO A. MELLANDER
President, Passaic Community
College
Author: *The United States in
Panamanian Politics*

PRÓLOGO

Este es un libro claro y documentado. Su propósito, en palabras del autor, es describir las consecuencias jurídicas que ha tenido la hegemonía de Estados Unidos sobre una zona geográfica de diez millas de ancho a lo largo del canal de Panamá, a partir del tratado Hay-Bunau-Varilla de 1903. Este fue negociado en circunstancias sospechosas y sumamente desfavorables para Panamá, por un individuo que ni era panameño ni tenía facultades para obligar al gobierno de esa nación. Asimismo el autor pronostica lo que ocurrirá a corto o largo plazo, pero inexorablemente, en vista de las señales diplomáticas que se advierten a partir de 1965 y que anticipan la desaparición de las equívocas bases que estableció el tratado de 1903 para que Estados Unidos dispusiera unilateralmente del Canal y de su Zona. Al verificarse la reversión plena de la zona a Panamá, se desarrollará un proceso jurídico y lingüístico a la inversa de lo que ha ocurrido desde 1903 y que tan magistralmente se expone en el libro que comentamos. En otras palabras, a partir de 1903 el sistema de Derecho Civil hispánico fue gradualmente desplazado por el sistema anglo-americano conocido como el "Common Law". Al recuperar Panamá el pleno ejercicio de su soberanía sobre la zona, retornará su sistema de Derecho, caracterizado por el autor como un retoño colombo-panameño de la rama española de la familia romano-germánica del Derecho. Esa rama española había fructificado en Panamá, antes de 1819, fecha de la independencia de Colombia, soberana de Panamá hasta que ocurre le secesión de 1903.

El desarrollo jurídico que ha tenido lugar en la Zona del Canal de Panamá desde 1903 hasta nuestros días, y la vuelta en redondo

---

PROLOGUE

This is a lucid and well-documented book. Its purpose, according to the author, is to describe the juridical consequences of United States control—which began in 1903 with the Hay-Bunau-Varilla Treaty—over a strip of land ten miles wide running the length of the Panama Canal. The treaty was negotiated in suspicious, and for Panama extremely unfavorable, circumstances by an individual who was neither Panamanian nor empowered to obligate the government of that nation. Thus the author foretells what will happen, sooner or later, but inevitably—to judge by indications of a diplomatic nature which signal the disappearance of the questionable bases for unilateral United States control over the Canal and the Canal Zone. When these revert wholly to Panama, the result will be a reversal of the juridical and linguistic process which Bray has set out so masterfully. In other words, from 1903 on, the system of Hispanic Civil Law was gradually displaced by the Anglo-American system known as Common Law. When Panama recovers full sovereignty over the Canal Zone, its legal system will again become effective. This Colombian-Panamanian offshoot of the Spanish branch of the Romano-Germanic family of law had already matured in Panama before 1819, when Colombia became independent, and continued in use under Colombian rule until secession in 1903.

Neither the legal developments of the Canal Zone from 1903 until the present, nor the about-face which will inevitably occur, can be fully understood without setting out the background of the actors, who range from flesh-and-blood people to nations. It

que ocurrirá inexorablemente, no pueden comprenderse a cabalidad si no se exponen los antecedentes históricos próximos y remotos de los actores, que en estos casos son desde personas de carne y hueso hasta entes nacionales. No era simplemente una nación relativamente pequeña y otra grande, Panamá y Estados Unidos, las que se estaban enfrentando en circunstancias muy peculiares en 1903. Era toda una herencia cultural-jurídica en una zona geográfica la que estaba envuelta. Panamá representaba una manifestación cultural del inmenso mundo hispánico, al igual que lo representó Puerto Rico en 1898, frente al expansionismo anglo-sajón representado por Estados Unidos en ese período histórico de fines del siglo XIX y principios del XX. Por eso, y con muy buen acierto, Wayne D. Bray comienza su libro relatando los sucesos inmediatos producidos por el expansionismo mencionado a partir de la guerra hispano-americana de 1898, para remontarse a renglón seguido a describir la génesis del Derecho vigente en Panamá en 1903, desde sus orígenes ibéricos.

El 26 de febrero de 1904 se creó la entidad jurídica llamada Zona del Canal. Bajo esta realidad Estados Unidos supuso que tenía facultades para desplazar el ordenamiento jurídico civilista que allí regía hacía 400 años. Estas facultades dependían de dos factores, a saber, el elemento de soberanía en el tratado Hay-Bunau-Varilla y la validez e interpretación del tratado. Se pregunta el autor si estas cuestiones son académicas o insolubles. O, nos preguntamos nosotros, si se trata de cuestiones de *realpolitik*. Como la llamada recepción del "Common Law" en la zona, o más bien el desplazamiento del Derecho Civil, ocurrió como consecuencia de la presencia allí de Estados Unidos y esta presencia depende del tratado, la controversia actual persistirá mientras persista el tratado de 1903. La mejor prueba de este aserto, dice el autor, es el hecho de que Estados Unidos se comprometió en 1964 (y ratificó ese compromiso en 1974) a abrogar el tratado de 1903 y a sustituirlo por otro en que el concepto de que Estados Unidos ejerce jurisdicción como si fuese soberano será abolido. El mismo Teodoro Roosevelt, el presidente que "tomó a Panamá," entendió, según se desprende de carta que dirigió al Secretario de la Guerra Taft el 18 de octubre de 1906, que Estados Unidos no ejercería funciones gubernamentales en exceso de las que fueran necesarias para construir, conservar y operar el canal bajo los derechos otorgados por

---

was not simply a matter of a small Panama and a large United States facing off in peculiar circumstances in 1903. The entire juridical and cultural tradition of a region was involved. Like Puerto Rico in 1898, Panama represented one cultural manifestation of the immense Hispanic World, in confrontation with Anglo-Saxon expansionism represented, in the late nineteenth and early twentieth centuries, by the United States. For this reason, and quite rightly, Bray begins his book by relating events which were the immediate results of this expansionism, the Spanish-American War of 1898, and then goes on to describe the origins of the legal system then in effect in Panama, beginning with its Iberian roots.

The juridical entity known as the Canal Zone was created on February 26, 1904. Given this fact, the United States presumed that it had authority to set aside the civil legal order which had been in effect for 400 years. This authority depended on two factors: the question of sovereignty in the Hay-Bunau-Varilla Treaty and the validity and interpretation of the treaty. Bray asks whether these are merely insoluble, academic matters. Or is it a question of *realpolitik*? As the so-called "reception" of Common Law in the Canal Zone—or rather replacement of Spanish Civil Law— occurred as a consequence of the presence there of the United States, and this presence depended on the treaty, the present controversy will persist as long as the treaty lasts. The best test of this, says Bray, is the fact that the United States committed itself in 1964 (and ratified the commitment in 1974) to abrogate the treaty and substitute for it one in which the provision under which the United States exercises jurisdiction as though sovereign is to be abolished. Judging by a letter to Secretary of War Taft, dated October 18, 1906, President Theodore Roosevelt himself, who "took" Panama, clearly understood that the United States was not to exercise governmental functions beyond those necessary to construct, preserve and operate the canal according to the rights granted by the

el tratado. Es precisamente lo limitado del aspecto técnico de la operación del canal lo que asombra por cuanto ello sirvió de pretexto para establecer un ordenamiento jurídico extraño en la zona del canal. En otras palabras, la zona se convirtió en un apéndice del canal.

Salvo que así lo hagamos constar, en este prólogo seguiremos el razonamiento del autor. Aunque un proceso de evolución presidió la recepción del "Common Law" y no empece que los forjadores de la política pública de la zona al principio no proclamaron abiertamente sus propósitos de conseguir la suplantación de un sistema jurídico por otro, lo cierto es que ciertos supuestos subyacentes, acerca de la presencia norteamericana, junto a un cambio drástico en la población de la zona, crearon unas condiciones que hicieron inevitable la recepción. Un factor importante que militó en favor del "Common Law" era el desarrollo superior que en esa familia jurídica, según el autor, había tenido el concepto de Derecho público, frente al cual el Derecho Civil estaba casi indefenso. La explicación que ofrece es la siguiente. Cuando los normandos conquistaron a Inglaterra en 1066, no eran portadores de un sistema de Derecho desarrollado, ni en el país conquis-

tado desplazaron un sistema de Derecho de tal naturaleza. Esto era así porque todavía en la Europa continental no se había operado la recepción plena del Derecho romano ni los anglo-sajones habían alcanzado ningún grado de refinamiento jurídico. También, en aquel tiempo remoto, Guillermo el Conquistador, igual que el Presidente Teodoro Roosevelt en 1904, declaró que el sistema de derecho de los conquistados se conservaría. Sin embargo, el talento administrativo normando creó unas condiciones que modificaron todo el Derecho, incluso el privado. Así, por ejemplo, los tribunales reales en Westminster, que originalmente se concibieron como un brazo de la Administración para salvaguardar los intereses de la Corona en asuntos fiscales y de tierras, poco a poco fueron ampliando el ámbito de sus actuaciones en el campo de la litigación privada. La impronta de los orígenes del Derecho público quedó indeleblemente marcada en el Derecho común del reino a que dió origen. Esta situación no se dió en el Derecho romano cuyas normas de Derecho privado se originaron independientemente de las de Derecho público.

Este elemento preponderante de Derecho público se manifestó en la Zona del Canal de Panamá a modo de punta de lanza en la

---

treaty. It is precisely the limitation to technical aspects of the operation of the canal which is startling for the degree to which it served as a pretext for establishing a legal system foreign to the Canal Zone. In other words, the Zone became an appendage of the Canal.

What follows is Bray's argument, unless stated otherwise: Though the reception of Common Law was evolutionary in nature and though policy-makers did not begin by declaring their intention of supplanting the existing legal system, it is certain that conditions were created which made reception of Common Law inevitable; these include the drastic change in population in the Canal Zone, and certain underlying assumptions in regard to the United States presence. An important factor which worked in favor of Common Law was its greater development of the concept of Public Law before which Spanish Civil Law was virtually defenseless. The explanation for this is as follows: When the Normans conquered England in 1066, they were not the bearers

of a fully-developed system of law, nor did they displace such a system of law in the conquered land. In continental Europe, Roman Law had still not yet been wholly absorbed, and the Anglo-Saxons had not reached a significant level of juridical refinement. Also, in that remote time, William the Conqueror, like Theodore Roosevelt in 1904, declared that the legal system of the conquered people was to be preserved. However, Norman administrative skill created conditions which modified all law, including Private Law. Thus, for example, the royal courts at Westminster, which were originally conceived of as a branch of the administration to safeguard the interests of the crown in fiscal matters and those concerning land, increased their range of activities little by little in the field of Private Law. The origins in Public Law left an indelible imprint on the Common Law of the realm to which it gave birth. This situation did not occur in Roman Law, in which Private Law and Public Law developed independently.

recepción del "Common Law" en la Orden Ejecutiva del Presidente de los Estados Unidos—Gobernante de la Zona a través del Secretario de la Guerra—de 9 de mayo de 1904. En ésta se proclama que las leyes del país, con las cuales los habitantes están familiarizados, quedarán vigentes hasta que sean modificadas por el gobierno, en este caso la Comisión del Canal del Istmo, por designación de los gobernantes de Washington, pero todo estaría sujeto a ciertos grandes principios de gobierno que han sido la base de la existencia de la nación. En este punto hacemos un paréntesis en nuestro tratamiento del contenido del libro que es objeto de este prólogo para intercalar un comentario sobre un asunto similar fuera del libro, aunque íntimamente relacionado con ese contenido. A tales propósitos conviene recordar que dada la casi coetaneidad de la expansión imperial de Estados Unidos en Panamá, a costa de Colombia, con la expansión de igual naturaleza en el Caribe y en el Pacífico a costa de España, en 1898, los precedentes del enfrentamiento de sistemas jurídicos en Puerto Rico y Filipinas constantemente eran tenidos en cuenta en la Zona del Canal de Panamá. A base de estas consideraciones véase la gran similaridad de los principios rectores de la mencionada orden ejecutiva de 1904 con el párrafo IX de la Orden General Núm. 1 del 18 de octubre de 1898, la primera dictada bajo el Gobierno Militar que se instaló en Puerto Rico el mismo día en que España cede Puerto Rico a Estados Unidos. Citamos la parte pertinente de dicho párrafo:

"Las leyes provinciales y municipales, hasta donde afecten la determinación de derechos privados, correspondientes a individuos ó propiedades serán mantenidas en todo su vigor, a menos que no resulten incompatibles con el cambio de condiciones realizado en Puerto Rico, en el cual caso podrán ser suspendidas por el Jefe del Departamento. Dichas leyes serán administradas materialmente, tales como existían antes de la cesión a los Estados Unidos."

Seguimos con el libro de Wayne D. Bray. Nos informa el autor que entre 9 de mayo de 1904 y 3 de marzo de 1905 el gobierno de la zona modificó el ordenamiento jurídico veinticuatro veces. De ellas, veintitrés

---

It was the dominance of Public Law which manifested itself in the Canal Zone in the Executive Order of the President of the United States—who was responsible for governing the Zone through the Secretary of War—dated May 9, 1904. That document states that the laws of the country, with which the citizens were already familiar, were to remain in effect until modified by the government—in this case, the Isthmian Canal Commission designated by Washington—but all such changes were to be in accord with certain great principles of government on which the existence of the nation was based.

Parenthetically, it should be added here that a matter beyond the scope of this book, yet intimately related to it, is the virtually simultaneous occurrence of United States imperial expansion in Panama, at the expense of Colombia, and in the Caribbean and the Pacific, at the expense of Spain, in 1898. These precedents for the confrontation of legal systems in Puerto Rico and in the Philippines were kept clearly in mind in the case of the Panama Canal Zone. On the basis of these considerations, one may observe the great similarity of the guiding principles of the Executive Order of 1904 comparing it to General Order Number 1, October 18, 1898, the first given under the Military Government which was installed in Puerto Rico on the same day that Spain ceded Puerto Rico to the United States. The relevant part reads as follows:

The provincial and municipal laws, in so far as they affect the settlement of the private rights of persons and property and provide for the punishment of crime, will be enforced unless they are incompatible with the changed conditions of Porto Rico, in which event they may be suspended by the Department Commander. They will be administered substantially as they were before the cession to the United States.

Returning to Bray's book, we are told that between May 9, 1904 and March 3, 1905, the government of the Canal Zone made twenty-four changes in the legal structure. Of these, twenty-three concerned Public Law, as did in part the remaining one. In sum, Common law was introduced by means of substantive and procedural provisions in Penal Law. Just as in the case of Puerto Rico, the new legal provisions were

aludían a asuntos de Derecho público y la otra en parte. En síntesis se introdujo el "Common Law" a través de disposiciones sustantivas y procesales de Derecho penal. Igual que en el caso de Puerto Rico las nuevas disposiciones legales se tomaron de California, un estado donde el Derecho Civil fue erradicado por fiat legislativo en 1849. En cuanto al Derecho privado civil, si bien es cierto que su aspecto sustantivo quedó vigente a través del Código Civil panameño traducido al inglés hasta 1933, lo procesal civil fue sustituído por un Código de Procedimiento Civil de orígen anglosajón en 1907. Nuevamente llamamos la atención al paralelismo con la sustitución de códigos que ocurrió en Puerto Rico en el período 1902-1904. Sin entrar en los méritos de los cuerpos legales envueltos,[1] durante el período mencionado en Puerto Rico había ocurrido casi lo mismo. Se sustituyeron el Código Penal y la Ley de Enjuiciamiento Criminal vigentes por los correspondientes códigos de California en 1902. Lo mismo sucedió en 1904 con la Ley de Enjuiciamiento Civil, sustituída por el Código de Procedimiento Civil de Califor-

nia. Es curioso, aunque no sorprendente, que la misma persona que tradujo al inglés las leyes vigentes en Puerto Rico al 18 de octubre de 1898 hizo la misma labor en la Zona del Canal de Panamá en 1905, a saber, Frank L. Joannini. Esta labor de traducción está reconocida como una de indiscutibles méritos, cualitativa y cuantitativamente hablando. Aunque el Código Civil panameño continuó vigente, el mismo fue desvirtuado por jueces y abogados formados en el "Common Law", desconocedores del genio que lo creó y del idioma en que está escrito. Lo mismo ha sucedido en otras jurisdicciones en donde se han dado las mismas condiciones, tales como Luisiana, Quebec, Filipinas y Puerto Rico. El libro que comentamos alude tangencialmente a estas situaciones y *mutatis mutandis,* con un poco de esfuerzo de imaginación, lo que se describe en cuanto a las vicisitudes, pasión y muerte del Derecho Civil panameño en esta época que toca a su fin y que culminará en el retorno triunfal del Derecho Civil y del idioma español a la Zona del Canal en un futuro próximo, es fácilmente visualizable en otros países. Sobre el enlace del idioma

---

taken from California, a state where Civil Law had been eradicated by legislative fiat in 1849. With regard to private Civil Law, though its substantive aspect remained in effect in English translation until 1933 via the Civil Code of Panama, Civil Procedural Law was replaced in 1907 by a Code of Civil Procedure of Anglo-Saxon origin. Once again, attention must be drawn to parallels with the substitution of legal codes which occurred in Puerto Rico between 1902 and 1904. Without going into the merits of the bodies of law involved,[1] it may be observed that virtually the same thing had happened in Puerto Rico. The *Código Penal* and the *Ley de Enjuiciamiento Criminal* in effect at the time were replaced by corresponding Californian codes in 1902. The same thing occurred in 1904 with the *Ley de Enjuiciamiento Civil,* which was replaced by the *Code of Civil Procedure* of California. It is a curious though not a surprising fact that it was Frank L. Joannini, the translator of

Puerto Rico's existing laws in 1898, who translated those of the Canal Zone in 1905. His work is held to be of unquestioned merit, both qualitatively and quantitatively speaking. Though the Civil Code of Panama remained in effect, it was undercut by judges and lawyers brought up on Common Law, who did not understand either the spirit which created it or the language in which it was written. The same was true in other areas where the same conditions obtained: Louisiana, Quebec, the Philippines, and Puerto Rico. Bray's book touches on these situations, and, *mutatis mutandis,* with a little imaginative effort what he describes is easily visualized in other countries: the trials, passion and death of Panama's Civil Law in this period which is coming to an end and will culminate in the imminent triumphal return of Civil Law and the Spanish language to the Canal Zone. Bray deals with the relations between language and the different kinds of law under consideration, and its inevitable involvement with matters of law. Section 12 of the *Code of Civil Procedure* of 1907 conclusively fixes English as the only official language of the

---

[1] Cf. Alfonso L. García Martínez, "Idioma y derecho en Puerto Rico," *Revista Colegio de Abogados de Puerto Rico,* XX. 183 (1960), pp. 194–6.

de los Derechos respectivos que estamos tratando y su inevitable vinculación con esta problemática jurídica trata el autor. La sección 12 del Código de Procedimiento Civil de 1907 dispuso terminantemente que el inglés sería el único idioma oficial de los tribunales. La exclusión del idioma español de todos los asuntos oficiales de la Zona del Canal de Panamá ha sido un hecho constante desde el comienzo. Reflexiona el autor al comparar lo que ocurrió en Puerto Rico con lo que ocurrió en la Zona, en cuanto a idioma se refiere, que habiendo recibido reconocimiento el idioma español en el primero, la recepción del "Common Law" no fructificó. Tenemos que resistir la tentación de acometer, para propósitos comparativos, la problemática linguística de Puerto Rico, por razones de espacio y propósito de este prólogo. El enfrentamiento de los idiomas español e inglés en Puerto Rico forma capítulo aparte en la historia de los pueblos hispánicos y del mundo.[2] Nos dice el autor en relación con el Código Civil de la Zona, citando un informe de 1932 del Senado de Estados Unidos, que éste, según el informe, no ha funcionado bien y que los tribunales se han visto obligados a recurrir a

interpretaciones forzadas de sus preceptos. En cuanto al Derecho procesal el mismo informe dice que en el período 1904-07 los jueces y abogados norteamericanos trataron de usar el Código Judicial de Panamá pero sin éxito. Si se examina la historia de Puerto Rico, en el período correspondiente, se encuentran expresiones similares.[3] Es un rasgo característico que han exhibido los gobernantes y personas influyentes norteamericanos—con honrosas excepciones—en su contacto con otras culturas, una resistencia a conocer, a penetrar el genio de otras formas culturales siendo como es la llave para ese descubrimiento el dominio del idioma en que se expresa esa cultura. Claro, ese rechazo se viste de cierto ropaje para paliar su rudeza. Así, en Puerto Rico, para justificar el desmantelamiento de los restos del gobierno autonómico que se creó a partir de 1897 se adujo que:

> Quedando plenamente demostrado, después de dos meses de concienzuda prueba, que la organización creada bajo el sistema español y continuada por los representantes del Gobierno de los Estados Unidos bajo la designación de Gabinete Insular, no es compatible con los métodos y progreso americanos,

---

courts. Spanish has in fact been constantly excluded from the very beginning. Comparing what happened in regard to language in Puerto Rico and the Canal Zone, Bray observes that where Spanish was accepted—as in Puerto Rico—Common Law did not develop fully. For considerations of length and the purpose of this prologue, one must resist the temptation to undertake a comparative discussion of Puerto Rico's linguistic circumstances. The confrontation of Spanish and English in Puerto Rico comprises a chapter apart in the history of the Hispanic peoples and of the world.[2] According to a report of the United States Senate in 1932, cited by Bray, the *Código Civil* of Panama had not functioned well, and the courts had been obliged to resort to forced interpretations of its principles. In regard to Procedural Law, between 1904 and 1907 United

States judges and lawyers tried to use the *Judicial Code* of Panama, but without success. If one looks at the history of Puerto Rico in the corresponding period, similar expressions may be found.[3] It is characteristic of American governors and influential persons—with honorable exceptions—that they are reluctant to enter into the genius of other cultural forms, as they fail to master the key to their understanding, which is the language in which they are expressed. Of course this rejection is clothed in such a way as to seem more acceptable, so that to justify the dismantling of the remains of the autonomous Puerto Rican government created after 1897, the following reasoning was given:

> It having become evident after a careful trial of two months that the organization created under the Spanish system and continued by the representatives of the United States Government, known as the

---

[2] Cf. Alfonso L. García Martínez, *Idioma y Política, El papel desempeñado por los idiomas español e inglés en la relación política de Puerto Rico-Estados Unidos* (San Juan, Puerto Rico: Editorial Cordillera, 1976).

[3] Cf. *Register of Porto Rico for 1926*, pp. 56, 57.

declárase disuelto dicho Gabinete Insular.[4]

Termina el autor explicando porqué el Código de Procedimiento Civil de 1907 en Panamá representó en lo jurídico un rompimiento con el pasado ya que en el Derecho Civil el Derecho procesal es un apéndice, mientras que en el "Common Law" es en sí un conjunto autónomo de normas generadoras de Derecho. Mr. Frank Feuille, Secretario de Justicia de Puerto Rico, a principios de siglo en su informe oficial al Gobernador de Puerto Rico en 1904 se refería de la siguiente manera a la influencia, no sólo procesal, que en todo el ámbito jurídico tenía el Código de Procedimiento Civil de origen anglo-sajón adoptado en Puerto Rico en 1904:

"Uno de los más grandes beneficios derivados de la nueva ley de procedimiento se encuentra en el impulso que la misma está dando al estudio del Derecho Norteamericano por los abogados nativos. Pocos de ellos están ahora sin libros norteamericanos de derecho, y en la selección de esos libros no se limitan a obras sobre procedimiento, sino que están extendiendo sus investigaciones a muchas otras ramas del Derecho norteamericano. El resultado ha sido un marcado cambio en el pensamiento legal en Porto Rico. La sabiduría de un sistema que confía en la sana discreción del Tribunal está siendo admitida cada vez más. Para poder leer el Derecho norteamericano, el abogado puertorriqueño ha tenido que aprender el idioma inglés, y merece el más grande encomio la dedicación de muchos de ellos en esa dirección"[5]

Mr. Frank Feuille fue más tarde Jefe del Departamento de Administración Civil en la Zona del Canal de Panamá y desempeñó un

---

Insular Cabinet, is not compatible with American methods and progress, the same is dissolved.[4]

Bray concludes by explaining why the *Code of Civil Procedure* of 1907 represented a break with the past in legal matters, because Procedural Law in the civil law system is a mere appendage of Civil Law, while in Common law it is, in itself, an autonomous body of norms capable of generating law. Mr. Frank Feuille, Secretary of Justice of Puerto Rico at the beginning of the century, in his official report to the Governor in 1904 referred to the more than procedural influence which the Anglo-Saxon *Code of Civil Procedure* had had on the whole legal situation.

On that point he said that one of the greatest benefits derived from the new Code of Civil Procedure is found in the impetus the same is giving to the study of American Law by the local lawyers. Now, very few of them are without American law books and in the selection of these books they are not limited to works on civil procedure but are broadening their research to other branches of American Law. The outcome has been a marked change in the juridical thought in Porto Rico. The wisdom of a system that places its trust in the sane discretion of the court of justice is being more readily admitted. To be able to read American Law, the Porto-Rican lawyer had to learn English and deserves the greatest praise for his dedication in the pursuit of such knowledge.[5]

Feuille was later head of the Department of Civil Administration in the Canal Zone, and played an important role in the development of its legal system.

At the beginning of the book, Bray warned the reader that though many books had been written on the relations between Panama and the United States in regard to the Canal and the Canal Zone, none had attempted to go deeply into the juridical consequences of what had happened there, and even less attention had been paid to what would happen when the process was reversed. Once his course is set, Bray fixes the limits of the incursions he will necessarily have to make into the historical events surrounding his subject in order to place it in the right perspective. Despite the restraint which this implies—fortunately—Bray is obliged to set out a wealth

---

[4] Párrafo 1, Orden General Núm. 12, Cuartel General, Departamento de Puerto Rico, San Juan, Febrero 6, 1899/ Paragraph 1, General Order Number 12, General Headquarters, Department of Puerto Rico, San Juan, February 6, 1899.

[5] Cf. Carmelo Delgado Cintrón, "Prólogo," *Idioma y Política, op. cit.*, note 2. [The Editors were unable to locate an original English version. It is paraphrased here from the Spanish.]

papel de importancia en el desarrollo del sistema jurídico de ésta.

Al comenzar el libro advirtió el autor que aunque se habían escrito muchos libros sobre las relaciones entre Panamá y Estados Unidos a propósito del Canal y de la Zona, ninguno se había dirigido a profundizar sobre las consecuencias jurídicas de lo que ocurrió y menos aún, de lo que ocurrirá cuando se opere a la inversa el proceso de panamanización. Una vez que establece su rumbo el autor fija el límite de las incursiones que en el campo de los sucesos históricos circundantes se verá obligado a hacer para situar el tema tratado en su justa perspectiva. No obstante las autolimitaciones que esto necesariamente implica, afortunadamente tiene que exponer una riqueza de datos e interpretaciones de índole diplomática, política, económica, demográfica, lingüística y otros que sería prolijo enumerar pero que es fácil imaginar. El resultado es un tratado completo, erudito, objetivo y revelador. El lector se da cuenta de que la obra no podía incluir menos de lo que incluyó. En cuanto al prologuista se

refiere hubiere deseado más, ya que independientemente del fondo, la forma y el estilo son agradables.

Si bien es cierto, como se ha señalado al principio de este prólogo, que la naturaleza de este libro es preponderantemente jurídica, la riqueza de datos de otra índole a que hemos aludido y que forma el trasfondo que imparte sentido al tema central permite al lector contar con los elementos de juicio necesarios para juzgar las motivaciones y actuaciones de los protagonistas del drama histórico-jurídico. El veredicto de culpabilidad, inocencia o de otra índole que en la conciencia de cada lector se formule sobre lo que sucedió, es parte de ese terrible, severo e impersonal juicio de la historia. Cuando los pueblos, poderosos y débiles, desaparecen como tales del escenario del mundo, los libros que presentaron los sucesos en los cuales esos pueblos fueron actores, heroes y villanos, serán los jueces de última instancia de lo que sucedió. El libro *The Common Law Zone in Panama, A Case Study in Reception,* por Wayne D. Bray es uno de esos libros.

of diplomatic, political, economic, demographic, linguistic and other data and interpretation which would be too lengthy to list here, but can easily be imagined. The result is a thorough, learned, objective and revealing treatise. The reader will understand that the work could have included no less than it does; more would have been welcome since, quite apart from the content, it is a pleasant book to read for its style.

Though, as was pointed out earlier, the book is preponderantly concerned with juridical matters, the wealth of data of the other kinds mentioned, and which forms the background that gives the central theme its

meaning, provides the reader with the basis necessary to judge the motives and actions of the protagonists of this historical and juridical drama. The verdict as to guilt or innocence which each reader forms in his own mind about what happened is part of history's fearful, harsh, and impersonal judgment. When the peoples involved—both weak and powerful—disappear as such from the world scene, the books which present the events in which peoples were the actors, heroes and villains, will be the final judges of what happened. Bray's book, *The Common Law Zone in Panama, A Case Study in Reception,* is such a volume.

ALFONSO L. GARCÍA MARTÍNEZ
School of Law,
Inter American University of Puerto Rico
Author: *Idioma y Política*

FOREWORD

Yet another agonizing reappraisal of a United States foreign policy position has been going on intermittently since 1964 and is now past the point of no return. For several years it went on quietly, overshadowed by more visible and dramatic reappraisals in the Middle and Far East, without attracting much attention in the United States. Even the aborted 1967 draft treaties, which fell victim to domestic politics and never reached the ratification stage, stirred only a mild flurry. The ending of the Vietnam War and the renewal of active Panama Canal negotiations, dramatized by the Joint Statement[1] issued on February 7, 1974 by Secretary of State Henry A. Kissinger and Panamanian Foreign Minister Juan Antonio Tack, has changed all that.

The Joint Statement explicitly sets forth agreements in principle to abrogate the 1903 Hay/Bunau-Varilla Treaty, put a definite time limit on any new treaty which replaces it, return control of the present Canal Zone to Panama, and eventually turn over operation of the Canal itself to Panama. This renewed commitment by Secretary Kissinger —which in fact is not much different in intent and purpose from commitments previously made in 1964 by President Johnson, with the prior assent of former Presidents Hoover, Truman, and Eisenhower[2]—has stirred up intense controversy, ensuring that matters will now move to a decision whose repercussions will be felt far beyond the tiny country of Panama where the *res* is located.

The foreign policy position now being reappraised—the essence of which is unyielding insistence on continuing to exercise "in perpetuity" all the rights in the Canal Zone, granted in the Hay/Bunau-Varilla Treaty, which the United States would possess "if it were the sovereign"—has been held for more than seventy years. Though increasingly untenable as its premises are reexamined in a changing world,[3] it is emotionally charged and passionately defended by stand-patters invoking appeals to patriotism, national pride in a great engineering accomplishment, military security considerations, and *machismo*.

In the Hay/Bunau-Varilla Treaty, "negotiated" in 1903 under highly questionable circumstances, the United States acquired a unique and anomalous kind of *de facto*

---

[1] 70 Department of State Bulletin 184 (February 25, 1974).

[2] 65 Department of State Bulletin 731, at 732 (December 27, 1971).

sovereignty over a ten-mile-wide Zone splitting the Republic of Panama in two.[4] The treaty has since been amended several times, mostly to withdraw various kinds of American intervention into Panamanian affairs even beyond the Zone; but the basic position of exclusive United States suzerainty over the entire Zone, and all that goes on within it, has not changed. Since 1964 the executive branch of the United States Government, at least, has agreed that this position should be abandoned and the territory involved returned, incrementally, to the unrestricted sovereignty of Panama provided satisfactory new arrangements can be made for the protection and maintenance of the canal and its continued, uninterrupted use.[5]

In offering this book I am assuming—in full awareness that the assumption could turn out to be wrong—that a new treaty with Panama encompassing the above-stated objectives and commitments will eventually be achieved.[6] Seeing that as a desirable aim in itself, I have given it a helping hand, wherever appropriate, by illuminating the record and attempting to dispel certain harmful misconceptions. I must emphasize, however, that the original, and still the principal, motivation for the book was the discovery—and so, naturally, the abhorrence —of a vacuum in the middle of Canal Zone history.

In all the mass of literature on the engineering and strategic aspects of the Canal and on the legal and political aspects of sovereignty in the Zone, I could not find any full-dress study of the jurisprudential consequences flowing from the turnover of jurisdiction in the Canal Zone to the United States in 1904.[7] Still less anything suggesting the necessity of examining anticipated jurisprudential consequences of a return of the area to Panamanian control in the future. If what is past is prologue, the story of how the Common Law came into the Zone (on little cats' feet?) must contain some

---

[3] Panama succeeded in having the issue brought to a vote at a special meeting of the United Nations Security Council held in Panama City March 15–21, 1973. The resolution formally putting the United Nations on record as urging the abrogation of the 1903 treaty was defeated only because the United States representative used his right of veto. Of the fifteen members of the Security Council, including several countries normally friendly to the United States, not one supported the United States. Only the United Kingdom abstained.

[4] To get an idea of how this situation looks to the people of Panama in 1977, imagine a strip of land extending five miles on each side of the Mississippi River within which a foreign power, by virtue of treaty rights granted under suspicious circumstances in 1783, exercises complete control as "if it were the sovereign" and through which a resident of Illinois must pass to go to Missouri, during which passage he is subject to arrest by a foreign power and trial in a foreign court under a foreign system of laws. Obviously, the Mississippi River is not being compared to the Panama Canal as an interoceanic waterway. What is being compared is the political and juridical effect of alien control of the territory, and I think the comparison is a fair one.

[5] Despite the many flare-ups of Panamanian nationalism over the years, so far the only serious interruption of traffic which has ever resulted from man-made causes occurred in early 1976 when American pilots went on strike for several days in a labor dispute. Panamanian employees remained on the job and kept the Canal functioning at a low level of activity.

[6] Perhaps it should be explained that the United States did not veto the Security Council resolution because of any serious disagreement with the ultimate objectives and aspirations expressed, but because of the tactics employed by Panama; viz., throwing into the United Nations arena—and casting a stigma by inference on the United States—a matter which the United States considers of legitimate concern only to the two countries directly involved and who were already seized with it in bilateral negotiations.

[7] The nearest thing to it is an article by Lawrence Ealy entitled "The Development of an Anglo-American System of Law in the Panama Canal Zone" which appeared in the *American Journal of Legal History*, II (1958), pp. 283–303. This is an excellent work but limited in length, detail, and objective; I do not believe it negates the need for a full treatment in historical context, with legal analysis, which I have provided. An adaptation of the above article appears as chapter 9 in a book entitled "Yanqui Politics and the Isthmian Canal" by the same author published in 1971. See also a short but illuminating article by John O. Collins entitled "Canal Zone Changes to Common Law System" which appeared in the *American Bar Association Journal*, v. 20 (1934) pp. 233–34; and a longer, rather specialized article by William K. Jackson, a former prosecuting attorney of the Canal Zone, entitled "The Administration of Justice in the Canal Zone" which appeared in the *Virginia Law Review*, vol. IV, no. 1 (October 1916) pp. 1–20.

lessons as the time approaches for the Civil Law to return, as it presumably will when the Zone, as such, disappears and the territory reverts to the jurisdiction of Panama.

To avoid redundancy and superfluity I have rigorously sought to exclude incursions into general history—as well as the preserves of diplomatic, political, economic, and social history—except insofar as I felt it indispensable to put the legal history and analysis into meaningful relationship with these other factors. If my judgment as to how much was indispensable is questioned, I can only plead that none of these disciplines exists in a vacuum and the making of boundaries between them is far from an exact science. (In a few instances, not very space-consuming, I have simply yielded, I must confess, to irresistible impulse. Truth is sometimes not only stranger but funnier than fiction.)

As to those parts of the book which are undiluted legal history and analysis, beyond any reasonable doubt, I had to make another kind of decision: how much detail. While trying to be rigorously spare in this respect too, I am sure that I have supplied in some places more about a particular topic, particularly in the footnotes, than some people will want to know. They can skip over it; others will be as fascinated (I hope) as I was. My reason for choosing to err, if indeed I have, on the side of too much is that I want the book to be as useful a tool as possible (though not claiming to be definitive in this first edition) for the serious scholar in this relatively neglected facet of Canal Zone history. There is nowhere else available between two covers so much material bearing on the subject; and much of it is drawn from sources inconvenient, to say the least, for some people to find, and sometimes in such poor physical condition as to be in danger of being lost. Indeed, some important parts of the record seem to be lost already, as I have indicated in occasional footnotes.

Concluding, I repeat, in the possibly vain hope of assuaging any partisan passions that may already have been aroused, this is a book about the reception of the Common Law in the Panama Canal Zone, a legal history, not a polemic on the current controversy over a new Panama Canal treaty. Of course, as admitted, I have opinions about the latter, and that they are exposed from time to time, but only as a distinctly secondary theme and only because they seem to me to follow, as logically and inevitably as the night the day.

I did not start the book with the opinions ready-formed; they simply grew alongside as I read and studied and thought and wrote. Even now, I am sadly lacking, as always, in the missionary instinct. I would probably be embarrassed if I converted anybody. What I do have in full measure, which I find impossible to rein in, is a sort of non-utilitarian investigative, or detective, instinct which—whether regrettably or fortunately, I am never quite sure—becomes a self-justifying and self-destructing end in itself. Having discovered the truth or ascertained the right, as nearly as may be, and said so, I tend to sink into complacency, caring little whether others choose to see the light so plainly revealed.

It occurs to me—and I had better stop this psychoanalysis right now before I lose my reader, or readers if more than one—that the reason I could never be a successful crusader is that, behind this bold facade of self-assuredness, there is always a tiny gnawing doubt. Could I somehow be wrong? I would not, for example, care to stake my life on prophesying that the new treaty will usher in a golden age of harmony and end all problems with the Panama Canal. But I agree with Ambassador Bunker that:

> The real choice before us is not between the existing treaty and a new one but, rather, between a new treaty and what will happen if we should fail to achieve a new treaty.[8]

---

[8] Address made on December 2, 1975 by Ambassador at Large Ellsworth Bunker, Chief United States Negotiator for the Panama Canal Treaty, before the World Affairs Council at Los Angeles, California.

TABLE OF CONTENTS

CHAPTER I

THE GHOST OF RECEPTION PAST

Except for three small enclaves of Common Law jurisdiction, the Civil Law [1] brought to the New World by the Conquistadores and their societal kinsmen still holds unbroken sway in the entire Western Hemisphere mainland south of the Rio Grande. Those three exceptions, judicial sore thumbs so to speak, are: (a) the British dependency of Belize (formerly British Honduras), (b) the former British dependency of Guyana, and (c) a strip of land (and land under water) ten miles wide and fifty miles long in the middle of the Republic of Panama known as the Panama Canal Zone.

Though alike in their apartness, there are striking differences historically in the way these legal aberrations came about. In the first, clearly, the Common Law was simply imposed by conquest on a sparsely populated territory inhabited by a primitive society with no competitive legal system of its own. In the second, the Common Law was also imposed by conquest; but in an area where the Civil Law (Roman-Dutch variant) had been established for two hundred years.[2] Moreover, the replacement of Roman-Dutch law took place very gradually between 1814 [3] and 1917 when it was abolished, with some important reservations.[4]

The third, the importation of the Common Law to the Panama Canal Zone, was yet a different kettle of fish:[5] there it displaced peacefully and relatively swiftly a fully developed Civil Law system in force for four hundred years, perhaps the most extraordinary legal acrobatics of the twentieth century.[6]

---

[2] Other areas where Roman-Dutch law still prevails are the Union of South Africa and Sri Lanka (formerly Ceylon).

[3] The territory now known as Guyana was ceded to Great Britain by the Anglo-Dutch Convention of 1814 following its capitulation to British forces in 1803.

[4] Roman-Dutch law still governs personal status and real property disputes.

[5] No play on words intended, but I am reminded by the metaphor that the word "Panama," of Indian origin, is said to mean "abundance of fishes."

[6] Even the importation of the Common Law to British India in the eighteenth century is

---

[1] As used in this book the term "Civil Law," which has other meanings, is equivalent to the "Romano-Germanic family" as defined by David and Brierly. Rene David and John E. C. Brierly, *Major Legal Systems in the World Today* (London: The Free Press, Collier-MacMillan Limited, 1968).

That what occurred in the Canal Zone was another instance of "reception" cannot be doubted. But what kind of reception? The reception of legal ideas has taken innumerable forms in the history of the world and they have been characterized or categorized by legal scholars in many different ways. Such terms as "total," "partial," "gradual," "eclectic," "systematic," "deliberate," "unconscious," "imposed" and others come to mind. Each case, one may suppose, however characterized, is unique in some respect, given the infinite variety of the human condition; but surely none is more peculiar, in both meanings of the word, than that of the Canal Zone.

The more we look back at how it happened, and reexamine past circumstances and events with a cool objectivity (somewhat difficult to maintain in view of the present controversy over the future), the more difficult it is to find an apt characterization. It was not exactly reception by conquest, yet coercive aspects were not lacking.[7] At the present time it is more nearly complete than in Puerto Rico (reception by conquest), or even in Louisiana (reception by purchase?), yet enough remnants of the Civil Law remain to trip an unwary visiting lawyer from one of the states.[8] It was gradual, as compared to the instantaneous method by which Civil Law codes are received, but it was not just the usual gradual accumulation of practice and precedent by bench and bar.

An unusual factor facilitating reception in this case, certainly by way of rationalization and probably containing the seeds of inevitability, was the radical change which occurred in the composition of the population; to such an extent, in fact, that one might justifiably question whether it was actually a change in territorial law so much as a modern case of personal law brought in on the backs of invading settlers who became the dominant class.

Today the winds of change are rising again. Diplomatic negotiations under way, in response to the pressure of growing Panamanian nationalism and world opinion, foreshadow a return of the Civil Law, perhaps coincident with a reverse shift in the nature of the population. Is it not possible that, in the long view, the most accurate characterization of the Common Law reception in the Canal Zone may turn out to be "transitory"?

---

not comparable as it never actually displaced the Islamic and Hindu laws.

[7] Indeed, as will be explained later in more detail, Panamanian international lawyers have almost from the beginning contested the legality of the whole process by which the Hay/Bunau-Varilla Treaty was consummated and a full-fledged apparatus of civil government set up in the Zone.

[8] The United States District Court for the Canal Zone, in Playa de Flor Land and Improvement Co. v. United States, 70 F. Supp. 281 at 287 (1945), said: "We realize that the appellate court has but few cases to review from this jurisdiction, furthermore that such court could not possibly be familiar with the law, practice, and procedure because *it is entirely different from that existing in the United States* [emphasis supplied] . . ." While I consider that a slight exaggeration, even in 1945, it makes the point.

CHAPTER II

THE SPANISH-AMERICAN WAR
AND ALL THAT

The interaction of Spanish and American law which began in the Canal Zone in 1904 did not take place in a vacuum, but in the political and juridical fallout from the military collision of 1898. The absorption of the last remnants of the Spanish overseas empire in the last gasp of Manifest Destiny had set off an earlier interaction of the same general nature whose consequences were still hovering in the air. Moreover, the acquisition of the Zone, which led to the interaction, could fairly be described as, in some degree at least, a strategic corollary of the absorption.[1]

Had not the Hay/Bunau-Varilla Treaty followed so closely in the wake of the Spanish-American War, American legislators and jurists would have had no recent precedents for coping with the associated juridical problems.[2] However, the Treaty of Paris of 1898 had ceded the Philippine Islands and Puerto Rico to the United States and left Cuba temporarily under American control. Immediately before them was the record of five years of intense, if sometimes ill-advised or frustrating, experience in the amalgamation of the Common Law with the centuries-old Spanish law in those territories.

There were differences, of course, in the situations of the three former Spanish territories; but the overriding similarity was compelling enough to lead to a similarity in

---

[1] Though not a direct result, it was more than coincidental that the Canal Zone was acquired so soon after the sudden annexation of new territories, separated by a narrow land barrier, in the Caribbean and in the Pacific (the Oregon was remembered as well as the Maine). There is no evidence in either case, however, that the resulting private law problem was the subject of any premeditation; rather it was simply a by-product of strategic considerations.

When Secretary of War Elihu Root conceived and drafted the Platt Amendment in 1901, it is clear that he was already envisaging the future canal as the cornerstone of the post-war United States Caribbean policy and was taking steps to ensure that approaches to the canal would be safeguarded. See "A Caribbean policy for the United States," *The American Journal of International Law*, Vol. 8, No. 4 (October 1914), pp. 886–89.

[2] In the more distant past, of course, and under conditions so dissimilar as to afford limited guidance, there had been some experience with mingling, most notably in Louisiana but also in Florida, California, and other states which had been part of the Spanish empire. The California experience of 1846–50 was put to some advantage later on, as will be shown in chap. VII, but it lacked the immediacy of the 1898 examples. Also, these were mainland territories expected to become part of the Union. The Supreme Court later held in the Insular Cases that the Constitution did not automatically "follow the flag" in its extracontinental forays, and neither, it seems, did the private law.

3

approaches, solutions, and even institutions. And some of this similarity was carried over into the Zone. What happened there cannot be fully appreciated without some allusion to it. The landmark Canal Zone cases involving conflicts and comparative law are studded with citations to Philippine and Puerto Rican precedents.

It is one of the many little ironies of history that Cuba, ostensibly the seed-bed of the war, never came under the rule of an American civil government (though temporarily ruled by "civil orders" promulgated by the military government) and hence played little part in the after-effects of the war on Canal Zone developments.[3] Instead, the Philippine Islands and Puerto Rico, almost incidental acquisitions, became the proving grounds for the great experiment in Spanish and Common Law coexistence.

Writers of text books and law review articles have paid some attention to the conflict of systems in the legal histories of the Philippine Islands and Puerto Rico since 1898, less to the same conflict in the legal history of the Canal Zone since 1904. To the best of my knowledge, nobody has made a serious study of the influence by example of the former on the latter. I am not attempting to do that here in any definitive way, but many peripheral references thereto will appear as the subject of this book is developed in later chapters.[4]

I am not unmindful of the discrepancies between the Spanish Civil Law encountered in the Philippine Islands and Puerto Rico in 1898 and that encountered in the Zone in 1904. In the first case the territories concerned were an integral part of the Spanish colonial empire at the time of transfer; while in the second case the territory had been part of the Republic of Colombia, and thus independent of Spain, since 1819.

It was after 1819 that Spanish legal history entered the so-called period of the modern codes, making a radical break with all previous legal tradition (as to form).[5] These modern codes consequently did not extend to Colombia,[6] but were in effect in the Philippine Islands and Puerto Rico. They were, principally:

1. The Spanish Civil Code of 1888
2. The Spanish Code of Commerce of 1885[7]
3. The Spanish Penal Code of 1870, revised in 1876
4. The Spanish Law of Civil Procedure, substantially amended in 1881
5. The Spanish Law of Criminal Procedure, amended in 1879, 1882, and 1888

---

[3] Despite our Government's ritual disclaimer of territorial ambitions in Cuba, the European powers were unanimously amazed when we kept our word and turned Cuba loose (more or less). No such avowal had been made with respect to the Philippine Islands and Puerto Rico both of which were thought, for various reasons, not to be ready for independence.

[4] The influence was exerted in several different ways, not all of which were obvious. E.g., Charles E. Magoon was appointed Governor of the Canal Zone in 1905 (and also Minister to Panama) mostly because of his previous experience as law officer, Bureau of Insular Affairs, where he had "specialized in those legal problems emanating from United States acquisition of Cuba, Puerto Rico, and the Philippines. . . ." As the only person ever to occupy both positions concurrently, Magoon formulated policy and instituted precedents which were followed by the United States Government for many years. G. A. Mellander, *The United States in Panamanian Politics* (Danville, Illinois: The Interstate Printers & Publishers, Inc., 1971) p. 74. For a thoroughly-researched and balanced analysis of Magoon's role, drawing largely on contemporaneous news-

paper stories, see, Gustavo Adolfo Mellander, "Magoon in Panama" (unpublished M.A. thesis, The George Washington University, 1960).

[5] For the first time Spanish law was broken down into homogeneous parts (civil, civil procedure, criminal, criminal procedure, commercial) after the manner of the Napoleonic Code. All previous codes had been compilations without differentiation. See following chapter on "The Civil Law in Force When Reception Began."

[6] Which by that time had a code of its own, as we shall see.

[7] The first of the (Spanish) modern codes in point of time was an earlier commercial code which went into effect in 1830. Schmidt, writing in 1851 while work on the Civil Code was still in progress, said:

"No country of modern Europe can furnish so rich and so complete a collection of laws as Spain, and from the materials thus accumulated, during the lapse of centuries, there can be no doubt that, without looking to any other source, a code may be formed superior to any yet enacted elsewhere.

"We understand that such an undertaking is now progressing, and from the specimen furnished of the capacity of the Spanish jurists to do it justice, as evinced in the 'Código de Comercio,' no doubt can be entertained, that, when completed, it will be a work of consummate ability." Gustavus Schmidt, *Civil Law in Spain and Mexico* (New Orleans: privately printed, 1851).

Also a part of the law of Puerto Rico (but not of the Philippine Islands) was the daring Autonomic Charter of 1897. This was a last desperate attempt of the Spanish crown to hold Cuba and Puerto Rico by extending a substantial measure of self-government without actually relinquishing the reins of colonialism. It went into effect on February 11, 1898 (see José Trías Monge, "La carta autonómica de 1897," XLIII *Revista Jurídica de la Universidad de Puerto Rico*, p. 179, 1974, and Alfonso L. García Martínez, "La constitución autonómica de Puerto Rico de 1897,—un desarrollo no igualado en nuestra historia política," Núm. 35 *Revista Colegio de Abogados de Puerto Rico*, p. 387, agosto de 1974) but history did not allow it enough time to prove itself. The American expeditionary forces landed on July 25 of the same year.

Another subtle but potentially crucial difference is that the Philippine Islands and Puerto Rico were transferred in fee simple *including* sovereignty. The transfer to United States control of the Zone did *not* include sovereignty.[8]

To the above divergences must be added, of course, the additional differences created by Colombian legislation (and reception) between 1819 and 1903.[9]

Nevertheless, I would maintain that, in sum, the discrepancies were more superficial than essential. Even the radical new codes, though more logical and convenient, did not greatly change the substance of the Peninsular law, as extended to the colonies, nor did Colombian legislation before 1903 alter the intrinsic Spanish character of Colombian law. Colombian judges until 1903, like Philippine and Puerto Rican judges until 1898, continued to look to Madrid for enlightenment as to the origins and meaning of basic concepts in the inherited law (*derecho*).[10]

While a full recitation of the Puerto Rican experience with reception would be too much of a digression, a capsulized version may help to show how it saved, by bad example, the Zone lawmakers from attempting to change the legal system too abruptly. In my judgment it also tends to support the view that the almost complete reception eventually achieved in the Zone would probably not have succeeded, or at least not so smoothly, without a concurrent massive shift in the population (which did not occur in Puerto Rico).[11]

In Section 40 of the Foraker Act of April 12, 1900 (providing for the establishment of a civil government in Puerto Rico) Congress ordained, unwisely it would seem, that a commission of three members, at

---

[8] Exactly what kind of a facsimile of sovereignty the United States acquired through the Hay/Bunau-Varilla Treaty has been in dispute since the moment the ink was dry on that document. To oversimplify, the Panamanian position is that the United States received, at most, a kind of waiver to permit the exercise of simulated sovereign power while the real, residual sovereignty always remained with Panama. Sovereignty over the Canal Zone is an immense subject in its own right and not to be disposed of in a footnote. See chap. IV for fuller discussion of the subject.

[9] See chap. III, p. 15 et seq., infra.

[10] Here again, though, the difference between a colony and an independent country must be noted, and a distinction made between (a) general enlightenment as to the law (*derecho*) and (b) the interpretation of specific code provisions (*leyes*). While both looked to Madrid with respect to (a) above, decisions of the Spanish Supreme Court with respect to (b) had little or no effect on Colombian law after 1819 but continued to have a direct effect on Puerto Rican and Philippine law right up to the Spanish-American War. Then, by a strange alchemy of reception in Puerto Rico, the effect was actually strengthened by the change of sovereignty on October 18, 1898. The Puerto Rican Code adopted by the Insular Legislature in 1902 was almost entirely copied from that of Spain. The District Court for Puerto Rico held, in Olivieri v. Biaggi (17 Puerto Rican Reports 676 (1919), that ". . . on October 18, 1898, the Civil Code of Spain, as it then stood with the judicial interpretation already put upon it by the Spanish courts, became the local law of Porto Rico under American rule [owing to the application of Common Law doctrine] . . . ." Consequently,

"Spanish decisions, which under the civil law doctrine may have had no binding force in Spain, and which were not binding in Puerto Rico when it was a Spanish possession, thus became binding precedents under American rule." *

This kind of result could not have been reached in the Canal Zone. There were, of course, many Canal Zone cases wherein recourse was had to interpretations put upon the Code by the courts of Colombia, but only for their persuasive force; to the best of my knowledge no assertion was made that such interpretation had "become the local law . . . under American rule."

[11] See Domingo Díaz A. et al v. Patterson, cited in chap. VII, infra, p. 113.

* Rudolf B. Schlesinger, *Comparative Law* (Mineola, New York: The Foundation Press, Inc., 1970) p. 412.

least one of whom should be a native of Puerto Rico, be appointed by the President "to compile and revise the laws of Puerto Rico." It met for the first time on September 8, 1900, and its report was due in Congress on April 12, 1901. Thus, as Professor Rodríguez has pointed out,

> (i)n a period of seven months, two Americans and one Puerto Rican were to lay the foundations for the harmonizing of the differences between the Civil Law and the Anglo-American law in Puerto Rico.[12]

Apparently recognizing the impossibility of the task, as well as the lack of any clear and present need for it,[13] the Commission took full advantage of "the purpose of Congress to bring the institutions of the island into closer harmony with the American system . . . without any sudden changes . . ." It limited its recommendations to pruning and "harmonizing" around the edges. By the time the report was referred to the Insular Legislative Assembly in 1902 another commission had been created by that body in substitution of the former and both reports, neither of which made any basic changes, came before the assembly for revision.

As Professor Rodríguez says, with reference to the choices before the assembly, "(t)he adoption of the common law system by legislation would have been an obvious negation of the common law," whereas legislative abolition of the Civil Law or simultaneous recognition of both systems would have been equally unacceptable. In the end, the Spanish Civil Code of 1888 (extended to Puerto Rico, Cuba, and the Philippine Islands in 1889) was left substantially in force after some tinkering, mostly with the language of Book One on "Persons," to bring it more into conformity with

the provisions of the Civil Code of Louisiana.[14]

The pressure of the new ruling culture could not be denied, but it could be deflected or absorbed. The result was that the institutions of the island were brought into "closer harmony," not in one fell swoop by Congressional dictate, but by piecemeal legislation of the Puerto Rican Assembly, and later of the Legislature, borrowed mostly from the laws of one or another of the states, and, for the most part, relatively inconsequential in their effect on the legal method.[15]

(Any work dealing with reception, by the very definition of the subject, tends to emphasize conflicts and change; but it is well to remember, and this seems as good a place as any to do so, that reception in the Zone—as well as in the Philippines and Puerto Rico—was relatively easy as compared, say, to the reception of the Swiss civil code in Turkey because the Anglo-American and Spanish private laws are not all that dissimilar in most of their basic precepts. The eminent Hispanic-American law scholar Clifford Stevens Walton,[16] writing in 1900, had no trouble finding the

---

[12] Rodríguez, "Interaction of Civil Law and Anglo-American Law in the Legal Method in Puerto Rico," vol. XXIII *Tulane Law Review* No. 1 (1948) p. 14. In contrast, as we shall see, the Congress did not ordain a new Civil Code for the Canal Zone until 1928, and it was not ready for publication until 1933.

[13] As the Commission itself observed: "With the exception of the revision of the organic act (the Foraker Act), all of the subjects intrusted to the commission are within the competency of the local legislative assembly, and unless Congress is prepared to enact a complete code of laws for the island, the revision of the legal system will have to be carried out by the insular assembly," Rodríguez, "Interaction of Civil Law," p. 17.

[14] Professor Rodríguez cites the unpublished notes on the history of Puerto Rican law of Dr. Luis Muñoz Morales, Professor Emeritus of the College of Law of the University of Puerto Rico, as authority for the observation that the pertinent provisions were taken from the Louisiana Code of 1870, which was not only older than the Spanish Code of 1888 but also out of touch with the mores of Puerto Rico, so that even this attempt was later abandoned and most of the Spanish Code re-established.

[15] To this day the fundamental provisions of the Spanish Civil Code of 1888 survive in the Puerto Rico Civil Code and form the basis of Puerto Rico Civil Law. Officially, the Spanish Civil Code of 1888 was superseded by the Revised Civil Code of 1902, enacted by the legislative Assembly of Puerto Rico, created by the first organic act of 1900, commonly known as the Foraker Act. In 1930, a new official edition of the Civil Code was approved, which is the legislative basis of later amendments. The Code of Commerce of 1885 has suffered greater erosion owing to the fact that bankruptcy and other commercial matters fall exclusively under U.S. federal jurisdiction.

[16] Clifford Stevens Walton, *The Civil Law in Spain and Spanish-America* (Washington, D. C.: W. H. Lowdermilk and Co., 1900) p. 112. For all his undoubted scholarship, however, I regret to have to say that Walton lifted whole paragraphs verbatim from Schmidt (see note 7, supra) without attribution.

Spanish Civil Code, with some adjustments in the public law sector, acceptable for continued use in an Americanized Puerto Rico.)

It was almost inevitable, given the historical confluence, that American policy makers, particularly in the early stages, would look upon the newly-acquired Spanish dependencies and the Canal Zone as pretty much of a piece with respect to the treatment of private law. We see the same general attitudes and even, to a considerable extent, the same language being used.

After the capitulation of Spanish forces in Cuba the policy line was enunciated in the following excerpt from a letter of the President to the Secretary of War dated July 13, 1898, (published in General Order No. 101 dated July 18, 1898):

> Though the powers of the military occupant are absolute and supreme and immediately operate upon the political condition of the inhabitants, the municipal laws of the conquered territory, such as affect private rights of persons and property and provide for the punishment of crime, are considered as continuing in force, so far as they are compatible with the new order of things, until they are suspended or superseded by the occupying belligerent and in practice they are not usually abrogated, but are allowed to remain in force and to be administered by the ordinary tribunals, substantially as they were before the occupation. This enlightened practice is, so far as possible, to be adhered to on the present occasion.[17]

The effect of the order was extended to Puerto Rico a few days later.

On April 7, 1900, the President wrote a letter to the Secretary of War, for transmission to the Philippine Commission, containing these words:

> The main body of the laws which regulate the rights and obligations of the people should be maintained with as little interference as possible.[18]

Now consider, from President Theodore Roosevelt's Executive Order of May 9, 1904, following ratification of the Hay/Bunau-Varilla Treaty:

> The laws of the land, with which the inhabitants are familiar, and which were

in force on February 26, 1904, [effective date of transfer of control] will continue in force in the canal zone and in other places on the isthmus over which the United States has jurisdiction until altered or annulled by the said [Isthmian Canal] commission, but there are certain great principles of government which have been made the basis of an existence as a nation which we deem essential to the rule of law and the maintenance of order, and which shall have force in said zone.

The obvious intent of the first part of this provision was the same as that evinced in the immediately preceding military occupations; viz., to conform to the customary law of nations respecting the civilian population of occupied or ceded territory when such population has been accustomed to living under a different legal order from that of the occupier. Some new language has appeared, "The laws of the land, with which the inhabitants are familiar . . . ," which would later have the unintended result of a curious legal paradox.

The final clause, reserving "certain great principles," was followed by a list of those principles borrowed almost verbatim from the President's letter to the Secretary of War dated April 7, 1900, cited above, respecting the governance of the Philippines. In effect they amounted to a restatement and extension to the Canal Zone of the Bill of Rights of the United States Constitution.

Thus, the approach to reception had a strain of marked similarity in Puerto Rico, the Philippines, and the Canal Zone: initial preservation of existing private law subject to American principles of public law.[19]

---

[17] House Document No. 1484, 60th Cong., 2d sess., p. 2177.

[18] *A Compilation of the Acts of the Philippine Commission* (Manila, P.I.: Bureau of Printing, 1908) p. 14.

[19] Aside from the customary international law on the subject, the English Common Law view seems to have been laid down in a 1795 case in the Court of King's Bench, Blankard v. Galdy,* reaching the Court from Jamaica:

"1st, In case of an uninhabited country newly found out by English subjects, all laws in force in England are in force there; so it seemed to be agreed.

"2dly, Jamaica being conquered, and not pleaded to be a parcel of the kingdom of England, but part of the possessions and revenue of the Crown of England, the laws of England did not take place there, until declared so by the conqueror or his successors."

As noted in chap. I, the laws of England were not declared to take place in British Guiana until more than a century after the conquest.
* 2 Salkeld 411 (1795).

CHAPTER III

THE CIVIL LAW IN FORCE WHEN RECEPTION BEGAN

When we say that the Civil Law was in force in the Zone on February 26, 1904, we are correct but not very precise. Specifically, it was the law of the Republic of Panama. But the Republic of Panama was born of secession from Colombia in November of the preceding year and had not as yet seen fit to make any changes in the internal law. So we really mean the law of Colombia. And the law of Colombia was the law of Spain extended to its overseas empire, as amended by legislation since 1819. So the first question becomes: What was the law of Spain?

The common lawyer who has never encountered it tends to think of the Civil Law as an unfamiliar monolith. Unfamiliar it may be; monolithic, no. The Civil Law— i.e., the Romano-Germanic family—comprises a number of family members with a common ancestor. We are talking about the Colombian/Panamanian offshoot of the Spanish branch of the family. Long before 1819 the Spanish branch had developed its own distinctive character the roots of which lay deep in Spanish history.

Fortunately, we can ignore the legal systems of all the pre-Roman peoples who inhabited the Iberian peninsula (Iberians, Celts, Greeks, Phoenicians, Carthaginians, et al.) as the traces which they left in the Spanish legal system [1] are too obscure to follow through the Spanish conquest of the New World. For all practical purposes it seems to be generally agreed that Spanish legal history, as such, begins with the Gothic invasions. This proposition depends for its validity, of course, on the assumption that Roman law in Spain up to that point was not distinguishable from the mainstream law of the empire. [2] Granted.

The law of the Visigoths when they came into Spain consisted of unwritten Germanic tribal custom. It was first reduced to writing in the Code of Euric (466-484) completed at Tolosa in 480. The forms of this first code, and in fact its very creation, owed much to the influence of the superior Roman civilization. Some scholars even believe that it was written in Latin, though that is disputed by others. Whatever the language or style, it seems clear that the law was almost undiluted Gothic and strictly personal, not applicable to the conquered Roman people who were allowed to keep their own jurisprudence.

---

[1] John Thomas Vance, *The Background of Hispanic-American Law* (New York: Central Book Company, 1943), p. 31.

[2] Or, at most, was simply the law of Spain as a Roman province.

8

In order to clarify the latter, and make the existing legal dualism more manageable, Alaric II (484-507) ordered a similar compilation of the Roman law which, despite the length of Roman rule, had never been unified. The result was the *Breviarium* of Alaric promulgated in 506. The *Breviarium* drew heavily on the Theodosian code[3] but included also selections from the Gregorian and Hermogenian codes, the Institutes of Gaius, and other sources of imperial law.[4]

Thus began a competition of several centuries from which the Roman element would eventually emerge triumphant over the Gothic, though never to its extinction.

The personality of the Gothic law is already seen to be eroding in the reign of Leovigild (572-586) when the Code of Euric was drastically revised and modernized, and in the succeeding reign of Recarred (586-601) three laws at least have been found which ignore the distinction between Goths and Romans. The merging process was facilitated by the conversion of Recarred, the first Catholic king, from Arianism to orthodox Christianity bringing about a uniformity in ecclesiastical discipline which paved the way for entry into the law of the canonical element (which has been a mark of Spanish law ever since).

The Councils of Toledo, which played an enormously important role in the formative period of Spanish law, were in origin purely ecclesiastical and considered religious affairs only. The first Councils were attended only by bishops and abbots; but after the conversion of Recarred, which occurred during the Third Council, the nobility were added and the resolutions of the Council referred to both the religious and civil orders. In the first case the Council continued to enjoy complete authority, but in the second the king reserved an absolute veto power and also could legislate without

the Council if he chose. In practice the clergy, by sheer force of superior learning if for no other reason, gradually enlarged its sphere, the turning point in the intrusion of the clergy into all affairs probably coming during the Fourth Council presided over by the illustrious St. Isadore of Seville.

The trend toward a general law for the Visigoths and the conquered people was especially noticeable in the Eighth Council and culminated in the landmark work of the Sixteenth Council, during the reign of Egica (687-700), known as the *Fuero Juzgo*.[5] The *Fuero Juzgo* contains fifty-four titles, subdivided into five hundred and seventy-eight laws, of which one hundred and eighty-three are attributed to Euric and Leovigild, one hundred and twenty-four to Sisenand and St. Isadore, two hundred and thirty-three to various other kings, and nineteen to the Councils of Toledo.[6] There can be little doubt that it was written in Latin.

While space does not permit a detailed account here of its known contents, it can be said in general that it accomplished its purpose of ending the legal dualism, that it was far ahead of its time in many respects,[7] and that it built so well that even a conflicting stricture of the renowned *Las Siete Partidas* half a millenium later did not wash away its authority.[8] For all the theo-

---

[3] Theodosius, though ruling in the Eastern Empire, was born in Spain.

[4] Though officially in force for only a hundred and fifty years, its influence continued much longer and even into Frankish and other Germanic territories where it was copied and applied. "To the *Breviarium* may be ascribed the merit of having preserved, at least in part, the imperial Roman law and part of the classical jurisprudence, by having combined the elements that entered into its formation in a more skillful manner than had been done in the Edict of Theodoric and other similar compilations." Vance, *Background*, p. 46.

[5] This work was known by several names, among them *"Fori Judicum,"* of which *Fuero Juzgo* is a thirteenth century corruption which has stuck.

[6] As will be noted by the alert mathematician, this leaves a few unaccounted for.

[7] "[It] includes in reality one of the earliest written constitutions in Europe. . . . The student will be surprised at the modern principles embraced in these laws; they are especially noted for their common sense and practical application and would, in some respects, serve as good examples for legislators of the present age." Walton, *Civil Law*, p. 52.

[8] In an important decision of the Spanish court of last resort in 1779, in the reign of Charles III, it was held that "as said law of *Fuero Juzgo* is not derogated by any other, you should abide by it on determining on this or similar business, without attaching much importance to those from the *Partidas.*" Walton, *Civil Law*, p. 57.

"The *Fuero Juzgo* is the most ancient code of Teutonic origin which has preserved its influence even to this day. The laws of the Franks, Burgundians, Lombards, etc., have disappeared . . . while the Visigothic law still

cratic spirit injected into it by its clerical drafters, and the compromises with the *Breviarium,* the *Fuero Juzgo* is predominantly Gothic, erected on a multitude of purely Germanic institutions such as conjugal community property (*gananciales*) and advantages (*mejoras*) which have retained their importance in Spanish civil legislation. In land law, provisions are laid down respecting accession and prescription which have likewise retained their relevance into the twentieth century and which are essential to a full understanding of some of the conflicts which have occurred in the Canal Zone.[9] On the other hand, some of the titles concern matters, such as wills and testaments, which are purely Roman and unknown to the Gothic law.

Almost immediately after the promulgation of the *Fuero Juzgo* another invasion of Spain, this time from the south, upset all calculations and launched a new phase of Spanish legal history which was to last nearly eight centuries and become known as the Period of Reconquest. First crossing the Strait of Gibraltar in force in 711, it

took the Arabs only two years to overrun almost the whole of the peninsula. A small Christian enclave held out in the mountains of Asturia and in this tiny area the *Fuero Jugzo* remained in force as the general law of Spain. As the Christian-held area slowly enlarged through the long stretches of the Middle Ages the general law flowed back.[10]

But things could never be exactly the same again. The short-lived unity of the Gothic kingdom had been broken, and the reconquest was accompanied by a new fragmentation and a spirit of separatism, manifested in the law by the phenomenon of the *"fueros."* It must be explained here that the word *"fuero"* in Spanish law has an incredible number of meanings, only two or three of which we need be concerned with in this chapter. In its most widely understood acceptation it means (a) a compilation or code, and in this sense it is used in *Fuero Juzgo* (and, as we shall see a little later, in *Fuero Viejo* and *Fuero Real*). It also means, however, (b) the customs and usage of a province, and (c) a kind of special franchise or charter or exception, and it is in a combination of these latter significations that the *fueros* account for that separatist strain in Spanish law which surfaced early in the Reconquest and persists to the present time, acquiring renewed vitality since the death of Franco.

In the precarious conditions of the Reconquest the Gothic king needed all the help he could get. One method of keeping up enthusiasm for the cause was to enlist the self-interest of all leading combatants by generous grants of semiautonomy and special privilege (*fueros*) in the recovered territory. From a legislative point of view, consequently, the Reconquest is known as the period of local or foral law. There was no more general legislation, comparable to the *Fuero Juzgo,* until the *Fuero Real* in 1255.[11]

---

governs a large portion of the civilized world." Schmidt, *Civil Law,* pp. 29-30.

[9] Let me give two examples. (1) One class of accession was "by planting." In an almost comic repetitive pattern, Panamanian peasants will go into unoccupied parts of the Zone and plant crops, eventually be discovered by Zone officials, and adamantly defy eviction orders because, regardless of any other considerations, they have "planted." (They may not be aware of the origin of their belief in the power of positive planting, but they come by it honestly.) After much delicate negotiating, with an eye to avoiding an international crisis, the trespasser will be permitted to stay until he has harvested his crop. Both sides have saved face. At the next growing season the same formula will be followed. (2) Several cases in the Zone have involved tracing private land titles back to a point where old maps show the land in dispute as property of the crown and there is no record of divestiture. The Spanish law that recognizes prescription even against the crown, upon which claimants have relied, is founded in the *Fuero Juzgo* and is not well understood by common lawyers in the Zone or anywhere else. In the monumental case of Playa de Flor Land & Improvement Co. (see chap. I, note 8), at p. 324, the court found it necessary to correct attorneys for the Panama Railroad Company for "their erroneous assumption that the lands could not be acquired by prescription against the [Spanish/Colombian] Government."

[10] Strictly speaking it had never left, the Saracen rulers allowing the Romano-Gothic population to keep their own law and customs in what amounted to a return of legal dualism. It was in a subordinate position, however, and inevitably absorbed some Islamic ideas which in due course modified the returning pristine general law. The most lasting Arabic influences were felt in the laws concerning agriculture, irrigation, and riparian rights.

[11] Walton (*Civil Law,* p. 66) would extend the foral period to the *Ordenamiento de Alcalá* in 1348, but I can see no justification for this

It is interesting, and perhaps a bit para-doxical, that feudalism in Spain never took quite such deep roots as in other countries of Western Europe—e.g., the direct line of authority from monarch to subject was never interrupted, at least in theory—yet regional legislative independence took deeper roots and lasted longer.[12] Somewhat as in France, however, the crown dispensed charters to the rising towns (*fueros municipales*)[13] as a means of off-setting the threatening power of the nobility and clergy.

Alarmed at the increasing power of other elements in society, the nobility demanded of the king that their *fueros* be confirmed. Instead of "confirming," Alfonso VIII merely ordered that their *fueros* be collected and unified. The resulting *Fuero Viejo*, the old law, of 1212 was little more than a holding action[14] until Alfonso X, the Wise, (1252-1284) could come out with his own version of what was needed in the public interest, the *Fuero Real* of 1255. The *Fuero Real*, the king's law, tried to bring the multiplicity of statute laws into unity and, as noted, was promulgated as a general code for the whole realm. It established fundamental rules for the regulation of legal relationships and consisted of seventy-two titles containing five hundred and fifty laws.

Alfonso X is credited with a second code and still another collection of laws,[15] but he is best remembered for a work which is essentially a treatise and of less immediate legislative force than the *Fuero Real. Las Siete Partidas*, in addition to its somewhat

uncertain value as law in the Austinian sense,[16] is such a thesaurus of wisdom, philosophy, literature, and vivid thirteenth-century history that the temptation must be resisted to linger over it disproportion-ately. Any reader whose interest has been stimulated, but who has not the time and language accomplishment to read it in the original, is directed to the delightful sum-marized translation with commentary by Madaline W. Nichols of Dominican College, San Rafael, California.[17]

Las Siete Partidas, written between 1256 and 1265, formalized the predominance of Roman and canon law over the Gothic element which had already been reached in the legal practice. Reflections of the Gothic law and of the local *fueros* are, however, not lacking. While the authors have never been definitely identified, they were unques-tionably familiar with the work of the Bolognese glossators on the *Corpus Juris* of Justinian. Alfonso, in fact, regarded himself as the Spanish Justinian and the claim is recognized by scholars as not without merit.[18]

As its name implies, the *Partidas* is di-vided in seven parts, each part beginning with a letter of Alfonso's name; it has eighty-two titles comprising two thousand four hundred and seventy-nine laws. The First Part, from which the standing of the church in the order of things may be de-duced, deals with matters spiritual and obedience to God and the "holy Catholic faith." But a random dip into the Second Part, which deals with "emperors, kings and other great lords," reveals a leavening of temporal realism:

> In his marriage, the king should see to it that his wife is of good lineage, is beautiful, of good habits, and rich. When the king shall have obtained a wife that

---

as the *Fuero Real* was clearly promulgated as a general code and specifically intended to override the particularism which had gotten out of hand.

[12] Unlike the Napoleonic Code and other nine-teenth-century codes of Western Europe, the Spanish Civil Code of 1888 did not blanket the country but had full force only in areas where there was no conflicting foral law, which took precedence. (It also differs, of course, in not being a complete code but dealing only with one branch of the law.)

[13] The first is believed to have been the *Fuero de León*, authorized by Alfonso V in 1020. Leon was the first Christian kingdom formed in the Reconquest.

[14] Much opposed by the nobility, the *Fuero Viejo* was reformed with new dispositions added and promulgated as a general code by Pedro I in 1356. Walton, *Civil Law*, p. 70.

[15] The *Espéculo* and the *Ordenamiento de las Tafurerías*.

[16] It contains absolutely no enforcement pro-visions, for example.

[17] Nichols, "Las Siete Partidas," 20 *California Law Review* 262 (1932).

[18] "The famous law of the *Partidas* wrought a radical change, a revolution, in Spanish laws and jurisprudence. . . . It was made the ob-ject of general study by men dedicated to the legal profession, a subject for thoughtful men which soon made it the jurisprudence and common law of Spaniards . . . the most com-plete treatise of jurisprudence which had been published up to that time." Walton, *Civil Law*, p. 75.

possesses all these qualities, then should he thank God greatly for it.[19]

"The Partidas ends with a series of short miscellaneous provisions such as the following:

All judges should aid liberty.

He who does a thing that he does not know how to do or that is not suited to him is in great fault.

No one should grow rich at the harm of another.

He who is once proven evil is always held as such until he proves the contrary.

Laws should not be made on matters that seldom occur." [20]

The *Partidas* was not actually promulgated until 1348 and even then it was given effect only as "supplemental law" in Title 28 of the *Ordenamiento de Alcalá*.[21] Though in a subordinate position as to binding force, it was accepted as a fundamental reference work on doctrine, cited by legislators, and applied generally until the publication of the nineteenth century Civil Code (by which time it was already embedded in the law of Spanish-America).

As remarked by Max Radin in his admirable introduction to Miss Nichol's article, there seems to be more than a possibility that the *Partidas* exercised some indirect influence on the development of the English Common Law. Edward I of England, the English Justinian,[22] received knighthood from Alfonso, his older cousin and brother-in-law, and lived at Alfonso's court for several months at a time when the latter's pride in the *Partidas* could not have escaped his notice. Moreover, a certain historical parallel in their early growths can surely be discovered between the English Common Law—distinguished from the various local laws by being common to the realm—and the so-called Spanish general law—distinguished by its generality from the regional laws (*fueros*).[23]

Finally, *Las Siete Partidas* has one more claim to fame (which may be irrelevant but I can't bring myself to ignore it); it was the first important work published in the Spanish vernacular. Thus, it must be accorded a place in the subsequent development of the language comparable to that of *La Divina Commedia* in Italian.

A compendium known as the *Leyes de Estilo* appeared about 1300. It was purely doctrinal but attained some importance as a guide to application of the norms of the *Fuero Real*. Some of its doctrines acquired binding force centuries later by being included in the *Novísima Recopilación* (q.v.).

The *Ordenamiento de Alcalá* (1348), heretofore referred to as the vehicle on which *Las Siete Partidas* was carried to official recognition, was also a very important and comprehensive piece of legislation in its own right. That it does not stand out on the historical horizon is owing to (a) being overshadowed by the *Partidas* and (b) the fact that its provisions were incorporated in subsequent compilations which then came to be the ones cited. It is notable for its valiant efforts, even at that relatively early date, to bring some order out of the multiplicity of laws which had accumulated, both geographically and chronologically.

With the Reconquest completed (except for Granada which would fall soon), a new attempt was made at unity of the law, to match the unity of the country, but the result was not impressive. The *Ordenamiento de Montalvo*, completed in 1484,

---

[19] Nichols, "Las Siete Partidas," p. 268.

[20] Ibid., p. 285.

[21] Walton, *Civil Law*, p. 73.

[22] Statutes of Westminster, *De Denis, Quia Emptores*.

[23] Indeed, this general law is often referred to as common law (*derecho común*) by Spanish publicists themselves; Spanish legal historiography is replete with such titles as *"Historia del derecho civil español, común y foral."* The common law of Spain is often thought of as the law of Castile; but, to be accurate, the

law of Castile is as much foral law as that of the other provinces except that it is "first among equals" and many of its provisions have won general acceptance. Walton, *Civil Law*, p. 87.

The early parallel between the English and Spanish common laws soon disappeared, of course, as the English eliminated its competition while the Spanish did not. Also, the Spanish common law was always limited in content to the substantive civil law, exclusive of penal, procedural, and other branches.

As another scholar in this field has pointed out: "While the beauty and value of the old Roman Law has always caused it to be influential, it was never received in the sense that it was in France and Germany, and strictly speaking it is not the Common Law of Spain." "Germanic and Moorish elements of the Spanish civil law." *Harvard Law Review*, Vol. XXX, No. 4 (February 1917), p. 309, by Peter J. Hamilton of the "District Court of the United States for Porto Rico."

was a massive compilation; but it never received express sanction, had no effect on existing legislation, and became merely another of the many sources of Spanish law.[24]

The next labor brought forth, if not complete success, something much more than a mouse. The *Leyes de Toro,* published in 1505, was fully authoritative and enormously helpful in explaining, correcting defects, and supplying omissions in the unwieldy body of laws. One of its most notable features was the recognition and restoration of certain Germanic elements.[25] On the whole, it is one of the milestone enactments in Spanish law and was repeated verbatim three hundred years later in the *Novísima Recopilación,* the last significant legislative act before the independence of Colombia.

For all its virtues, however, the *Leyes de Toro* had regulated only the most important controversial questions, so that the beginning of the reign of Charles I[26] found the state of the law still in desperate need of unity. The familiar task was begun once more. By the time it was published in 1567, under the name of *Nueva Recopilación de las Leyes de España,* three successive authors had died on the job and Charles I himself had been succeeded by Philip II. Still the result was not satisfactory, primarily because it was lacking in necessary new approaches and did not tackle the problem of obsolescence but left almost all the old laws subsisting. It subsequently went through ten different editions, attracted several augmentations, and was the object of many commentaries.

The most important augmentation was the *Autos Acordados o Resoluciones del Consejo* of 1745. This was a collection of court decisions and resolutions of the Council passing on disputed questions and published in the form of laws (one hundred and ten titles and one thousand one hundred and thirty-four laws).[27]

Providing one more impressive demonstration of the Spanish genius for keeping an unworkable apparatus working, the *Nueva Recopilación* with its appendages remained in force until 1805, when it was replaced by something even more unwork-

able. In that year, during the reign of Charles IV, the *Novísima Recopilación* was promulgated. Intended to remedy the defects of the *Nueva Recopilación,* it was in fact subject to the same criticisms. "It was said to be incomplete, deficient as to system, and representing a chaos of all sorts of laws and decrees from the medieval period down to the time of compilation."[28] The following order of prelation was established:

(a) Laws issued after the *Novísima Recopilación* and its supplements.

(b) The laws included in the *Novísima Recopilación,* or in its additional laws on the basis of the principle of *lex prior,* provided they were *fueros* with the character of establishing fundamental rights.

(c) Those provisions of the *Nueva Recopilación,* the *Ordenamiento de Montalvo,* and other *fueros,* not reproduced in the *Novísima Recopilación,* provided they have not fallen into desuetude. The *Leyes de Toro* should be accorded precedence over the *Fuero Real* and the municipal charters.

(d) The *Fuero Juzgo,* the *Fuero Real* and the *fueros municipales,* insofar as the validity of their provisions was ascertainable (for the *Fuero Juzgo* the decisions of 1775 and 1785 of the royal council to be used as a basis); the *Ordenamiento de Alcalá* on the basis of the decision of the royal council of 1773 (in spite of the fact that the *Leyes de Toro* had embraced and covered it).[29]

One remarkable feature in the legislation of Spain should not be overlooked, to wit, that at no time was any attempt made, upon the promulgation of a new code, to abrogate the old one. Hence, all the different codes of Spain must be examined in order to determine the law on any given subject. This rule, however, is to be understood with this restriction, that the latest in point of time is first in authority. . . . In consulting these, there is no difficulty as to the authority of the [*Novísima*] *Recopilación,* which is the latest, as well as the highest authority. But when the *Recopilación* is silent, there exists some diversity of opinion as to

---

[24] Vance, *Civil Law,* pp. 115-17.

[25] Walton, *Civil Law,* p. 74.

[26] Charles V of the Holy Roman Empire.

[27] This seems to be the first reference to court decisions as a source of law, even though indirectly by being embodied in legislation.

[28] Vance, *Civil Law,* p. 126. It even included police regulations for the City of Madrid. Walton, *Civil Law,* p. 78. A facsimile reprint of the original 1805 edition, comprising twelve "books," was brought out in six volumes in 1975 in Madrid by *Boletín Oficial del Estado.*

[29] Vance, *Civil Law,* p. 127.

which of the remaining codes ought to prevail.[30]

In broad terms, such was the condition of Spanish Peninsular law at the time of Colombian independence.

To pick up the origins of the Colombian/Panamanian offshoot we now have to go back to 1505 when the *Casa de Contratación* (House of Contracts, or India House) was set up in Seville to handle matters of trade with the American colonies. An ordinance of 1510 delegated certain judicial functions to the *Casa de Contratación*. In 1524 a Council of the Indies was constituted and made superior to the *Casa de Contratación;* it was also authorized to settle judicial affairs in the name of the king. Further legislation in 1539 extended a large measure of both civil and criminal jurisdiction to the *Casa de Contratación,* with appeal to the Council of the Indies.

By the middle of the sixteenth century the Council of the Indies had clearly established itself as the body by which Spanish-America was governed, under the authority of the king. It had supervision over the *audiencias* (high courts) [31] of the Indies as well as all administrative institutions. Most importantly, for our purposes, it had almost plenary legislative powers. The ordinances of 1571 prescribed the form which the Council should follow in issuing laws and general provisions.[32]

The laws enacted in Spain for the government of the colonies were forwarded thither in the form of *cédulas, decretos, resoluciones, ordenamientos, reglamentos, autos acordados,* and *pragmáticas.*[33]

One of the principal objects of the Council of the Indies was the conversion of the Indians, and this object was inextricably associated with one of the most important and enduring institutions in Spanish colonial history, the *encomienda.* The *encomienda* figures in Canal Zone land title cases in its character as a royal grant of territory, but in its original concept the emphasis was not so much on the territory itself as on the right to collect tribute or exact services (in effect, enslavement) from the Indians inhabiting the territory "on condition that they should take good care of the Indians, both spiritually and physically." [34]

As early as the reign of Philip II, during whose time the *Nueva Recopilación* was published, the laws for the New World had already become so numerous and confusing that the king ordered a collection to be made. In 1680, in the reign of Charles II, the *Recopilación de Indias* was finally completed. An enormous compilation,[35] it piles

---

[30] Schmidt, *Civil Law,* p. 88.

[31] The *audiencias* had executive and consultative, as well as judicial, functions. In the latter capacity they were responsible only to the king, and at all times had the right of direct communication with Spain over the heads of local authorities. During the absence of a local ruler the *audiencia* assumed an executive role. The word *audiencia* is also sometimes used, by extension, to denote the territory over which the court had jurisdiction. Thus the existence, at various times, of an *audiencia* of Panama becomes significant in later quarrels with Colombia (and between Colombia and the United States) over the right of the province to secede and be recognized as a state in international law. (See chap. IV, note 65, infra.)

[32] "It provided that the laws should be made with great deliberation. The members of the council should be well informed; first, of what had been decided previously, and of what was to be newly enacted. Furthermore, it was required that the laws should be framed, having in mind the greatest possible information about the affairs and places where they were to be

enforced, including the advice and opinions of those who administered these laws." Vance, *Civil Law,* p. 136. It would be hard to improve on those instructions for legislators anywhere at any time.

[33] "*Autos acordados* and *cédulas* were orders emanating from some superior tribunal, promulgated in the name, and by the authority of, the sovereign.

Decretos were similar orders in ecclesiastical matters.

Ordenamientos and *pragmáticas* were also orders emanating from the king and differing from *cédulas* only in form, and in the mode of promulgation.

Reglamentos were written instructions given by a competent authority without the observance of any peculiar form.

Resoluciones were opinions formed by some superior authority on matters referred to its decision, and forwarded to the inferior authorities for their instruction and government." Schmidt, *Civil Law,* p. 93.

[34] The resulting slavery—much opposed by some clerical jurists (notably Bartolomé de las Casas), though upheld by others—gave rise to lively moral/legal arguments for generations, but it was a completely dead issue long before the beginning of reception in the Zone.

[35] Three times as long as it needs to be in the opinion of Schmidt, *Civil Law,* p. 94. Re-

law upon law, omitting nothing that has gone before even though abrogated or modified by later laws also included.

The significant fact about the *Recopilación de Indias* is, however, not its size but its nature. It is not in any sense a civil code, but rather a digest of public (including penal) law and political, military, and fiscal regulations. The private law of the Indies continued, for the most part, to be, in effect, the general law of Spain, with the *Recopilación de Indias* a supplementary source. (Technically, it was the other way round, the *Recopilación* providing—in Book 2, Title 1, Laws 1 and 2—that matters on which it is silent [which is to say, the bulk of private law matters] would be decided in accordance with the law of Castile, as defined in the *Leyes de Toro*.)

The general applicability of the Peninsular law to the colonies was modified, however, in another provision of the *Recopilación*—Book 2, Title 1, Law 40—which decreed that no law enacted for Spain should be obligatory in America unless accompanied by a *cédula* to that effect from the Council of the Indies. Thus, in recognition of the different conditions prevailing, not all Spanish laws were extended to the colonies; while on the other hand, some laws were enacted exclusively for the colonies and not applied to the Peninsula. *Autos acordados* of the *audiencia* of Lima are also thought to have had at least persuasive authority in the area which later became Colombia (then the vice-royalty of New Granada).

No further collection of the laws of the Indies was made after the *Recopilación de Indias* of 1680.[36] Piecemeal law in the form of the *cédulas, decretos,* etc., mentioned above continued to flow until about 1819. The *Novísima Recopilación* of 1805 was never declared by royal *cédula* to be in force in America, yet it was made so in large

measure by a dictate of the *Recopilación de Indias* making binding the *Nueva Recopilación*, which latter was almost entirely repeated in the *Novísima Recopilación*.

From 1819 to 1903 the territory now comprising Colombia went through a dazzling number of constitutions [37] (not to mention seventy civil wars) which, however, generally speaking, had little effect on the private law. The constitution of 1821 continued "in full force and effect [all existing laws] insofar as they do not conflict with this constitution or with decrees and laws which the Congress may enact." [38] A law of 13 May 1825 established the following order of prelation:

(1) Laws which the Legislative Power has enacted or may enact

(2) *Pragmáticas, cédulas, órdenes, decretos* and *ordenanzas* of the Spanish Government promulgated up to 18 March 1808 and which had been extended to the territory of the new Republic

(3) Laws of the *Recopilación de Indias*

(4) Laws of the *Nueva Recopilación de Castilla*, and

(5) Laws of the *Siete Partidas* [39]

From 1825 on the Congress did from time to time enact laws, some of which—in consequence of the above order—expressly or tacitly, in whole or in part, repealed existing laws.[40] Before long a sufficient body of indigenous law had been built up to justify compilation and this was accomplished in a work called "*Recopilación de las Leyes de la Nueva Granada*" which contained the laws enacted from 1821 to 1844.[41] It was later supplemented by an

---

flecting the fact that "[t]he colonies were regarded as a royal monopoly, as fiefs dependent on the crown, and their administration was an exclusive prerogative of the king" (Vance, *Civil Law*, pp. 128-29), the full title of the work was *Recopilación de Leyes de los Reynos de las Indias.* A facsimile reproduction of the edition of Julian de Paredes of 1681 was published in Madrid in 1973 by Ediciones Cultura Hispánica, with a prologue by the towering Spanish scholar of the 20th century, the late Ramón Menéndez y Pidal.

[36] A revision was ordered about 1777 but it was never completed.

[37] All of which are reproduced in: Manuel Antonio Pombo and José Joaquín Guerra, *Constituciones de Colombia* (Bogota: Biblioteca Popular Cultura Colombiana, 1951).

[38] "en su fuerza y vigor las leyes que hasta aqui han regido en todas las materias y puntos que directa o indirectamente no se opongan a esta Constitución ni a los decretos y leyes que expediere el Congreso." *Código Civil de Colombia* (Madrid, Instituto de Cultura Hispánica, 1963) p. 15.

[39] Ibid., pp. 15-16.

[40] This process of repealing Spanish laws (*leyes*), as distinguished from Spanish law (*derecho*), continued bit by bit until, in 1887, Law 153 (q.v., p. 17, infra) provided that: "All Spanish laws are abolished."

[41] Bolívar's original Gran Colombia had lasted

Appendix containing the laws from 1845 to 1850.

Perhaps the most significant, in long-range effect, of the laws enacted in this period were those precluding inalienability of property and irredeemable obligations, reforms which were confirmed in all subsequent constitutions. "Thus disappeared the odious perpetual family ownership of entailed property which the laws of Spain permitted." [42]

The next milestone in Colombian legal history rears its impressive silhouette in the period of the Federation, i.e., between 1858 and 1885, when a completely new code was adopted in several successive acts of deliberate and voluntary reception. [43] This "received" code, still in effect in 1903, was the famous 1855 Code of Chile, to which remarkable document we must now turn our attention, not only because of its tremendous impact on the whole of Hispanic-American jurisprudence, [44] but because it is thus seen to be the primal source, with some modifications during the Colombian reception, [45] of the first Civil Code of the Canal Zone which remained in force until 1933.

The Chilean Code was the twenty-year labor of one extraordinary savant, Andrés Bello, born in Caracas, mentor and associate, during the early part of his career, of his fellow *caraqueño* Simón Bolívar. Something of a renaissance man, Bello would have been remembered as a philologist and philosopher even if he had never

turned his hand to the law. His juridical formation, as we know by his own writings, was grounded in the *Siete Partidas*, which he also took as a model for language and the influence of which can be seen in the Code.

Before moving to Chile and commencing his opus, Bello lived for eighteen years in London. (As another indicator of cross-fertilization between the two bodies of law which met on the Isthmus in 1904, it is unlikely that Bello could have lived that long in London without absorbing a good deal of Common Law, which would have made its influence felt in the Code.) [46]

In describing the chaos which made a Spanish-American codification imperative, Bello was talking about Chile but his observations could just as well have been applied to Colombia:

Our codes are an ocean of shoals in which the most skilled and experienced pilots may shipwreck. Laws of the *Partidas, Leyes de Toro, Leyes de Indias, Nueva Recopilación*, ordinances of various kinds, advices of the senate, government decrees, laws of our congresses, views of the commentators, etc. Into this immense collection the judge must plunge in the hope of finding an authority which will support his decision. Can he expect not to run aground on a reef? [47]

Bello saw no help from the commentators who, he said, far from clarifying, had merely obscured the sense of the text more and, worse, had usurped the legislative power so that the judges no longer asked: "What does the law say?" but "What does Gómez (or other preferred author) say?" [48]

A man of vast erudition, Bello consulted many sources (including the code of Louisiana); but what he produced was something more than a synthesis, something new in kind as well as in degree, a new beginning for Spanish Civil Law jurisprudence in the New World. At the core, to be sure, he had kept the usable parts of the ancestral Spanish law—extracted primarily from his beloved *Siete Partidas*, the *Novísima Recopilación*, and the *Fuero Real*—but the inherited law as a whole had become static, stifling, and poorly related to actual conditions. [49]

only until 1830 when it was succeeded by the republic of New Granada, later known as the Republic of Colombia.

[42] "Desapareció así el odioso perpetuo dominio familiar sobre los bienes vinculados, que las leyes españoles consagraban." *Código Civil de Colombia*, p. 16.

[43] While the term "reception" generally connotes the importation of a body of law from outside the legal family, there seems to be no reason to preclude its use to describe such actions by independent countries within a family.

[44] The Chilean Code was "received" in several other Latin American countries besides Colombia and had some effect in almost all. It appears correct to say that it played a role in Latin America analogous to that of the French Code of 1804 in Europe.

[45] Most of which, it seems, were detrimental and unnecessary whims of the Colombian legislators. *Vigencia de Andrés Bello en Colombia* (Bogotá, Colombia: El Gráfico Editores, Ltda., 1966), p. 328.

[46] A kind of replay in reverse of the role of Edward I in bringing some Spanish influence into the Common Law. See p. 12, supra.

[47] *Vigencia*, p. 304 (translation by author).

[48] Ibid., pp. 304-5 (translation by author).

[49] Among the absurdities that Bello described,

The gradual metamorphosis of the Common Law in the liberated English colonies into a different species of the same genus was paralleled in Spanish-America by a similar drift, at least in philosophy and usage if not in the written norms, which ultimately found expression in Bello's code. "The idea that America has its own voices, that it has its own vital impulses, and that the good from other cultures should be adapted for this part of the world to the extent suitable was Bello's central motif." [50]

In form Bello's code consists of a Preliminary Title, containing basic definitions, and four Books, with the usual titles and laws. Book One deals with persons; Book Two deals with property, its ownership, possession, and use; Book Three deals with succession; and Book Four deals with obligations and contracts.

In style it is a literary masterpiece combining richness of language with simplicity of thought, with the conscious aim of making knowledge of the law available to Everyman and not just to lawyers (in this respect resembling the earlier French Code and unlike the later German). It is believed by many to equal in precision and clarity the work of Portalis.

Returning now to the chronology of the aforementioned "several successive acts" of Colombian reception, it is necessary to recall that Colombia from 1858 to 1885 had an extremely loose, indeed almost invisible, federal form of government with nine sovereign states, each with its own constitution and laws. One of these states was Panama, and Panama accepted the Bello code in 1860, thus anticipating by thirteen years its reception (in 1873) by the federal government of Colombia.

In 1885, following a civil war, the sovereign states disappeared in a unitary Republic of Colombia which forthwith adopted a new constitution. In 1887 the unitary Republic gave renewed sanction to the Bello code which, therefore, with some supplementary legislation, was the law which the seceding province of Panama took with it upon departure in November 1903, and which the Government of the

United States translated into English and adopted for the Canal Zone in May 1904.

To round out this last phase in the development of the Civil Law in force in 1904, there remains only to mention the most salient of the aforementioned supplementary legislation, Laws 57 and 153 of 1887.

Law 57 was intended to correct omissions and lacunae which practice had revealed in the Bello code, as well as abrogate some articles which had become obsolete. More than that, however, it introduced some new concepts: (a) in reversing the ancient Roman law principle which permitted the rescission of contracts for grave inequity (*"por lesión enorme"*),[51] (b) in the sale of personal property, and (c) in public sales by court order. It also established modalities for the endorsement of negotiable instruments (*"para efectuar la cesión de créditos personales"*); expatiated on the meaning of "quasicontract," "quasidelict," "delict," "fault," and "community quasicontract"; and made some changes in the law of marriage.

Law 57 is further memorable for ordaining that Title III of the national constitution, which deals with civil rights and protection of liberties (*"Derechos Civiles y las Garantías Sociales"*), be added to and made a part of the Bello code.[52]

Law 153, passed only four months later, was intended to correct the errors and omissions of Law 57 (one such omission being failure to end definitively the binding force of Peninsular laws) and consequently much of it goes over the same subject matter. Its transcendental importance, however, lies not with its treatment of specific omissions but with its general approach to the problem of remaining gaps in the Code. Articles 8, 13 and 48 form, in effect, a single rule telling the judge how to interpret and, if necessary, create the law.

Article 8 says that if no applicable law can be found the judge will use analogy, either *legis*—i.e., to a law intended for a similar situation—or *juris*—i.e., to a previ-

---

"[t]here were handwritten royal *cédulas* which had never been published and which were preserved, like holy relics, 'in various offices, the ignorance of which was no excuse.'" Ibid., p. 303 (translation by author).

[50] Ibid., p. 322 (translation by author).

[51] A complete exposition of this overruled principle, which goes back at least to the *Corpus Juris Civilis* of Justinian, can be found in: *Enciclopedia Jurídica Omeba*, (Buenos Aires, Editorial Bibliográfica Argentina S.R.L., 1964) Tomo XVIII, pp. 229-33.

[52] Roughly equivalent to the addition of the Bill of Rights to the codified private law of the United States if such existed.

ous decision in a factually similar situation. (It will be noted that analogy *juris* is coming very close to *stare decisis*.) [53] Article 13 says that absent an applicable law that can be stretched to fit, the judge will have recourse to custom, with certain safeguards to ensure that the custom is general and in accord with Christian morality. Article 48 is the linchpin which says that the judge must decide the case; he cannot avoid his duty by pleading that the law is silent.[54]

Methods of interpretation open to the judge under this liberalizing Colombian law are discussed briefly by the authors of one part of *"La Vigencia de Andrés Bello en Colombia."* [55]

The first method, they say, is that of the glossators, sometimes called exegesis, which seeks to interpret the norm by a meticulous analysis of the literal wording of the Code (in which it is assumed all the law can be found) without regard to its spirit. It is this method which dominated the thinking of Colombian judges and jurists at least until 1887.

The next method to which they advert is that, after Savigny, which seeks to interpret the norm by examining the purposes which the legislator had in mind.

Lastly, they consider the "logical objective" or "historical evolution" method which seeks to interpret the norm in the light of current social and economic realities so as to solve the actual problem justly without much regard to what the legislator may have had in mind. It is the last method which seems to have their approval and which they say is legitimized in Articles 8, 13 and 48, taken as a whole, even though not spelled out explicitly.

In any case, the total effect of Laws 57 and 153, it seems clear, is to move the Spanish/Colombian/Panamanian Civil Law closer conceptually to the English/American Common Law it was soon to confront on the Isthmus.

---

[53] See chap. VII, p. 99-101, infra, for more on Law 153 and *stare decisis*.

[54] Undoubtedly showing the influence of the French Code of 1804 (Preliminary Title, Article 4) which broke ground on this point.

[55] *Vigencia*, pp. 341-43.

CHAPTER IV

LEGAL FOUNDATION OF UNITED STATES "PRESENCE" AND EXERCISE OF "SOVEREIGNTY"

During my first exposure to life in French Morocco, as a soldier during World War II, I was much impressed by the ubiquity, and no less by the felicity, of the phrase *"la présence française."* It seemed to offer, with Gallic *delicatesse*, a noncontroversial explanation of the fact of French control behind the appearance of undiminished trapping and dignity of the Moroccan kingdom.

The *présence* and all it connoted was completely legitimate in international law, deriving from a treaty [1] wherein His Sherifian Majesty clearly yielded all his sovereign power (over his whole realm, not just a strip of it) to France. But the French overlords understood that, to be tolerable, the *présence*—even though sweetened by economic gains, health services, better roads, and the like—should not seem based too starkly on legal rights enforced by power. In *"la présence française"* there was always an aura of partnership, however unbalanced. [2]

It is perhaps idle now, but interesting, to speculate on whether the United States presence in the Canal Zone might have taken a less abrasive form if more thought had been given to preserving at least the appearance of a shared sovereignty. It would seem that the real purpose of the presence could have been accomplished without pushing to the limit all prerogatives permissible under the doctrine of *pacta sunt servanda*, especially as the "pact" was so bizarre in origin and so unconscionably favorable to our side. [3]

The "pact," of course, is the Hay/Bunau-Varilla Treaty on which the claims of the legitimacy of the United States presence

---

[1] The Treaty of Fez, March 30, 1912.

[2] Even so, of course, it finally came to an end as the trend of history since World War II seems to teach that all such *présences* sooner or later must.

[3] In a personal letter written to the Secretary of War on October 18, 1906, President Roosevelt expressed his desire not to exercise any greater rights than necessary to build and maintain the canal (see note 92, infra). "This is an extremely revealing letter, for the Roosevelt credo indicates very clearly that the writer did not consider himself or the United States lord and master of Panama. Instead, he was obviously very desirous of guaranteeing Panama her full sovereignty over her native isthmus. His were not the words of an imperialist bent upon aggrandizement; quite the contrary, he fully hoped that it would not be necessary for the United States to exercise the full extent of her legal treaty rights." Mellander, *United States in Panamanian Politics*, p. 118.

necessarily rest, and which has been the prime target of opponents of that presence. Before looking at the specific questions which have been raised about it, however, it would be appropriate (by the same token that prompted a review of the genesis of the Panamanian Civil Law in force in 1904) to consider the prologue to the "pact."

The first thing to notice about the prologue, as distinguished from the consequences, is that it has nothing whatever to do, except indirectly and accidentally, with either private law or reception. It is concerned primarily with interoceanic communication (in other words, geopolitics rather than law), and secondarily with sovereignty (public international law).[4] Even the Treaty itself touches on the private law problem only scantily and by inference. The object was to get firm control of enough space to build, maintain, and protect a waterway. That the space contained people, who would have to be governed, under some system of law, was (and still is) simply a nuisance from an engineering and strategic point of view.[5]

In 1517 the first ships—four brigantines built in an improvised shipyard in the Gulf of Darien—crossed the Isthmus of Panama from the Atlantic to the Pacific. They were knocked down and carried in pieces through the jungle and over the mountains on the backs of captive Indians, two thousand of whom died on the way; and when they arrived the timbers were found to be useless from the borings of the shipworm. There had to be an easier way. The idea of a canal was born and it never died during the next four hundred years.

This is not the place to recount the long story, or even list the highlights, of all the dreams and schemes;[6] but finally, as growing technology seemed to bring the project nearer and nearer to practicability, the chief impetus began to come, first from the rising United States of America, then France, then again the United States. Several specific sites along the narrow waist of the Western Hemisphere were considered besides the one finally chosen.[7] Though diplomatic efforts were made to keep various options open, the Nicaraguan route was actually the one most favored by United States experts and public opinion up until almost the last minute.

As early as 1825 the "Central American and United States Atlantic and Pacific Canal Company" was organized, one of its directors being De Witt Clinton, flushed with the recent success of another canal called the Erie. In 1835 the Senate voted for the first time, but not the last, to construct a canal by way of Nicaragua. And one of the objectives (unachieved) of the treaty negotiations ending the war with Mexico in 1848 was to acquire a "right of transit" across the Isthmus of Tehuantepec.

All these, and many other, unproductive initiatives may be left aside as ultimately irrelevant. The chain of events which led to the existing canal, with its corollary of a Common Law enclave in the middle of civilian law Panama, started with the "General Treaty of Peace, Amity, Navigation and Commerce Between the United States of

---

[4] After the territory passed from the control of Spain, the weak successor states often raised the question of sovereignty respecting actions taken by foreign powers in pursuit of interoceanic communication. The extreme sensitivity of Panamanians on this issue thus has deep historical roots. Though temporarily suppressed by expediency in the first flush of independence and the canal, it soon re-emerged and with a volatile new element added. For none of the earlier encroachments on sovereignty, however much resented for other reasons, was seen to threaten the very existence of the indigenous legal system. Not until after the Hay/Bunau-Varilla Treaty began to be implemented did any foreign power ever set up its own courts for the adjudication of private law disputes having no relation to inter-oceanic communication (and not until the Hay-Herrán Treaty draft of 1903 was the idea even introduced).

[5] The United States, in the negotiations for a new treaty since 1964, has narrowed its objectives to retaining—for a temporary period, the length of which is one of the conditions being negotiated—only enough land on each bank of the canal to meet engineering and strategic requirements. See chap. VIII, infra.

[6] The earliest documentary evidence, found in a book printed in 1555, shows that a Spanish explorer and lieutenant governor of Vera Cruz named Alvaro de Saavedra Cerón, who died in 1529, was intending to propose to the king of Spain the digging of a canal in one of four places: (1) through Darien from the Gulf of San Miguel to Uraba, (2) from Panama City to Nombre de Dios, approximately the route of the present canal, (3) through the Lake of Nicaragua, or (4) through Tehuantepec in Mexico. David Howarth, *Panama* (New York: McGraw-Hill Book Co., 1966), pp. 56-57.

[7] Principally the same ones suggested by Saavedra.

America and the Republic of New Granada" signed at Bogota on December 12, 1846.[8] Likewise, the threads of contemporary legal controversies over the legitimacy of the enclave lead back to the same convention.

This might have been a routine commercial treaty, of no more note than scores of similar protocols, except for Article XXXV in which fateful commitments were made by both parties respecting rights and interests in the Isthmus.[9] The operative parts are:

(a) The Government of New Granada guarantees to the Government of the United States, that the right of way or transit across the Isthmus of Panama, upon any modes of communication that now exist, *or that may be, hereafter, constructed,* [emphasis supplied] shall be open and free to the Government and citizens of the United States, and for the transportation of any articles of produce, manufactures or merchandize, of lawful commerce, belonging to the citizens of the United States, . . .

and

(b) [I]n order to secure to themselves the tranquil and constant enjoyment of those advantages, . . . the United States guarantee positively and efficaciously to New Granada, by the present stipulation, the perfect neutrality of the before mentioned Isthmus, with the view that the free transit from the one to the other sea, may not be interrupted or embarrassed in any future time while this treaty exists; and in consequence, the United States also guarantee, in the same manner, the rights of sovereignty and property which New Granada has and possesses over the said territory.

From that date and continuously since (not just from 1903), the United States has exercised some attributes of sovereignty over the Isthmus and, conversely, the sovereignty of the Republic of Panama and predecessors has been less than absolute.

The guarantees in the above excerpts, while not intended by New Granada to be exclusive, were never in fact entered into with any other government and gave the United States a powerful leverage in what it was now perceiving as a passage possibly vital to its future development.[10] The protectorate-type responsibilities assumed in excerpt (b) provided a legal basis for warning off other powers and thus leaving the plum on the tree until the day of harvest.[11] The Government of New Granada never foresaw, of course, that, after providing shelter for many years against both external and internal threats, Article XXXV would be reinterpreted at a critical point in history to ensure the success of an internal uprising.

However, lest United States policy makers be credited (or debited) with more cunning and prescience than was in fact the case, it must be added that Article XXXV was not sought by, but rather was pressed on, the American envoy, Mr. Bidlack, by the Government of New Granada. At the time, the latter was more alarmed by the clear and present aggrandizements of Great Britain in the area than apprehensive about the future appetite of its new protector. Bidlack, indeed, was somewhat leary of entering into such an alliance, exceeding his authority, but he rightly guessed that Polk and the Senate would recognize its advantages.

Nevertheless, the ratification mills ground slowly and the treaty was not finally perfected until June 10, 1848, by which time certain intervening happenings had enor-

---

[8] Although several unilateral actions had been taken, and many informal exchanges of view had occurred, this was the first actual treaty made by the United States in which the subject of isthmian transit was specifically mentioned.

[9] This treaty was also probably the most radical departure up to that time from the traditional policy of non-entanglement laid down by Washington.

[10] The United States had just acquired territorial sovereignty in Oregon by treaty with Great Britain. Moreover, President Polk was determined to have California as well and was already at war with Mexico to that end.

[11] Shortly after work was started on the French canal, Colombia attempted to bring the European powers into a broadened pact guaranteeing the neutrality (and Colombian sovereignty) of the canal area. Secretary of State Blaine promptly dispatched a note to all United States diplomatic offices declaring that: "In the judgment of the President, this guarantee [of 1846] . . . does not require reinforcement, or accession, or assent from any other power." The European chancellories took the hint. Dwight Carroll Miner, *The Fight for the Panama Route* (New York: Columbia University Press, 1940), p. 67. The Blaine note in its entirety may be found in 3 Moore International Law Digest 17.

mously increased its importance. The Treaty of Guadalupe Hidalgo, transferring California to the United States, was signed on February 2, 1848. That same week (though unknown to any of the governments involved until after ratification) a new era in the long history of Panama was opened by a gold miner panning at Sutters' mill several thousand miles away. As Edwards wrote: "The man who discovered gold in California indirectly affected the Isthmus more profoundly than any person since Columbus, who discovered it." [12]

Before the year was out the first wave of 49'ers were already swarming up the Chagres River, then striking overland for the last eighteen miles by the ancient, overgrown and abominable Las Cruces Trail.[13] In April 1850 a New York corporation, headed by the American shipowner William Henry Aspinwall, obtained a concession from Bogota to build a railroad.[14]

This concession was fraught with delayed-action legal bombshells and gave birth to an extraordinary creature, the Panama Railroad (P.R.R.), which soon be-

came inextricably intertwined with, successively, the French and American canals in all their ramifications. (Under a law passed in 1950 the P.R.R. was made an agency of the Panama Canal Company. As the Governor of the Canal Zone is also ex officio President of the Panama Canal Company, the P.R.R. thus continues in tandem with the Canal and the civil government. Curiously, the P.R.R. has remained throughout, as it started, a private corporation, though its stock has been wholly owned since 1905 by the United States Government.) [15]

Though granted to a private corporation, the concession of 1850 to all intents and purposes was the beginning of effective implementation of the Treaty of 1846. Aside from this central point, probably the two most significant features of the concession were those relating to (a) a future canal and (b) reversionary rights.

(a) Article VI reads as follows:

While the exclusive privilege granted to the Company, or persons engaged in the enterprise of building the Railroad from one Ocean to the other, continues in force, the Government of the Republic agrees neither itself to build, nor to grant to any other company whatever, under any title whatever, the right of building any other railroad on the Isthmus of Panama; and it is likewise stipulated that, while the said privilege continues in force

---

[12] Albert Edwards, *Panama* (New York: The MacMillan Company, 1911), p. 397. For most of the 16th and part of the 17th centuries the jungle trail across the isthmus from Panama City on the Pacific to the ports of Nombre de Dios and Puerto Bello on the Atlantic was the richest trade route in the world. When the gold and silver mines played out the isthmus sank back into tropical torpor and traffic had dwindled to a comparative trickle.

[13] This was an alternate route the Spaniards had used, for incoming cargo only, in the rainy season when the all-land route ("el camino real") was too difficult. A once-paved mule path said to have been built by Pizarro, parts of it are still traversable—and even traversed on occasion by Boy Scouts and other modern-day adventurers.

[14] Exhibit E: Contracts between the Republic of New Granada and the Panama Railroad Company, made in 1850 and 1867, and modified in 1876, 1880, and 1891. In Report of Joseph L. Bristow, Special Panama Railroad Commissioner to the Secretary of War, June 24, 1905. Published by Office of Administration, Isthmian Canal Affairs. Washington, Govt. Print. Off., 1906. ([U.S.] 59th Cong., 1st sess. Senate Doc. no. 429, pp. 209-37.) This concession must be considered as the starting point because it was the first to become operative; it superseded two previous concessions, one to a French company, which were allowed to lapse and never went into effect.

[15] The total number of shares of the Panama Railroad Company, which never varied, was 70,000. As a result of the Hay/Bunau-Varilla Treaty, the United States Government in 1904 acquired all the holding of the French canal company which amounted to 68,887 shares. The remaining shares, held by various individual owners, were bought up by the Isthmian Canal Commission (see chap. V) during 1904-5. During congressional debate over the bill (S. 6539, 59th Cong., 1st sess., 1906) which placed the P.R.R. fully under United States Government control, opponents argued that this could not be legally done because the Railroad was a New York corporation. Senate Report No. 5179 (59th Cong., 2d sess., 1907) was devoted in large part to rebutting that argument and it was overriden. In 1945, however, Congress enacted the Government Corporation Control Act which prohibited the continued existence of any wholly owned government corporation created by or under the laws of any state. Accordingly, the Panama Railroad Company was reincorporated under a federal charter with authority to continue its operations as before.

the New Granadian Government shall have no power to undertake, nor to permit any other person to undertake, without the concurrence and consent of said Company, the opening of any maritime canal to unite the two Oceans across the said Isthmus of Panama.[16]

(b) In Article II the Government of New Granada reserved the right to redeem the concession and take full possession of the Railroad at the expiration of twenty years after completion upon payment of $5,000,000 indemnification, at the expiration of thirty years upon payment of $4,000,000, and at the expiration of forty years upon payment of $2,000,000.[17]

All these activities and portents had the undesirable side effect of increasing the danger of a conflict with Great Britain. Already holding a virtual protectorate over the whole Mosquito Coast, the British tightened their grip in January 1848 by seizing the Nicaraguan town of San Juan at the Atlantic terminus of what was then considered the most plausible route for a canal. In June 1849 Polk's diplomatic agent to Central America signed a treaty with Nicaragua, even stronger than the one with New Granada, granting the United States the exclusive right to construct, fortify, and control a canal or railroad or both and establishing a protectorate over the country. Other treaties quickly followed, both American and British, with Honduras and Costa Rica, all pointing toward a diplomatic impasse of explosive potential.

Other elements in the situation, however, were conducive to compromise. President Taylor, who had succeeded Polk in March 1849, wanted a neutral canal with United States rights assured but he did not at the time see any need for exclusive control, and above all he had no wish to provoke a military showdown with Great Britain which he knew he could not win. Palmerston, on the other hand, was willing to share control of a future and conjectural canal in exchange for an easing of relations with the United States (he had problems elsewhere) and a legalization of the British foothold in Central America.

None of the above-mentioned Central

American treaties was ever ratified, but instead the issue between the Anglo-Saxon powers was resolved by the Clayton-Bulwer Treaty of 1850.[18] It provided in Article I that:

> The governments of the United States and Great Britain hereby declare that neither the one nor the other will ever obtain or maintain for itself any exclusive control over the said ship canal, agreeing that neither will ever erect or maintain any fortifications commanding the same or in the vicinity thereof, or occupy, or fortify, or colonize, or assume, or exercise any dominion over Nicaragua, Costa Rica, the Mosquito Coast, or any part of Central America; . . .

Some other aspects of the treaty, including its effect on the Monroe Doctrine, are interesting [19] but the real thorn in the side of United States canal diplomacy for the next half century was the stipulation never to maintain or obtain any exclusive control over the waterway.[20] As United States policy started tilting toward control, various efforts were made to break out of the bind, including even a plea of *rebus sic stantibus* advanced by Secretary of State

---

[16] Records of the Panama Canal, Washington National Records Center, Archives Branch, Record Group No. 185, Entry No. 94.A. Also in Exhibit E (see note 14 supra).

[17] *Ibid.*

[18] 9 Stat. 995.

[19] A Panamanian legal scholar, analyzing the treaty in a monograph for the London School of Economics and Political Science in 1911, concluded that Mr. Clayton failed insofar as he was attempting to thwart the intrusion of Great Britain into American affairs. "It was feared that if the point at issue was not settled by means of an agreement between the two powers, the Monroe Doctrine would suffer a serious blow at the hands of the British Government. But the administration, considering itself to be placed in a dilemma, adopted a line of action that actually ran counter to the principle which it was sought to maintain. For every word of this treaty, so to speak, constituted a violation of both the spirit and the letter of that policy which had been consecrated by all North American statesmen." Harmodio Arias, *The Panama Canal, A Study in International Law and Diplomacy* (London: P. S. King and Son, 1911), p. 31. (Reprinted in New York by Arno Press (1970) in its American Imperialism series.) Arias later became president of Panama.

[20] An American authority, writing just before its abrogation by the Hay-Pauncefote agreement, called the Clayton-Bulwer Treaty "the most serious mistake in our diplomatic history." John W. Foster, *A Century of American Diplomacy* (New York: Houghton Mifflin Co., 1900), p. 457.

Blaine in 1881 in "one of the most remarkable state papers ever penned." [21]

Meanwhile, back on the Isthmus, actual construction of the American railroad began in May 1850 and simultaneously, as one result thereof, a new town was born at the Atlantic terminus which is now the second largest city in Panama and is called Colón (Spanish for Columbus). At first, until the Government in Bogota had time to react, adversely, to this Yankee presumptuousness, it was named Aspinwall for the obvious reason.[22] Navy Bay (also known as Limon Bay), the site chosen for the terminus, had sheltered Columbus from a storm on Christmas Day, 1502, but had not been used much since because of marshy shores. Of the debarkation points in more recent usage, the mouth of the Chagres was rejected because of lack of a harbor, and the port of Puerto Bello was rejected—according to stories current at the time—because one of the American entrepreneurs involved, shipowner George Law, had bought up all the land around and was holding it for an exorbitant price.

The fantastic hardships and cost in human life of building the railroad have been told in several books [23] but are still less familiar to the general reader, even in America, than the more publicized heroics of the French canal builders twenty-five years later (who had at least the benefit of a railroad in being, if not in top condition, almost parallel to their projected digging). The worst of the railroad job was the first eight miles after which something like solid ground was reached at Gatun in October 1851. The 49'ers started using it before it was even finished, first as far as Gatun, then to whatever point had been reached at a given time.[24] The first train crossed from ocean to ocean on January 28, 1855.[25]

Many years of rainy seasons
And malaria's countless treasons
Are among the several reasons
    Why he's gone.

"Close the sunken eyelids lightly
    He is gone.
Bind the shrunken mouth up tightly
    He is gone.
Chinese gin from Bottle Alley
Could not give him strength to rally,
Lone, to wander in Death's Valley
    He is gone.

"In his best clothes they've array'd him
    He is gone.
In a wooden box they've laid him.
    He is gone.
Bogus Hennisey and sherry
With his system both made merry.
Very hard he fought them—very!
    But he's gone!"

[24] One of those who used it in crossing in 1852 was Captain Ulysses S. Grant, on his way to garrison duty in California.

[25] One effect of the railroad was a quantum leap in the cultural clash—still an intangible but real factor in the legal conflicts—caused by the sudden dumping of uncontrollable numbers of North Americans in the capital city of the Panameños. Many American inhabitants of the Zone today are inclined to take a disapproving view of the "natives" because of their sometimes riotous and violent behavior, forgetting the other side of the coin as recounted, for example, by an English traveler in the 1850s. "The old city was literally astounded by the influx of noisy Yankees who paraded the town, armed with bowie-knives and revolvers, which were from time to time made use of in the excitement caused by gambling and the liquor of the impromptu drinking-saloons. From these early emigrants, and from such men as accompanied Walker in Nicaragua, the South Americans derived their first knowledge of the Americans of the northern States. The impression created was far from favorable." Edwards, *Panama*, p. 416.

---

[21] Arias, *Panama Canal*, pp. 47-48. Arias ridiculed Blaine's argument that ". . . the convention had been made over thirty years ago, under exceptional and extraordinary circumstances which had entirely ceased to exist . . ." concluding that ". . . though he had scarcely any ground for the controversy . . . nevertheless he plunged into the struggle for the abrogation of the treaty." One may reasonably speculate that Arias might not be quite so ready to dismiss *rebus sic stantibus* if he were alive today and involved in the struggle for abrogation of the Hay/Bunau-Varilla Treaty.

[22] Most Americans on the isthmus continued to refer to it as Aspinwall for a good many years after the name was changed on official maps.

[23] The most vivid story of the horrifying mortality among the laborers is found in a contemporary account by journalist Robert Tomes, *Panama in 1855* (New York: Harper and Brothers, 1855), pp. 114-122.

A more lyrical, but no less grisly, account of the health hazards of the era is captured in an "old chant" or ballad, which has been preserved for posterity by Edwards (*Panama*, pp. 530-31):

"Close the door. Across the river
    He is gone.
With an abscess on his liver
    He is gone.

At a cost of nearly eight million dollars (for forty-seven miles of track) it was possibly the most expensive railroad ever built, but certainly one of the most profitable. By carrying goods and passengers part way it had earned approximately one-third of the cost before completion, and for about fifteen years after completion continued to show fabulous profits.[26] Present-day visitors from the States see only a kind of jungle Toonerville Trolley tootling back and forth with its nondescript commuters between Panama City and Colón, but there was a time when the P.R.R. was a force to be reckoned with. It ran steamships on the high seas, monopolized the world's most coveted transit route on land, negotiated with governments, held the key to canal building concessions, and kept the peace.[27] Mr. Anthony Sampson has recently written a book called "The Sovereign State of I.T.T." In the late nineteenth century a similar book might well have been named "The Sovereign State of P.R.R."

Later a combination of unfavorable developments—not the least of which being the last spike in the Union Pacific Railroad —brought the halcyon days to a close and the line fell into a sad state (described by one observer as "two streaks of rust") until revived by Ferdinand de Lesseps for his own purposes. Even at the lowest point of its fortunes as a physical object, however, it continued to hold certain vested legal rights (stemming from the concession of 1850, as amended) ranging from transcendently important to vexatious, and affording much employment to lawyers.

By the terms of Article II of the 1850 concession the Government of New Granada would have the right to purchase, in 1875, for $5,000,000, a railroad which had cost $8,000,000 to build. In 1867, while the Railroad was still at the height of prosperity and paying a dividend of 24 percent, this dread eventuality was forestalled by a renegotiation in Bogota which extended the franchise for ninety-nine years (from 1875, hence expiring in 1974) in exchange for a lump sum payment of $1,000,000 in gold and a promise of annual payments of $250,-000 (and some other considerations). Article II of the 1867 agreement modified the canal provision of Article VI of the 1850 concession by specifying the area of the Company's consensual power as that "west of the line of Cape Tiburón on the Atlantic and Point Garachine on the Pacific"; moreover, it stipulated that:

[T]he right which is conceded to the Company to give its consent does not extend to its opposing the construction of a canal across the Isthmus of Panama (except on the actual route of the railroad itself), but only to its exacting an equitable price for such privilege, . . .[28]

The legal histories of both (a) the French Era on the Isthmus and (b) the stormy railroad-canal marriage (or adoption, or whatever it was) can be dated from a single event: the so-called Wyse concession of 1878.[29] Lt. Lucien Napoleon-Bonaparte Wyse of the French Navy, an illegitimate son of a daughter of Napoleon's brother Lucien, was one of the directors of a private company, the Société Civile du Canal Interocéanique du Darien, which had undertaken a "definitive" exploration of canal routes. By traveling horseback across the Andes on the double, he managed to reach Bogota in time to get the agreement signed on March 20, 1878, just days before President Parra, whom Wyse knew to favor the canal project, was due to leave office.

---

[26] The first-class passenger fare at opening was set at $25.00 in gold in a deliberate attempt to discourage traffic until facilities were a little better organized. Would-be travelers were not dissuaded by this almost prohibitory tariff, however, so the railroad corporation saw no reason to lower it and it remained in effect for twenty years.
[27] "The impotent government of New Granada . . . has delegated full powers to the Company. Accordingly the Railroad officials have taken into their hands the [policing] of the Isthmus, and exercise it with no weak sway. An armed guard, to the number of forty, was enrolled, and placed under the command of Ran Runnels, the famous Texas ranger . . . With Runnels at their head they have cleared the Isthmus of robbers, and kept the thousands of unruly laborers in wholesome subjection . . . Whipping, imprisonment, and shooting down, in an emergency, have been liberally inflicted in the exercise of the powers delegated by the government of New Granada to the Company, which has the power of life and death on the Isthmus without appeal." Tomes, *Panama in 1855*, pp. 122-24.

[28] Same as footnote 16.
[29] Exhibit C: Concession of 1878 and extensions. Wyse Concession, March 20, 1878. Reproduced in Attorneys General Opinions, Vol. 24 (1903), pp. 337-54.

The contract gave the Wyse company an exclusive privilege to excavate a maritime canal across the territory of the Republic, together with the grant of a strip of land *200 meters wide* (emphasis supplied) on each side of the canal, and to operate it for ninety-nine years after completion. The canal was to be completed within twelve years after the "formation of the universal anonymous company which shall be organized to construct it." The contract of concession was transferable to another private company but in no case to a foreign government. Should the canal be located west of the Tiburón-Garachine line, the company was obligated to come to an amicable agreement with the P.R.R. and pay the latter a satisfactory indemnity.[30]

With the valuable concession in his pocket but lacking the necessary capital to act on it, Wyse promoted an international congress on the subject which met in Paris in May 1879 and in which twenty-three countries were represented. Almost the only sensible proposal made during the conclave, by a French engineer named Godin de Lepinay,[31] was ignored; and the following resolution, presented by De Lesseps, was adopted:

> The congress believes that the excavation of an interoceanic canal at sea level, so desirable in the interests of commerce and navigation, is feasible; and that, in order to take advantage of the indispensable facilities for access and opera-

tion which a channel of this kind must offer above all, this canal should extend from the Gulf of Limón to Panama Bay.[32]

On July 5, 1879 De Lesseps signed a provisional contract to buy the Wyse concession, dependent on the organization and financing within two years of a company to undertake the project. During the next twenty months he was extremely busy at the ultimately successful endeavor, much of his activity being aimed at allaying hostility in the United States. March 8, 1880 found him in Washington explaining his case before the House Interoceanic Ship Canal Committee. On the very same day President Hayes declared in a special message to the Senate:

> The policy of this country is a canal under American control. . . . No European power can intervene for [its] protection, without adopting measures on this continent which the United States would deem wholly inadmissible. If the protection of the United States is relied upon, the United States must exercise such control as will enable this country to protect its national interests. . . . An interoceanic canal . . . will essentially change the geographical relations between the Atlantic and Pacific coasts of the United States, and between the United States and the rest of the world. It will be . . . virtually a part of the coast line of the United States.[33]

With more optimism than objectivity, De Lesseps cabled his son Charles the next day:

> The message of President Hayes assures the political security of the canal.

On March 3, 1881, the *Compagnie Universelle du Canal Interocéanique* (afterwards known as the Old Panama Canal Company) was formally incorporated.[34]

As the route chosen by De Lesseps for his "sea level" canal lay west of the Tiburón-Garachine line, the *Compagnie Universelle* could not turn a shovelful of dirt without the "amicable agreement" of the P.R.R., which was obtained by the expedient of buying up nearly all its outstanding shares at the exorbitant price

---

[30] Art. 3 of the Wyse concession (cited in 24 Attorneys General Opinions 144 at p. 339).

[31] "De Lepinay urged the adoption of the Panama route but argued long and earnestly against the sea level project and in favor of a lock canal. He proposed to dam the Chagres near the Atlantic terminus and the Rio Grande close to the Pacific, thus creating an immense artificial lake about 80 feet above sea level. . . . His proposed system of locks, dams, and artificial lake comprised all of the essential elements of the design actually executed by the builders of the present Panama Canal, and it also formed the basis of the compromise plan accepted by the French company in 1887 in a last desperate effort to avert failure. Had it been adopted at the beginning in 1879 the canal might well have been completed by the French instead of by the United States Government." Gerstle Mack, *The Land Divided: A History of the Panama Canal and Other Isthmian Canal Projects* (New York: Alfred A. Knopf, 1944), p. 294. (Reprinted in New York in 1974 by Octagon Books.)

[32] Ibid., p. 295.

[33] Senate executive document 112, 46th Cong., 2d sess., pp. 1-2.

[34] Mack, *Land Divided*, chap. 26 *passim*.

demanded by the stockholders.[35] As hereinbefore noted, the change in ownership of the stock did not affect the legal status of the P.R.R., which remained an independent New York corporation with its own executives and directors and never completely subordinated its own interests to those of the "parent" French company. (Indeed, the *Compagnie Universelle* decided to build a completely new town—now called Cristóbal, Spanish for Christopher—for its Atlantic terminus, deeming Colón undesirable for the purpose because its site belonged to the P.R.R.)[36]

The struggles of the Old Panama Canal Company from 1881 to 1888 have been oft told and the period can be passed over here except for brief mention of three topics bearing on the continuity of the overall theme.

(a) The civil war which broke out on the Isthmus (as well as in the rest of Colombia) in 1885 led to one of the major United States military interventions (an actual occupation that lasted several weeks) carried out under the auspices of the Treaty of 1846. The legal justification was that right of transit had been "interrupted" by depredations on the property of the Railroad (committed by "rebels") and the government in Bogota, far from complaining, was in fact the principal beneficiary thereof. The same year, with the insurrection suppressed, the semi-autonomy that Panama (and the eight other states) had enjoyed was abolished by the new unitary government.[37]

(b) This event might well, it seems, have caused some uneasiness to the stockholders and backers of the French company if they were alert to its full meaning. It illustrated the harsh fact that their canal concession, even with its 200 meters on each side, lay in the midst of a territory whose security depended in the end on the Government of the United States, which Government was more concerned with the New York Railroad than with the French canal, and, moreover, was still making plans for its own

canal through Nicaragua and hence could hardly have much enthusiasm for the French competitor.

(c) The French company provided no commissaries for its employees who were thus forced to live completely on the local economy, often paying excessive prices for the limited selection of foodstuffs and other goods available.[38]

By 1888 the *Compagnie Universelle* was so bogged down in mud, financial scandals, and pessimistic prognostications that it could not raise the money to keep going. In February 1889 it was placed in charge of a liquidator by the civil tribunal of the Department of the Seine, and work was finally suspended in May.

The twelve years allowed by the Wyse concession for completion of the canal would expire on March 3, 1893, and it was now evident that the deadline would not be met. In this critical situation, Wyse, who had been virtually excluded from participation while the project was rolling, was recalled to active duty. On December 10, 1890, he signed a new agreement, with Colombian Foreign Minister Antonio Roldán, granting an extension of ten years on condition that a successor company should be organized and working not later than February 28, 1893. The liquidator promised to pay Colombia 10,000,000 francs, and some other considerations, perhaps the most interesting of which was a contribution of 40,000 francs per month "to the maintenance of a garrison of 250 Colombian soldiers to protect the canal

---

[35] The French directors paid $250 a share for 68,887 shares, of 70,000 outstanding (see note 15, supra). Only two years before the Railroad had offered the shares to Wyse at $200, but Wyse lacked authority at the time to sign a contract.

[36] Mack, *Land Divided*, pp. 315, 322.

[37] See chap. III, p. 17.

[38] The first commissary was established on the isthmus in 1894 by the P.R.R. to supply groceries to the heads of its departments only. In 1896 commissary privileges were extended to all employees of the railroad, all steamship lines, warships of any nationality, diplomatic and consular officers living on the isthmus, and officials of the French canal company. When the United States Government bought the Railroad in 1904, it also acquired the commissary, which was rapidly expanded to provide for the hordes of new workers. Ever since, the commissary system has been an irritant in relations with Panama whose merchants feel that they have been deprived of much of the benefit they expected from the building of the canal.* The elimination or drastic reduction of commissary activities and their replacement by Panamanian enterprises is one of the points which Panama insists should be included in any new treaty.

* Edwards, *Panama*, pp. 566-67.

line." [39] If the new company failed to comply with the terms of the extension, the canal and all its appurtenances would revert to Colombia without compensation.

The task of forming a new company was enormously complicated by continuing reverberations from the collapse of the old company, which had shaken French investors like nothing since the Mississippi Bubble, and the time allowed by the Wyse-Roldán agreement proved too short. In another cliffhanger, the agent of the liquidator in Panama was sent off to Bogota where he signed, on April 4, 1893, a supplementary prolongation which allowed until October 31, 1894 for incorporation of the new company with the ten-year period to run from that date. Other provisions, notably the reversionary clause, remained the same.

(While a bit tedious, the above explanation is necessary to an understanding of the significance which the date October 31, 1904 later assumed in the eyes of the Colombian Government during the treaty negotiations of 1901-3.)

The *Compagnie Nouvelle du Canal de Panama* (afterwards known as the New Panama Canal Company) was incorporated on October 20, 1894, eleven days before the expiration of the prolongation. During its ten-year life construction was resumed on a small scale, 11,400,000 cubic yards of dirt were excavated, and the equipment was preserved. By 1898, however, the directors no longer had any hope of success and began turning their primary attention to salvaging what they could by sale of the canal. It was evident that the canal would never be built with anything less than the resources and commitment of a national government, and the only government that could be convincingly envisaged in the role was that of the United States (by coincidence having just acquired from Spain new reasons for being interested in a canal).[40]

Principal obstacles to such a sale, not necessarily in order of magnitude, were: (a) disagreement over the value of what the French company had to sell, (b) the Clayton-Bulwer Treaty, (c) restrictions on alienation in the Wyse concession, as prolonged, and (d) the predilection of the United States for a Nicaraguan canal.

All these obstacles were eventually overcome, and more or less subsumed as it were, in a new game of international law and diplomacy beginning about 1898 and involving four sovereigns in shifting and sometimes overlapping adversarial relationships. Loosely, but tenably, the game might be said to have played itself out in four phases as the spotlight moved from one relationship to another: first on that between the United States and Great Britain, then between the United States and Colombia, then between Colombia and Panama; and finally, as Colombia accepted the *fait accompli* of Panamanian independence and Panama refused to accept that of the Hay/Bunau-Varilla Treaty, the continuing conflict between the United States and Panama.[41]

That the game took the course it actually did was owing largely to the skill and ruthlessness in the crucial years between 1898 and 1904 of two remarkable men, who worked separately toward the same goal and could hardly stand the sight of each other, the French engineer Philippe Bunau-Varilla and the American lawyer William Nelson Cromwell (both of whom we shall meet later).

---

[39] Mack, *Land Divided*, p. 375. An assertion of sovereignty? An attempt to prevent any justification for another United States intervention under the Treaty of 1846?

[40] The connection between the Spanish-American War and the future of the isthmus did not escape the notice of perceptive Colombians. Dr. Uribe, writing in August 1899, remarked prophetically: "The negotiations between the English and North American diplomats con-

cerning the abrogation of the Clayton-Bulwer Treaty, the sole guaranty of our sovereignty in the Isthmus of Panama, and, in general, the tendencies of the imperialist party in the United States, now in charge of the Government, justifies the fears which we manifested at the beginning of the Spanish-American War, in the sense that, after Spain, those principally threatened will be ourselves, because of the exceptional situation of our territory." Antonio José Uribe, *Colombia y los Estados Unidos* (Bogota: 1931), p. xxvii.

[41] From the Panama Revolution of November 1903 to the perfection of the Thomson-Urrutia Treaty in March 1922 (wherein Colombia settled its quarrel with the United States and recognized Panama as an independent nation) there was an untidy overlapping of the last three phases. Since March 1922 the fourth phase has had a clear field.

There can be little doubt that had it not been for the activities of [these] men the Nicaragua canal would be in operation today while the abandoned excavations at Panama would represent only a melancholy monument to failure . . .[42]

The first fruit of the new diplomatic game period, corresponding to the above-mentioned first phase, was the proclamation on February 22, 1902 of the second Hay-Pauncefote Treaty. By this convention, which explicitly superseded the Clayton-Bulwer Treaty, Great Britain effectively withdrew all restrictions on complete control by the United States of any canal it might build.[43]

The second fruit (which, as it turned out, never ripened) was the Hay-Herrán Treaty signed on January 22, 1903 by John Hay, the Secretary of State who conducted all the canal negotiations of this period, and Tomás Herrán,[44] the Colombian *chargé d'affaires* in Washington. As a matter of Realpolitik, the abortive Hay-Herrán Treaty, which dominated the above-mentioned second phase, is important only because its rejection by the Colombian Senate provided the essential impetus for the Panamanian Revolution and the corollary Hay/Bunau-Varilla Treaty. As a matter bearing on the legal history of the Canal Zone, however, it is important per se as a link in the continuum of juridical questions underlying United States presence and exclusive administration of justice.

The conditions precedent for the negotiation of an agreement to take over the French canal were satisfied by the diplomatic and legislative ground-clearing operations of the Hay-Pauncefote Treaty and the Spooner Act.

It is, of course, axiomatic in international law that a treaty cannot be made which contravenes an existing treaty, and this obstacle was removed by the Hay-Pauncefote Treaty. (Whether or not the Treaty of 1846 with New Granda constituted an obstacle to the Hay/Bunau-Varilla Treaty of 1903 is another matter, which will rear its ugly head in due course.)

The passage of the Spooner Act of June 28, 1902 [45] was more complicated; involving, as it did, all the other three—(a), (c), and (d)—of the obstacles adduced above. Though plenty of hazards and pitfalls still lay ahead, the Spooner Act was the turning point in "the fight for the Panama route," [46] not only because it provided the legislative authority, but also, and perhaps more importantly, because it epitomized the shift in presidential policy and public opinion which Cromwell [47] and Bunau-Varilla had worked so hard to bring about.

The Spooner bill authorized the President to proceed with the construction of a canal through Panama provided he could obtain from the New Panama Canal Company a satisfactory title to all its assets (including the concession and the Railroad stock) for not exceeding $40,000,000 and from the Republic of Colombia "perpetual"

---

[42] Mack, *Land Divided*, p. 417.

[43] The first Hay-Pauncefote Treaty in 1900 was rejected by the Senate, largely because it prohibited the erection of fortifications.

[44] Herrán was the son of Pedro Alcántara Herrán who had negotiated for New Granada the ratification of the Treaty of 1846. Though a graduate of Georgetown University and *simpático* toward the United States, there is no reason to doubt that he represented Colombian interests, and he was a skilled diplomatist, with complete loyalty. He found himself locked in, however, by commitments already made by his predecessors, as well as by governmental instability at home, and the most he could do was obtain an increase in the monetary compensation to Colombia. Actually he had almost nothing to do with the writing of the treaty which bears his name.

[45] Sometimes called the Spooner Amendment. Technically, it was an amendment to the Hepburn bill which would have authorized the construction of a canal through Nicaragua. Though bearing the name of Senator Spooner, it was pushed through Congress by the power of Senator Marc Hanna of Ohio, whose conversion to the Panama route was claimed by both Cromwell and Bunau-Varilla.

[46] The book of that title by Miner (see note 11, supra) provides the best account of this phase of Canal history.

[47] Cromwell, who had been general counsel (as well as a stockholder and director) of the P.R.R. since 1893, was employed for the concurrent representation of the New Panama Canal Company in 1896. Though his efforts ultimately benefited both entities, the primary beneficiary was himself, as stockholder and as claimant of enormous legal fees. His hand was everywhere, even at times composing cables for the Colombian emissaries to send to their own government. Bunau-Varilla, equally skilled as a manipulator in his own way, had no authority at all to represent the Company and also represented primarily himself, though partly from idealistic commitment to a cause.

control of a strip of land not less than six miles wide; if these conditions could not be secured within a "reasonable" time, he was to go back to the original plan of a canal through Nicaragua.

Obstacle (a) had been overcome when the Canal company directors suddenly reduced their asking price (under pressure from Cromwell and Bunau-Varilla). Obstacle (d) had been overcome by the "lobbying" of Cromwell and Bunau-Varilla and their converts.[48] Obstacle (c) was removed, in a manner of speaking, by a piece of consummate legal trickery on the part of Cromwell, which the Government of Colombia (GOC) ultimately refused to swallow and which played a part in the rejection of the Hay-Herrán Treaty.

The Wyse concession, by its own terms, could be alienated to another private company but not to a government. Hence, the sale by the New Panama Canal Company of its assets to the Government of the United States (GOUS) could not be legally consummated without the consent of the GOC through a new convention. The GOC contended that, in addition to payment for the grant of a six-mile strip of land (as stipulated in the Spooner Act), it was also entitled to exact a price (to come out of the $40,000,000) for waiver of the bar against alienation to a government. The GOC argued, not without logic, that this was a valuable property right, without which the New Company's assets were worthless. On the other hand, if the waiver could not be obtained within a "reasonable" time, the GOUS would go to Nicaragua (is required by the Spooner Act) and the property right of the GOC would be as valueless as the New Company's assets.

As a matter of simple justice, it would seem that Colombia was entitled to a share of the $40,000,000, much of the consideration for which, be it remembered, lay in the concession which would expire on October 31, 1904.[49] If the negotiations could be

protracted inconclusively until that date, the New Company would have nothing to sell and the GOC might reasonably ask for all of it. But Cromwell, who was determined not to share, was busily ensuring (in Article I) that the Hay-Herrán Treaty would commit Colombia to the waiver without promise of indemnity and without further delay.[50] Faced with an ultimatum from Hay on January 21, 1903, Herrán signed on January 22 at Hay's residence.[51] The only other person present was Cromwell.

The inadequacy of monetary compensation, from the Colombian point of view, was a factor in arousing opposition to ratification, but not the major factor. Though the Roosevelt administration, ably abetted by the orchestrated propaganda of Cromwell, professed to see no motive nobler than greed, unbiased historians have concluded that infringement of sovereignty weighed more heavily in the decision of the Colombian solons.[52] The specific infringements

---

[48] "The significant point is that the Panama route was not adopted because of its obvious merits as a canal site. The energy and resourcefulness of a few men served to reverse the 'deliberate judgment' of both houses of Congress in the face of an overwhelming partiality for Nicaragua. . . . the Spooner Act of June 28, 1902, deserves to rank with the masterpieces of the lobbyists art." Miner, *Fight*, p. 75.

[49] Another extension had been granted in

April 1900 which would have advanced the expiration date to October 31, 1910. The constitutionality of this grant, made by presidential decree in the midst of a civil war without the consent of Congress, was seriously questioned, however. While the ratification of the Hay-Herrán Treaty was under consideration by the Colombian Senate in 1903, there can be little doubt that the senators expected the property of the New Panama Canal Company to revert to Colombia on October 31, 1904.

[50] President Marroquín considered Article I, as well as other articles, subject to revision during the ratification process even if the treaty were signed. Cromwell correctly calculated that refusal of the Colombian Senate to approve the treaty verbatim could be sold to American public opinion as a double-cross.

[51] Three days later Herrán received a cable from President Marroquín ordering him not to sign the treaty, but to await new instructions. "There is no record that Herrán ever informed Hay of the contents of Marroquín's cable." Miner, *Fight*, p. 200.

[52] "Of [the objections to the treaty], the sovereignty question was by far the most skilfully presented. Colombia, as a weak nation forced to rely to the full on such protection as international law afforded, had produced a distinguished group of scholars in that field, many of whom were actively engaged in the discussions of those months. Consequently, the Bogotan who kept abreast of the news was likely to be much better informed on such theoretical matters as the 'attributes of sovereignty' than his contemporary in New York or Chicago. . . . [The] concept of 'sovereignty' was endowed

which seemed most galling, and also happen to be the ones most pertinent to the continuum of juridical questions carried over into the Hay/Bunau-Varilla Treaty, were those concerning (a) perpetuity, and (b) the court system in the strip.

(a) Colombian lawyers believed that the "perpetual control" demanded by the Spooner Act would amount to an alienation of part of the national territory and thus would violate the constitution which nowhere granted any such power to either the executive or the legislature.[53] Hay was sufficiently impressed by this point to attempt to work out an accommodation. The treaty, therefore, (Article III) did not use the word "perpetual" but spoke of "a term of one hundred years, renewable at the sole and absolute option of the United States, for periods of similar duration so long as the United States may desire, . . ." Colombian lawyers, understandably, found this wording a distinction without a difference.

(b) Article XIII created a three-tier system of courts for the administration of justice within the concession area.

The first would be Colombian, with jurisdiction over all cases between citizens of Colombia or between citizens of Colombia and those of foreign countries other than the United States. The second type would consist of United States courts, with jurisdiction over suits between United States citizens or between citizens of that nation and foreigners other than Colombians. These latter courts would dispense justice according to the laws of the United States "without diminution of the general sovereignty of Colombia over the said zone." They would also have jurisdiction over "all controversies growing out of or related to the construction, maintenance, or operation of the canal, railroad, and other properties and works." Finally, a series of mixed tribunals, whose

members would be appointed by the two nations, would be instituted to handle cases arising between citizens of the United States and Colombia or between citizens of countries other than the treaty powers. These courts would also administer criminal and maritime law within the zone in accordance with such codes as the two governments should draw up.[54]

The propositions of perpetual control and separate courts not under Colombian law represented a drastic departure from all previous protocols regulating the activities of foreign enterprises, governmental or private, in the Isthmus.[55] The Railroad and the French canal had seemed to get along without them.

The dilemma in which Colombia saw itself over the Hay-Herrán Treaty—to ratify and accept the loss of sovereignty and national honor, or not ratify and possibly lose the Isthmus entirely—was not made any easier by the inflexible insistence of the State Department that Colombia, because its representative had signed the treaty, was therefore bound to ratify it without amendment and without delay.[56] The absurdity

with particularly deep significance. It represented the Colombian people's moral right of dominion over their historic territory, regardless of their ability to maintain constant control. It was the chief symbol of national permanence and unity in a land of disorderly change." Ibid., p. 256.

[53] "[As the newspaper El Colombiano pointed out], Article 3 of the constitution fixed the national boundaries and made no provision for altering them except by the regular process of amendment. The basic charter, it continued, is not amended by means of public treaties, since these are subject to its terms." Ibid., p. 260.

[54] Ibid., pp. 160-61.

[55] "This radical change of aims on the part of the United States set Colombian publicists on the alert, and had far more influence in the rejection of the Treaty than the inadequateness of the compensation offered, notwithstanding that it was notoriously small." Ministry of Foreign Affairs, Protest of Colombia against the Treaty between Panama and the United States (London: Wertheimer, Lea & Co., 1904).

[56] Any wavering doubt that Roosevelt might have had as to the divine rightness of this position appears to have been dissipated by the John Basset Moore memorandum of August 1903 * in which Moore went so far as to argue that the Treaty of 1846—because it guaranteed the United States a right of transit over any present or future mode of communication—authorized the United States to take over and finish the French canal even without the Hay-Herrán Treaty. As Miner and other historians have suggested, if Roosevelt had been a little less impetuous and less disdainful of international law, there is a good chance that the Hay-Herrán Treaty would eventually have been ratified in some acceptable form and an enormous amount of Latin ill-will against the "colossus of the north" avoided. The constitutional impediment could have been removed by amendment, as was done in Nicaragua and Costa Rica. It also seems that a project which

* Miner, Fight, appendix D.

of that interpretation of international law needs no demonstration.

Though publicists in the rest of the country were nearly unanimous in their condemnation of the treaty, there is no gainsaying that sentiment of Colombian lawyers in the Department of Panama was just the opposite. Perhaps this is a small point in support of the Marxist tenet of the economic interpretation of history. Perhaps, too, it gives aid and comfort to cynics who say that the only purpose of studying international law is to be able to make a legal case for actions which would be taken anyway out of self-interest. Be that as it may, Isthmian lawyers, no less than Isthmian merchants, could see how bleak the future with no canal, and the vision inspired scholarly briefs in favor of ratification.[57]

Probably the best, as well as the most extreme, pro-treaty exposition was that of Dr. Pablo Arosemena published in June of 1903.[58] Though holding a doctorate of law from the National University in Bogota and a former minister of the Bogota government, Arosemena was a native of the Isthmus and, like others, had come to think of himself as an Isthmian first and a Colombian second.[59] He conceded that Articles III and XIII of the treaty diminished the sovereignty of Colombia in the immediately affected territory,[60] but belittled the extent of the diminution (adding that it was already diminished anyway by the Treaty of 1846) and maintained that it was offset by United States guarantees to protect the sovereignty of the Isthmus as a whole. In any case, he said, the treaty should be judged by the larger standards of international comity and world needs, which take precedence over Colombia's parochial claims of "sovereignty," rather than in the "Procrustean bed of the civil code."[61] With regard to the allegation of inadequate monetary compensation, he said that, on the contrary, the economic benefits to the nation of having the canal would be so great that Colombia, if its financial condition permitted, should pay the United States for building it there.[62]

(Alas, what a difference a revolution makes. The same statesmen who in 1903 could take such an ecumenical view of the attributes of national sovereignty, when it belonged to Colombia, in 1904 suddenly discovered that the same sovereignty, now belonging to Panama, was much more important than they had previously thought. Their sons and grandsons have not wavered from the truth of that revelation.)

The epochal Congress which convened in Bogota in June 1903 was newly elected after a campaign in which the treaty was the major issue. There is no reason to doubt that it was reasonably representative of the public will on the question. Even the American envoy, who was counting on the "dictator" to ram the treaty through, had written in a dispatch on April 15: "This fact is clear, that if the proposed convention were to be submitted to the free opinion of the people it would not pass."[63] On October 30 the Senate voted unanimously to suspend any further consideration of the treaty, and on October 31 the Congress

---

had waited centuries to be started and would take many years to finish could have been delayed a few more months to let the New Canal Company concession die and the financial benefits thereof go to Colombia.

[57] A more corporeal source of inspiration was Cromwell who, alarmed by the anti-treaty statements of some prominent Isthmians such as Pérez y Soto, was using all his influence to produce articles and petitions favoring ratification. Several of the inspired writers, including Arosemena (see note 58, infra), were attorneys in the employ of the Railroad.

[58] Pablo Arosemena, *La Causa Inmediata de la Emancipación de Panamá* (Panamá: Imprenta Nacional, 1933) p. 151 et seq.

[59] He did not approve of the secession movement but after independence was proclaimed he took an active part in the political life of the new Republic, and was the president of the constituent convention which drew up the first constitution of Panama.

[60] "Como este escrito es un trabajo de buena fe, comienzo declarando honradamente que las cláusulas III y XIII del Tratado Herrán-Hay, si merman la soberanía de la República sobre la zona de terreno que se determina en el artículo III." *Estudio Jurídico* . . . Arosemena, *Causa Inmediata*, p. 151.

[61] "No juzgo admirable que se coloque este pacto en el lecho de procusto del Código Civil." *Estudio Jurídico* . . . Ibid., p. 154.

[62] "*La Estrella de Panamá*, the newspaper which published Arosemena's essay, was the principal organ of the pro-treaty forces. It was owned and edited by José Gabriel Duque, a native of Cuba and a naturalized citizen of the United States, whose son was in business in the Colombian capital with the son of former [United States] Minister Hart." Miner, *Fight*, p. 291. *La Estrella* is still owned by the Duque family.

[63] Ibid., p. 251.

adjourned. Five days later word arrived that the Department of Panama had declared its independence.

The circumstances of the secession and almost simultaneous consummation of the Hay/Bunau-Varilla Treaty have been amply chronicled and need not be retold, even in summary, except insofar as essential to following the threads of legal controversy over the legitimacy of the Canal Zone.

Despite Roosevelt's famous boast that "I took the isthmus" made in a speech at Berkeley, California on March 23, 1911,[64]

___

[64] Although this phrase, with its surrounding context, is one of the most often quoted (and misquoted) passages from a speech in all of American political history, there is a mystery about it which will probably never be solved. The crucial phrase has been variously quoted as "I took the isthmus," "I took the Canal Zone," and "I took Panama"; and there are many different versions in print of the surrounding wordage.

As reported by the *San Francisco Examiner* of March 24, 1911, Roosevelt said:

. . . if I had followed the traditional . . . method I should have submitted an admirable state paper . . . detailing all the facts to Congress . . . In that case there would have been a number of excellent speeches . . . in Congress; the debate would be proceeding at this moment with great spirit and the beginning of work on the canal would be fifty years in the future. Fortunately the crisis came at a period when I could act unhampered. Accordingly I took the isthmus, started the canal and then left Congress not to debate the canal, but to debate me.

As reported by the *New York Times* of March 24, 1911 (in an inconspicuous spot on page 1 at the bottom of column 6), Roosevelt said:

I am interested in the Panama Canal because I started it. If I had followed traditional, conservative methods I would have submitted a dignified state paper of probably 200 pages to Congress and the debate on it would have been going on yet; but I took the Canal Zone and let Congress debate; and while the debate goes on the Canal does also.

On its editorial page of March 25, 1911 the *Times* repeated the above words and called it a "belated confession" of a most perfidious action.

Down through the years since 1911 the quotations and misquotations have poured from the presses, and doubtless will continue to do so. *TIME* magazine of August 23, 1976 (p. 18) quoted Roosevelt as saying: "I took the Canal Zone." Richard Hudson (identified as "a writer

the type of zone in which the United States could act as "if it were the sovereign" was the unanticipated prize of a Revolution for which he was not solely responsible. Granted it would not have succeeded at that time, or even been attempted, without assurances of his benevolent and protective gunboat "neutrality," the Revolution, in the long view, was the final success of a genu-

___

who specializes in international affairs"), in the *New York Times Magazine* of May 16, 1976 (p. 18) quoted Roosevelt as saying: I took Panama. He was only following one of the versions which has been used by innumerable others before him. One of the best known congressional documents dealing with the Panama Canal (see bibliography, *The Story of Panama*) resulted from the Rainey resolution which commences:

Whereas a former President of the United States [Theodore Roosevelt] has declared that he "took" Panama. . . .

In our search for truth, the next item to be considered is the original typewritten draft of the speech in the Theodore Roosevelt Papers (microfilm), Library of Congress (reel 421) which reads:

Naturally the crisis came when I could begin the work unhampered. I took a trip to the Isthmus, started the canal and then left Congress not to debate the canal, but to debate me and in portions of the public press the debate still goes on as to whether I acted properly in getting the canal, but while the debate goes on the Canal does too and they are welcome to debate me as long as they wish, provided that we can go on with the canal now.

Theodore Roosevelt scholars at the Library of Congress tell me that Roosevelt when delivering his speeches often departed from the prepared text. In this case I think it is obvious that he did so, because, for one reason, the text as written is nonsensical. To say "I took a trip to the Isthmus" is quite a long way from saying "I took the Isthmus"; but in any case it is a known historical fact that he did not take a trip to the Isthmus, and start the canal, in that order. His first trip to the Isthmus was in November 1906, long after the canal was started.

As there is no audio recording of his speech, there would appear to be no way of proving what he actually said. It is my personal opinion that the *San Francisco Examiner's* version is the correct one. I will not take the space to give all my reasons, but, for one thing, there was no "Canal Zone" at the time of the "taking"; whereas the word "isthmus" had been applied to the area concerned for centuries.

ine, deep-rooted Panamanian separatist movement.[65] In the short view, the fact that it actually came off, exactly when and how it did, (as well as the generosity of the prize) owes more to Philippe Bunau-Varilla than to any other one person.[66]

While the separatist movement was genuine and indigenous enough, the community of its cause with that of the Panama Railroad had more than a little to do with the momentum it developed after the Hay-Herrán Treaty started to founder. The acknowledged earliest leader of the revolutionary conspiracy, in the spring of 1903, was another Railroad attorney, José Agustín Arango.[67] The original junta consisted of

himself,[68] his three sons, his three sons-in-law, and C. C. Arosemena.[69] The group soon came to include a few others, one being Dr. Manuel Amador Guerrero, the Railroad medical officer. The Governor of the State of Panama, José de Obaldía, an avowed separatist, was living in the Amador household at the time, but apparently was not privy to the revolutionary meetings held there.

By July a slightly reorganized junta had gained enough confidence to hold relatively open meetings at which revolution and the creation of an independent republic under the protection of the United States were discussed. A guest at one of these meetings was Hezekiah A. Gudger, United States Consul-General in Panama (later to be a Chief Justice of the Supreme Court of the Canal Zone).

In late August of 1903, by which time it was obvious that Colombia was not going to ratify the Hay-Herrán Treaty, Dr. Amador was sent by the junta to Washington to sound out the Roosevelt administration on the chances of securing at least tacit support for Panamanian secession. Unable to see either Roosevelt or Hay, Amador had several conversations with Cromwell and was beginning to feel encouraged until suddenly Cromwell refused to see him any more.[70] He was about to leave the country empty handed when he ran into his old friend Bunau-Varilla who had just arrived from France. It has never been proved that Cromwell arranged for a change of handholders; but it is a fact that Bunau-Varilla, having no official connection with anything, was invulnerable to Herrán's threats.

The last chief engineer on the French canal (the first three having died with their boots on), Bunau-Varilla had devoted his life ever since the collapse to a crusade for

---

[65] Panamanian separatism is of truly ancient origin, beginning with the establishment of the first *audiencia* (see chap. III, note 31) of Panama in 1535. Abolished by the New Laws of 1542, placing Panama under the vice-royalty of Peru, the *audiencia* was re-established in Panama in 1563-64. Abolished once again in 1718, it was soon restored in 1721, retaining its separate existence until placed under the government at Santa Fe de Bogotá in 1751. In 1774 a new *audiencia* was established at Panama City, nominally under the vice-royalty of Santa Fe. During the Wars of Liberation against Spain, Panama won its independence (proclaimed on November 28, 1821) entirely by its own efforts, then voluntarily chose to unite itself with Bolívar's new state of Gran Colombia (which action was soon and often regretted). It was apparently this episode to which Hay referred (p. 46, infra) when he justified precipitous recognition on the ground that the people of Panama had only "resumed their independence." The Colombian Minister of Foreign Affairs made a strong case, however, that there was never actually any break in Panamanian allegiance to Bogota.[*] However that may be, there were certainly several periods, totaling many years, between 1821 and 1903 when the ties connecting the Isthmus of Panama to Colombia were gossamer thin. During all this time, too, the isthmus was utterly inaccessible from the "mainland" of Colombia except by sea.

[66] "One of Panama's leading historians has called Bunau-Varilla the most important personage in Panama's history during the early part of the twentieth century. Yet he hastens to add that he is now roundly and understandably hated by all Panamanians." Mellander, *United States in Panamanian Politics*, p. 44.

[67] And still another will show up later as the highest authority of the Bench and Bar at the beginning of the Common Law reception. (See chap. VI, p. 84, infra.)

[*] Protest of Colombia, (note 55, supra), p. 3.

---

[68] According to press reports, the absurd statements about the Panama Canal Zone with which Ronald Reagan made political hay in the presidential primaries were inspired by one Philip Harman, a California businessman who claims to be the "grandson-in-law of the founder of the Republic of Panama." The factual basis of Harman's claim is that he is married to the granddaughter of José Agustín Arango.

[69] Miner, *Fight*, p. 337.

[70] Herrán, who had been tipped off about the revolutionary plotting, warned Cromwell that if he had anything to do with it the Railroad concession would be canceled. Discretion was indicated.

completion of the project. His motives were a mixture of (a) financial self-interest —holdings of canal and Railroad stock plus fees for services—and (b) a determination to vindicate his professional judgment as an engineer and to rescue the honor of France. Notably absent from the mixture was any concern for Panama, on whose soil he had not set foot for several years.[71]

Bunau-Varilla was a close friend of Undersecretary of State Francis B. Loomis and other influential Washingtonians.

[B]y a series of suspicious, although reputedly accidental, meetings with high United States Government officials (including President Roosevelt and Secretary Hay) and by stint of his own dynamism and determination, Bunau-Varilla was able to guarantee Dr. Amador that the United States would permit a revolutionary uprising to succeed in Panama. This was to be accomplished by preventing Colombian reinforcements from landing and by precipitous recognition of the new republic. Events show this is [almost] exactly what happened.[72]

On November 3, 1903, a few days after Amador's return to Panama, the Revolution came off according to Bunau-Varilla's scenario, though owing much also to the courage and decisiveness of Amador and his wife. With the U.S.S. Nashville standing by in the harbor, the Colombian troops which had landed in Colon were prevented by Panama Railroad officials—with the backing of the United States military— from crossing the Isthmus (while the garrison already stationed in Panama City under General Huertas was neutralized by other means, mainly bribery).

Though a number of other factors were important, and it was a close thing whether

they would all mesh, the key to the whole undertaking was precisely this suppression of any military movement along the line of the railroad. It was the last in a series of interventions covering more than half a century pursuant to the Treaty of 1846, and the first to be denounced by Colombia as a violation thereof.[73] Though executed with tongue-in-cheek impartiality—that is, applied equally to the battle-ready government forces and the non-existent revolutionary soldiers—the transparent effect was not to "guarantee the rights of sovereignty and property which [Colombia] has and possesses over the said territory"[74] but to guarantee the loss of those rights. The best reply the United States Government was able to make to the Colombian complaints was the rather weak contention that the Treaty of 1846 guaranteed the protection of Colombian sovereignty in the Isthmus against external, but not against internal, threats. It is true that the Attorney General gave an opinion in 1865 that Article XXXV did not oblige this Government to protect the Isthmus of Panama, on behalf of the central government at Bogota, against internal insurgency[75] (although it did so, in effect, several times for the primary purpose of keeping transit open). What happened in 1903, however, went beyond simply refusing to help, and amounted to preventing the central government from acting in its own behalf.

While Roosevelt's long arm held off the Colombian armed forces (to that extent justifying his boast), the separatist Revolution was started and finished in one day and

[71] Incredible as it may seem, he explained to Amador that what he wanted was for only the strip of territory comprising the canal area to declare its independence with the rest of the isthmus remaining loyal to Colombia.* The mind boggles at contemplation of what kind of international law entity this would have created, especially after the independent strip transferred all its sovereign powers to the United States. Despite their dependence on Bunau-Varilla, this was one suggestion the revolutionaries refused to accept.

[72] Ibid., pp. 15-16.

* Mellander, *United States in Panamanian Politics*, p. 20.

[73] All the previous interventions had consisted of putting down rebellious activities or sometimes simply banditry, which were interfering with transit, and the effect had been to shore up the precarious hold of the Bogota Government on the wayward province. True, there had been one disturbing experience during the bitter civil war raging in the isthmus in 1902. On one occasion in that year United States authorities had forced Colombian federal troops to disarm before being transported on the railroad. Colombian legalists rightly saw in this action a dangerous precedent, but did not press the point to a crisis because they ruefully recognized that the rebel Liberals would probably have won control of the isthmus had not the United States taken even harsher measures against them.

[74] Treaty of 1846, article XXXV.

[75] 11 Attorneys General Opinions 391.

was virtually bloodless.[76] The "governing" body which proclaimed the independence of the "Republic of the Isthmus" [77] at about 6 p.m. on November 3 was a Provisional Junta composed of José Agustín Arango, Federico Boyd, and Tomás Arias. It seems that the first official act of the Junta, within minutes, was to send a written assurance to the superintendent of the Panama Railroad that the new government would guarantee its contractual obligations (concession agreement) therewith and protect the Railroad property.[78]

---

[76] The only casualty was a Chinese noncombatant killed at his dinner table in Panama City, victim of a shell lobbed in by the Panamanian gunboat, Bogota. So far as I know, no monument has ever been erected to Mr. Wong Kong Yee who never knew what hit him, much less why.

[77] The name suggested by Bunau-Varilla. It was not entirely original with him, however. In 1841, during one of the many revolts against the government at Bogota, the territory formally seceded and a constitution was drawn up by Colonel Tomás Herrera which provided that Panama and Veragua should become the "sovereign state of the Isthmus."

[78] Mellander, *United States in Panamanian Politics*, p. 27. On the one hand, the action can be viewed as a confession of the new government's subservience to its plutocratic midwife. On the other hand, it can be cited as evidence of willingness to assume the legal responsibilities of a successor state in accordance with the norms of international law. The latter motivation is not completely convincing, however. At the transfer of sovereignty over the Philippine Islands from Spain to the United States, the Manila Railway Company, Ltd., incorporated in Great Britain, was the holder of a railway concession from the Government of Spain. When the company contended that the United States was bound to respond to the obligations of the Spanish Government under the concession, the Attorney General of the United States replied that a concession was in fact a contract, not a servitude, and he denied that the contract obligations of ceding sovereigns pass to cessionaries.* In arriving at this decision he accepted the argument of the same Magoon, then law officer of the Bureau of Insular Affairs, who was to become governor of the Canal Zone and minister to Panama in 1905 (see chap. II, note 4, supra). While Panama was not, strictly speaking, a cessionary, the analogy would seem to be pretty close.

* Ernst H. Feilchenfeld, *Public Debts and State Succession* (New York: The Macmillan Company, 1931), pp. 344-45.

Later in the evening the Panama City Municipal Council, the first legislative body to consider the change in status of the territory, met for ten minutes and agreed to (a) send a telegram to President Roosevelt declaring the Council's support for the separatist movement and requesting United States recognition, and (b) call an open meeting (*Cabildo Abierto*) for the following afternoon at the Presidential Palace to discuss the matter. On November 4 the *Cabildo Abierto* approved the separation without dissent, but hooted down Bunau-Varilla's suggested name for the new country and decided instead to call it the "Republic of Panama." [79]

The Council then, in what amounted to the Republic of Panama's first election, sanctioned the three-man Junta as the Provisional Government "and granted it, in the name of all the municipal councils of the Isthmus, the enabling powers to execute normal government functions. The triumvirate's tenure was to last until the creation of a constitutional republic." [80] The Junta promptly notified Hay by cable that the "Republic of Panama" had been created and requested recognition. Colombian troops were still in possession of Colón at the time but embarked for Cartagena the next day on a Royal Mail steamer, their commanding officer the richer by $8,000 in gold (supplied by Bunau-Varilla) and two cases of champagne.[81]

On November 6 the diplomatic die was cast in the form of three cables. The first, from the Junta to Hay, read:

> Colon and all the towns of the Isthmus have adhered to the declaration of independence proclaimed in this city. The authority of the Republic of Panama is obeyed throughout its territory.
> Arango
> Arias
> Boyd.

The second, from the U. S. Consul General to Hay:

> The situation is peaceful. Isthmian movement has obtained so far success. Colon and interior provinces have enthusiastically joined independence . . . Bunau Varilla has been appointed officially con-

[79] Mellander, *United States in Panamanian Politics*, pp. 31-32.

[80] Ibid., p. 32.

[81] Miner, *Fight*, p. 367.

fidential agent of the Republic of Panama at Washington.

And the third, from Hay to the Consul General:

The people of Panama have, by an apparently unanimous movement, dissolved their political connection with the Republic of Colombia and *resumed their independence* [emphasis supplied]. When you are satisfied that a *de facto* government, republican in form, and without substantial opposition from its own people, has been established in the State of Panama, you will enter into relations with it as the responsible government of the territory and look to it for all due action to protect the persons and property of citizens of the United States and to keep open the isthmian transit in accordance with the obligations of existing treaties governing the relation of the United States to that territory.[82]

Thus was the new republic recognized before Bogotá even had reliable information that an outbreak had occurred. There had obviously not been enough time for the "government," if there was one, to demonstrate whether it was in substantial control of the country. It is almost equally obvious that the Government of Colombia, had it not been prevented from doing so by the American shield, could easily have regained its hegemony over the rebellious province.

On November 10 Dr. Amador and Federico Boyd sailed from Colón as delegates of the Junta for the purpose of negotiating a canal treaty with the United States. They carried written instructions subordinating Bunau-Varilla to their orders.

Apprised, Bunau-Varilla was not about to risk losing everything (or anything) after coming this close. By threatening to block essential credits he had arranged, he forced Arango to cable him plenipotentiary powers. On November 13 he was received by President Roosevelt as Panamanian Minister. On November 15 Hay sent him the draft of a proposed treaty, modeled on the Hay-Herrán Treaty.

Working feverishly, Bunau-Varilla finished on November 17 a draft treaty of his own. He told Hay he was willing to accept either one but preferred his own because it "has the advantage of conferring upon the United States in broad and general terms

the rights she is entitled to have . . ."[83] Hay agreed, though he had not thought it prudent to ask for so much.

Bunau-Varilla impressed upon Hay the necessity for haste.

So long as the delegation has not arrived in Washington, I shall be free to deal with you alone, provided with complete confidence and absolute powers. When they arrive, I shall no longer be alone. In fact, I may perhaps no longer be here at all.[84]

At 6:40 p.m. on November 18, at Hay's residence (see illustrations A and B), Bunau-Varilla and Hay signed what was essentially the Bunau-Varilla draft. "The deal was consummated without the presence, advice or consent of a single Panamanian."[85] Later in the evening Bunau-Varilla greeted Amador and Boyd at Washington's Union Station with the news, which almost caused Amador to swoon on the platform.[86] The next day the Panamanian delegates attempted to reopen negotiations with the State Department but failed.[87]

General Rafael Reyes, the strongest political leader in Colombia and assumed (correctly) to be in line for the presidency, told the American chargé in Bogotá on November 6 that he would guarantee ratification of the Hay-Herrán Treaty if the United States would preserve Colombian

<hr/>

[82] Ibid., pp. 369-70.

[83] Ibid., p. 376.
[84] Mellander, *United States in Panamanian Politics*, p. 40.
[85] Ibid.
[86] Miner, *Fight*, p. 378.
[87] Mellander, *United States in Panamanian Politics*, p. 41. Also on the next day a curious story appeared in the *New York Times* (p. 2) which indicated that the Panamanians were not the only ones who wanted to reopen negotiations. Datelined Galveston, Texas, Nov. 19, 1903, the dispatch reported the arrival in Galveston, on their way to Washington, of a special embassy of three diplomats appointed by President Marroquín of Colombia to "request the Washington Government to rescind its action in recognizing the Government of Panama, and *who are also authorized to make a canal treaty with the United States at once on the latter's own terms*" [emphasis supplied]. Nobody could say that this offer, if correctly reported, was too little; but it does seem to have been too late. I was unable to find any further trace of the "special embassy" which, in any case, was quickly superseded by a higher-level Colombian mission under General Reyes (see continuing text).

sovereignty in the Isthmus. Failing to obtain such assurance, he headed a mission to Washington, which arrived on November 28, with the aim of restoring the status quo ante.[88] The Reyes mission stayed in Washington for some time and employed a lawyer to organize a campaign against ratification of the Hay/Bunau-Varilla Treaty.

Bunau-Varilla, realizing that he was not yet out of the woods, pressured the Junta into sending a cable on November 26 promising, sight unseen, to ratify the treaty as soon as it arrived. On December 2, less than twenty hours after it reached Panama City, the thirty-one page typewritten document, in English version only, was ratified by the Junta.

On February 23, 1904, after a bitter debate in which Senator Morgan of Alabama led a last-ditch fight for Nicaragua, the U.S. Senate advised ratification by a vote of 66 to 14. On February 26 the Hay/Bunau-Varilla Treaty was proclaimed.

While the ratification process was going on in Washington the Republic of Panama was getting itself organized as a nation. On December 27, 1903, thirty-two delegates were elected to attend a constitutional convention which met on January 15, 1904. On the same day the Junta relinquished its legislative powers to the convention.[89] The president of the convention was Pablo Arosemena (see notes 58, 59, supra) and the 1863 Colombian Constitutional Convention was used as a model for procedure.

Contrary to the wishes of William Insco Buchanan, the United States' first Minister to Panama, whose advice was often sought on other subjects, the convention assumed the authority to write, ratify, and promulgate a constitution without any reference back to the people. Contrary to the wishes of Secretary Hay (Buchanan's attitude in the matter is not entirely clear), an article

(No. 136) was included in the constitution giving the United States the right to intervene "in any part of the Republic" if necessary to restore peace and order, provided the United States guaranteed by treaty the "independence and sovereignty" of the Republic.[90] Though repealed many years later, it is highly pertinent to recall that this article, voluntarily and unilaterally waiving one important aspect of sovereignty, was part of the constitution promulgated on February 16, 1904, ten days before proclamation of the Hay/Bunau-Varilla Treaty.[91]

The constituent convention then transformed itself into the nation's first National Assembly and, as such, elected Dr. Amador the nation's first president. Amador was inaugurated on February 19.

Seven days later, as we have seen, the Canal Zone became a juridical entity within which the United States was assumed to possess powers and privileges broad enough to sanction the displacement of the four-hundred-year-old legal system prevailing therein. Whether the assumption was justified depends on (a) the meaning and measurement of sovereignty as an element in the Hay/Bunau-Varilla Treaty, and (b) the validity and interpretation of the treaty. Both are still unsettled questions. It might even be said that the questions are academic after so many years, as well as insoluble, but this would not be quite true.

As the displacement (reception) followed from the nature of the United States presence, and the presence derived from the treaty and what, if any, effective disposition it made of sovereignty in the Zone, these questions have refused to go away. And the best evidence that they cannot be ignored, even if they cannot be solved, lies in the very fact that the United States Government has been committed since 1964 (and recommitted in 1974) to the abrogation of the treaty and its replacement by a drastically different one in which the (if-it-were-the-sovereign) Zone concept will be abolished.[92]

(While much more is involved, of course, my purpose here is to explore these ques-

---

[88] At an emergency open meeting on November 12, the Government of Colombia had almost declared war on the United States, and on November 20 the Reyes mission had been prevented from landing at Colón. The State Department, apparently in a Freudian slip, had cabled the Colombian Minister of Foreign Affairs on November 11—five days after recognition of Panama—that Colombian troops would not be permitted to land on the isthmus as "such a course would precipitate *civil war* [emphasis supplied]." Miner, *Fight*, p. 374.

[89] One point still troublesome is how such powers could have included the right to ratify an international treaty.

[90] Mellander, *United States in Panamanian Politics*, pp. 52-53.

[91] It seems to be pretty well documented that several of the Founding Fathers, including Amador and Arias, would have preferred annexation of the whole country to the United States.

[92] It is arguable that even Roosevelt would not embrace the zone concept if he were alive

John Hay residence (corner building in foreground) in which both the Hay-Herran and Hay/Bunau-Varilla Treaties were signed. (*Photo courtesy of Adams National Historic Site, U.S. Department of the Interior, National Park Service*).

Philippe Bunau-Varilla and John Hay in latter's residence on November 13, 1903.

tions only insofar as they relate to the preconditions of the Common Law reception, the peculiarity of that reception, and the ineradicable cloud on its future. Exhaustive and able arguments between the two governments over sovereignty and treaty interpretation did indeed take place during the formative period of Canal Zone jurisprudence,[93] but they were almost always precipitated by clashes over such commercially-tinged matters as customs, ports, and postal service. The creation of an exclusive, exotic legal system in the Zone does not seem to have aroused the same fervor of opposition at first (possibly because the Zone courts continued to apply the Panamanian Civil Code); but today it is universally seen by Panamanians as an intolerable affront.)[94]

To vary the angle of vision slightly, while remaining within the same parameters, the remainder of this chapter will examine suc-

cessively: (a) whether the assumption of the right to establish a Common Law legal system was justified within the four corners of the treaty, so to speak, supplemented by a certain amount of derivative presumption from actions of the parties, and (b) whether the treaty itself was a binding instrument in international law.

As a prelude to that examination it will be useful to keep in mind the following excerpts from the Hay/Bunau-Varilla Treaty:

Article II

The Republic of Panama grants to the United States in perpetuity the use, occupation and control of a zone of land and land under water for the construction, maintenance, operation, sanitation and protection of said Canal . . . .

Article III

The Republic of Panama grants to the United States all the rights, power and authority within the zone mentioned and described in Article II of this agreement and within the limits of all auxiliary lands and waters mentioned and described in said Article II which the United States would possess and exercise if it were the sovereign of the territory within which said lands and waters are located to the entire exclusion of the exercise by the

---

today. In a personal letter to Secretary of War Taft (see note 3, supra) he wrote:

"... There is ground for believing that in the execution of the rights conferred by the treaty the people of Panama have been unduly alarmed at the effect of the establishment of a government in the canal strip [*sic*] by the [Isthmian Canal] commission. ... The United States must avoid creating any suspicion, however unfounded, of our intentions as to the future. We have not the slightest intention of establishing an independent colony in the middle of the State of Panama, or of exercising any greater governmental functions than are necessary to enable us conveniently and safely to construct, maintain, and operate the canal under the rights given us by the treaty. ..." President Theodore Roosevelt, 18 Oct. 1906, to Secretary Taft, 234/18, Department of State, National Archives.

[93] See, for example, the correspondence between Mr. Hay and Sr. de Obaldía in *Foreign Relations of the United States,* 1904, pp. 595-630. No really new points favoring one or the other interpretation have been raised in the last seventy years, nor are we any nearer to agreement over the old points. What we may agree on is to let the argument become moot by starting over with a new treaty.

[94] From an article in the *Washington Post* of February 15, 1974:

"*Balboa, Panama Canal Zone*—In the little magistrate's court which sits between the police station and the Elks Lodge atop a hill here, almost everything was American, except the defendants. ... Few places in Panama better illustrate the basic issue that

gives rise to the tensions in and around the Canal Zone than the Balboa Magistrate's Court . . .

"Although the United States has offered to make concessions to Panama, probably by allowing the Republic more canal revenues and turning over some zone for needed urban expansion, many Panamanians say that American law prevailing over the 530 square miles of the Zone angers them most. . . .

"Some effort also has been made to diminish a harsh side of American law in the Zone. Forty of the Zone's 300 policemen are Panamanians, and so are many court personnel.

"Yet none of that satisfies Panamanians who hate the fact that American law governs a large area of their country.

" 'It's not right,' exclaimed a local newspaper editor recently, as he drove his car on Fourth of July Street, the Zone's boundary in Panama City.

" 'One minute I am in Panama. The next I can be picked up by a foreign policeman, tried in a foreign court and sent to a foreign jail—in my own country,' he said . . ."

Republic of Panama of any such sovereign rights, power or authority.

Article VI

The grants herein contained shall in no manner invalidate the titles or rights of private land holders or owners of private property in the said zone . . . .

Article XVI

The two Governments shall make adequate provision by future agreement for the pursuit, capture, imprisonment, detention and delivery within said zone and auxiliary lands to the authorities of the Republic of Panama of persons charged with the commitment of crimes, felonies or misdemeanors without said zone and for the pursuit, capture, imprisonment, detention and delivery without said zone to the authorities of the United States of persons charged with the commitment of crimes, felonies and misdemeanors within said zone and auxiliary lands.

It will also be useful to cite the most pregnant differences between the Hay/Bunau-Varilla Treaty and the ill-fated Hay-Herrán Treaty which, though never ratified, played a significant part in the continuum of Canal Zone legal history:

Sovereignty.

(a) The Hay-Herrán Treaty says (Article 4):

The rights and privileges granted to the United States by the terms of this convention shall not affect the sovereignty of the Republic of Colombia over the territory within whose boundaries such rights and privileges are to be exercised. The United States freely acknowledges and recognizes this sovereignty and disavows any intention to impair it in any way whatever . . .

(b) The Hay/Bunau-Varilla Treaty contains no such provision expressly saving Panamanian sovereignty (though a kind of lip-service reference thereto is made in the preamble). On the contrary, a simulated sovereignty ("if it were") over the territory is granted to the United States.

Length of Servitude.

(a) The Hay-Herrán Treaty, as heretofore noted, grants control for one hundred years, indefinitely renewable for similar terms at the sole option of the United States.

(b) The Hay/Bunau-Varilla Treaty grants "in perpetuity." Perhaps a metaphysician could explain the difference. Even a lawyer can see that this change did not improve the position of the concessionaire.

Size of Territory.

(a) The Hay-Herrán Treaty stipulates a Zone six miles wide (actually ten kilometers).[95] Certain small islands in the Bay of Panama may be used insofar as necessary for the construction, maintenance, and operation of the canal, but are specifically not included in the Zone. The cities of Panama and Colón are specifically excluded from the grant except for land already in possession of the New Canal Company or the Railroad.

(b) The Hay/Bunau-Varilla Treaty creates a Zone ten miles wide; including, without reservation, certain small islands in the Bay of Panama. In the cities of Panama and Colón the United States has the right of eminent domain as well as the right and authority to maintain public order. The United States also has the right *in perpetuity* to any other lands and waters *outside the Zone* which it deems necessary for the operation or protection of the canal.[96]

Courts and the Laws.

(a) The Hay-Herrán Treaty, as we have seen,[97] provides for a three-tier system of courts, one of which, with limited jurisdiction, would appertain exclusively to the United States, applying United States law and procedure, but "[s]ubject to the general sovereignty of Colombia over said zone . . ." A mixed tribunal would entertain suits between citizens of the United States and citizens of Colombia or about the canal, while a third would be exclusively Colombian. Obviously this arrangement would have opened the door to reception of a sort though nothing like what has happened. Still, it went considerably beyond any infringement of sovereignty attempted up to that time, and was the principal reason for rejection of the treaty.

---

[95] The Wyse concession, it will be remembered, was 200 meters on each side of the canal.

[96] Using the "plain meaning" rule of interpretation, there would seem to be nothing in this language to prevent the United States from extending its control to the Costa Rican border.

[97] See p. 31, supra.

(b) The Hay/Bunau-Varilla Treaty is (deliberately) silent on the subject. Hence, the legitimacy of the plenary-jurisdiction courts erected in the zone, without which the Common Law reception could not have occurred, depends entirely on exercise of the controversial "sovereignty" granted in Article III, the force of which in turn depends on the standing in international law of the Hay/Bunau-Varilla Treaty itself.

For all the countless words that have been written about it, it is still impossible to say just exactly what disposition was made of sovereignty in the Canal Zone by the Hay/Bunau-Varilla Treaty. Reasons for the continuing enigma are both general and particular. As a general preposition, all disputes over sovereignty tend to be inconclusive, and eventually resolved or put aside by some sort of extra-legal *modus vivendi*, because the word has never had any fixed or universally accepted meaning. Whatever chance there might have been that this particular dispute would yield up its secret to jural analysis was thwarted at birth by the impenetrable, unlegal, and unprecedented language of Article III. Bunau-Varilla was an engineer, not a lawyer.

As used by Bodin and his followers at the beginning of the nation-state era, the idea of sovereignty carried a heavy connotation of absoluteness and indivisibility. "Thus sovereignty was the expression in legal terms of what actually existed as a political fact."[98] By 1903-4, however, new and different theories—consonant with changing political realities—had become dominant, with various gradations and distinctions recognized, and some writers regarding sovereignty as no longer essential to the concept of a state. Both American and Panamanian publicists were and have been singularly slow to take advantage of the possibilities for compromise held out by the new schools of thought. On the Panamanian side, of course, one reason may be that the issue has always been in fact more emotional than legal, and no approach which fails to recognize that reality can have any lasting results.[99]

Hanrahan astutely observes:

In view of the social, political and economic ties between the two countries it seems hardly relevant to the successful conduct of *a canal operation* (emphasis supplied) to argue the question of sovereignty.[100]

By separating the canal operation from a dissolving Zone built on "sovereignty," he points a way out of the impasse which will probably be taken in the near future. This does not, however, lessen the relevancy of the "question of sovereignty" to the introduction of the Common Law legal system in 1904, nor betray any awareness that the abandonment of "sovereignty" is also the abandonment of the system.

It seems strange in retrospect but it is a fact that while the Panamanian Minister in 1904 was putting up a spirited fight in defense of other manifestations of sovereignty, he did not seem to attach much importance to the legal system. As Hay tellingly demonstrated from the record,[101] the Panamanian courts seemed positively eager to disclaim any jurisdiction in the Zone from the moment the treaty became effective.

In addition to the cases cited by Hay, which were in the lower courts, two decisions of the *Corte Suprema de Justicia de Panamá—J. N. Gris v. The New Panama Canal Company,* and *Carlos Carbone v. Juan Esquivel,* rendered on January 20, 1905, and January 25, 1905, respectively (*Registro Judicial,* Vol. II, pp. 59 and 61)— conceded the ". . . rights of the United States to organize, to the exclusion of the Republic of Panama, the Judiciary of the Canal Zone. . . ." The latter decision, however, took note of the contention of the *Procurador General* (Attorney General) of Panama that the Republic retained its rights of sovereignty [102] in the Zone and ". . .

---

[98] Hanrahan, "Legal Aspects of the Panama Canal Zone—in Perspective," 45 *Boston University Law Review* (1965), p. 79.

[99] There is even a tuneful folk song in Panama called "Panamá Soberana," recorded by the popular Lucho Azcárraga band, which lays claim to sovereignty over the Canal.

[100] Hanrahan, *Legal Aspects,* p. 81.

[101] *Foreign Relations of the United States,* 1904, p. 624 et seq.

[102] In the letter of Secretary of State Hughes to Panamanian Minister Alfaro of October 15, 1923 (Foreign Relations of the United States, 1923, vol. 2, p. 657) the Spanish word *soberanía,* in a quotation from the Carbone decision, is

therefore the Judges of Panama have not lost their jurisdiction in cases triable by them prior to the American . . . possession of the Canal Zone, though such cases may cover real-estate situated therein." (Translation by author)

The strange language of Article III has been said to mean, in effect, that the United States Government can do anything in the Canal Zone that it can do in the District of Columbia or any other part of the national territory (but doing "in" is not the same as doing "with"—see Afterword). If it "were the sovereign . . . to the entire exclusion of the exercise by the Republic of Panama" of sovereignty, Hay argued,[103] the United States Government would surely possess the right and authority to regulate commerce therewith, establish customs-houses therein, and provide postal facilities therefor. He did not mention creating an exclusive court system and providing a body of law and procedure, but how could a line be drawn against such actions if the above reasoning be admitted? And so the line was not drawn.

The Panamanian counter-argument, again without specific mention of the legal system, was that the grant of sovereign power in Article III must be read in the light of the general purpose of the treaty (stated in Article II to be "for the construction, maintenance, operation, sanitation and protection of said Canal . . .") and was therefore limited to the amount necessary for the accomplishment of that purpose.[104] It could

have been urged, therefore, and apparently was to a limited extent and without success, in *Gris v. The New Panama Canal Company*, that the displacement of Panamanian private law in the whole area of the Zone was not necessary. The "entire exclusion" clause would have made this argument a little more difficult, but not necessarily impossible, to sustain.[105]

After a careful study of the sovereignty problem in 1926, Dr. L. H. Woolsey, President of the American Society of International Law and a former Solicitor of the Department of State, found a great deal of merit in the Panamanian contention of a limited grant, and also came to the following general conclusion:

> It is not derogatory of the views entertained by either country to say that it was doubtless not the intention of either party that the United States should hold and administer the Canal Zone as an independent colony or possession of the United States. The Canal Zone is more in the nature of a great international right of way across Panama territory, of which the United States is the administrator and protector with power sufficient to carry out the great design of the parties.[106]

Intention notwithstanding, however, he also found that, with respect to police and judicial powers, the grant seems to be without effective limitation. Moreover, Article XVI (see p. 40, supra) by inference, "indicates that the United States shall exercise police and judicial powers within the Canal Zone

---

mistranslated as "eminent domain," thus making the *Procurador General's* claim of Panamanian sovereignty appear to be much more limited than it actually was.

[103] *Foreign Relations of the United States,* 1904, p. 615.

[104] In a memorandum of January 3, 1923 to Secretary of State Hughes, Panamanian Minister Alfaro attempted to renew the Hay-De Obaldía dialogue of 1904 (see note 93, supra) on this point. In the course of this argument he made the interesting statement that: "If the Canal were abandoned by the United States the United States would have no legal ground for occupying the zone, title to which it has not acquired either by purchase, transfer, or conquest." Hughes did not attempt to dispute the logic of that conclusion but contented himself with repeating that the Article III grant of power "as if it were the sovereign" . . . "is conclusive upon the question you raise." *Foreign Relations of the United States,* 1923, vol. II, pp. 645, 652-53.

[105] "In the Aspinwall Case, the Court said that 'where language is employed in a treaty which is susceptible of two meanings, that is to be preferred which is least for the advantage of the party for whose benefit the clause is inserted.' . . . One is impressed by the fact that the purpose of the Convention of 1903 as stated in the preamble is to 'secure the construction of a ship canal across the Isthmus of Panama . . .' Viewed objectively, the United States' declared purpose does not appear to be put in jeopardy by a restrictive interpretation of the treaty. Application of the International Law standards of interpretation could well result in such a construction." Hanrahan, *Legal Aspects,* pp. 84-85.

[106] Woolsey, "The Sovereignty of the Panama Canal Zone," vol. XX. *American Journal of International Law* (1926) 117 at p. 124. Woolsey undoubtedly took into consideration, among other evidence, the declaration made by President Roosevelt on October 18, 1906 (see note 92, supra).

to the exclusion of the exercise of such powers by Panama." [107]

Article XVI, of course, relates only to criminal law, and across-the-board reception still depended mainly on the "if-it-were" sovereignty of Article III, which sprang full blown from the brain of Bunau-Varilla. Even in the frantic haste of his efforts to find a way of giving the territory to the United States without seeming to do so, how could he come up with such an untenable formula? The short answer seems to be, as heretofore indicated, that Bunau-Varilla was not stupid, just untrained. He was in somewhat the same position as the apocryphal young inventor who "didn't know that it couldn't be done, so he went ahead and did it." He invented a sovereignty that was not sovereignty [108] and a cession that was not a cession. [109] His treaty defies interpretation by precedent or analogy because it is *sui*

generis, as is the exotic legal system which it spawned in the heart of Panama.

Out of all this confusion can any conclusions at all, then, be drawn from an examination of the four corners of the treaty? I would venture to say yes.

First, the territory of the Zone was not ceded to the United States in fee simple and therefore any powers exercised by the United States must have been expressly or impliedly granted in the treaty. Second, the power to set up an exclusive and independent legal system may reasonably be implied from the "if it were the sovereign" language of Article III, despite some inconsistency with the "general purpose" clauses of the treaty. Third, statements and actions of the parties suggest, however, that this was not their intention beforehand nor within their contemplation. Fourth, but statements and actions of Panamanian authorities in the period immediately after the promulgation of the treaty suggest acquiescence, or perhaps estoppel by condonation.

On balance it would seem that the United States has, by a slim margin, the better case, if the controversy be viewed as strictly a contractual matter—and if it be assumed that the validity of the treaty in international law is beyond question. Which takes a bit of assuming.

One historian, in summing up his account of Panama Canal diplomacy, casually disposes of the whole argument over validity in almost a throwaway line:

> Thus the start was made on the construction of the Panama Canal. The initial diplomatic steps were, I think, clouded by an attempt to make the action of the United States appear as justified by treaty. [110]

What might be called the morality factor—though perhaps with some misgivings about legality also discernible between the lines—is rather embarrassingly exposed in a personal latter from Secretary Hay to Senator Spooner while the treaty was pending before the Senate:

> As it stands now as soon as the Senate votes we shall have a treaty in the main

[107] Ibid., p. 123.

[108] Richard M. Weiner concludes a thoughtful study, updating the work of Woolsey, with the following quotation from Bunau-Varilla which may explain what the latter was trying to do and why: "After mature thought I recognized that if I enumerated in succession the various attributes of sovereignty granted, I ran the risk of seeing, in the United States Senate, some other attributes asked for. To cut short any possible debate I decided to grant a concession of sovereignty en bloc." Weiner, "Sovereignty of the Panama Isthmus," 16 *New York University Intramural Law Review* (1960) 65 at p. 75.

[109] Some writers have called it a "disguised cession" but it fails to pass the most elementary test of that characterization, even in disguise, as shown by Weiner. The first and most persuasive indication cited by Weiner is simply that, if cession had been intended, the treaty could so easily have been drawn to make that clear, as was done in the treaty with Spain ("Spain cedes to the United States the island of Porto Rico") and in the acquisitions of Louisiana, Alaska, et al. A second indication is the fact that domiciliaries of the territory did not become nationals of the acquiring state as would normally have occurred in case of cession in the absence of a special provision. "By act of Congress not only did prior domiciliaries of the Zone retain their alien status but even their children born in the Zone after 1903 are classified as aliens." And a third indication is the rent-like payments which would surely not be applicable to ceded territory, but rather suggest a lease (with reversion if the payments are not made).

[110] Alfred L. P. Dennis, *Adventures in American Diplomacy* (New York: E. P. Dutton & Co., 1928), p. 336.

very satisfactory, vastly advantageous to
the United States, and we must confess,
with what face we can muster, not so
advantageous to Panama.[111]

The various reasons which have been
alleged for vitiating the treaty as a binding
international instrument are based on a
number of charges which I shall arbitrarily
over-simplify and group under the headings
of (a) fraud, duress, and coercion, (b) violation of the Treaty of 1846, and (c) unconstitutionality.

(a) *Fraud, duress, and coercion.*

As a matter of undeniable historical fact,
the Hay/Bunau-Varilla Treaty was shot
through with enough fraud, duress, and
coercion, in one way and another, to shock
the conscience of a Godfather. Which is
not to say that it was necessarily illegal.

International law does not require that
treaties adhere to any particular form. Sub-
stantively, general contract principles are
applicable; but with some differences, most
significantly that consideration is not necessary and that there is a much higher tolerance of duress. As the Solicitor for the
Department of State wrote, respecting the
Versailles Treaty:

. . . Even though a vanquished nation
is in effect compelled to sign a treaty, I
think that in contemplation of law its
signature is regarded as voluntary.[112]

While Panama in November 1903 was not
a vanquished nation—indeed, there is reasonable doubt that it was a nation at all—
it stood in about the same position as one so
far as freedom of choice was concerned.
And with the same result "in contemplation
of law." [113]

A different view is taken when duress is
applied, not against the state, but directly
against rulers or negotiators acting for the
state.[114] Such cases are rare, but a classic

example often cited is that of the treaty for
renunciation of his crown signed by Ferdinand VII of Spain in 1807 while he was a
virtual prisoner of Napoleon and under
threat of being tried for treason. When this
test is brought to bear on the Hay/Bunau-
Varilla Treaty, however, the situation, as
Alice said, gets curiouser and curiouser.
Bunau-Varilla, far from being under duress,
stood ready, willing, and anxious to give
the United States negotiator more than the
latter expected—or perhaps even wanted.
The publicists have little to say that seems
applicable to that kind of a pass.

What about fraud?

In practice no instances of the actual
employment of fraud in the negotiation
of treaties are known, and there appear
to be no decisions either of national or
international tribunals involving the question. Nevertheless, it is altogether conceivable that fraud might be successfully
employed by a treaty negotiator, as it
has often been employed in the making
of contracts at private law. . . . Nearly
all writers on international law who have
discussed the subject conclude that the
effect of recourse to fraud by the representatives of a State with a view to in-
ducing another State to enter into a
treaty, either renders the treaty voidable
or void.[115]

This comes closer but also misses the point
as Bunau-Varilla used fraud, not to induce
another state to enter into a treaty, but to
induce the state he represented. Arguably,
there was something fraudulent in the way
the United States negotiator hurriedly
signed the treaty with an agent who was
patently not representing his principal in
good faith, knowing that two bona fide
agents were only hours away. Arguably
also, duress and coercion were employed by
the agent against his principal to obtain the
agency relationship. And what is to be said
about the fact that the Panamanian Junta,
exercising dubious authority, ratified, after
less than twenty hours "deliberation," a vital
treaty written in a foreign language?

Whether or not any or all of these things
meet the minimum requirements of international law for provable illegality, it is not

---

[111] Ibid., p. 341.

[112] Hackworth, *International Law* 158 (1943).

[113] "Although the Government of Panama has
intimated that the treaty was signed 'hastily,'
and United States interference at the moment
of revolution is a historical fact, an application
of the international law standard of duress does
not result in disturbing the validity of the
Treaty of 1903." Hanrahan, *Legal Aspects,* p.
84.

[114] "There seems general agreement that coercion or duress employed against the individual

plenipotentiaries negotiating and signing a
treaty, or against the persons ratifying it on
behalf of a state, may invalidate the treaty."
5 Hackworth, p. 159.

[115] Ibid., pp. 159-160.

the purpose of this author to pronounce. At the least, though, it would seem that, borrowing a phrase from real property law, they must leave a "cloud on the title," even without considering the legal effect, if any, of the remaining counts.[116]

(b) Violation of Treaty of 1846.

Colombian Foreign Minister Luis Carlos Rico on April 12, 1904 presented to the United States *chargé* in Bogota the definitive "Protest of Colombia" (see note 55, supra) against the Hay/Bunau-Varilla Treaty in the form of a follow-up to his note of November 12, 1903 which had listed acts already accomplished in the first flush of the Revolution in alleged violation of the Treaty of 1846. The "Protest," citing subsequent and continuing violations both of the treaty and of "the principles of International Law," is a masterful—one is tempted to say devastating—statement of the Colombian case.

Of course, Rico was no fool and he knew by April 12, 1904 that the events of which he complained would not be reversed by legal arguments, no matter how persuasive, addressed through diplomatic channels to the State Department. His objective was to lay a foundation for forcing the United States into arbitration proceedings, or raising a credible threat thereof, from which he hoped would come a generous "settlement" (an objective finally achieved, as we have seen, in 1922).

In pursuit of this point, Rico concluded the "Protest" by denying the United States' contention that Colombia's claims were of a purely political nature and insisting that they called for judicial decision because they were founded: "(1) In the violation, on the part of the United States of the Treaty of 1846," "(2) In the violation of the rules of neutrality established by the Law of Nations," and "(3) In the signing of an Agreement with the so-called Republic of Panama for the opening of the Inter-oceanic Canal, notwithstanding that a Treaty of Peace, Friendship, and Navigation between the Republic of New Granada (now Co-

lombia) and the United States was still in force."

He supported (1) simply with a terse statement (and citation) that "all questions of this kind are of a judicial nature."

He supported (2) largely on the basis of precedents established by the United States Government itself in the ALABAMA CLAIMS. The Treaty of Washington of May 8, 1871, agreeing to submit said claims to a Court of Arbitration, established that course as proper where a state fails to observe its duty of neutrality toward belligerents in a civil war.

He supported (3) with, in part, the following argumentation which, I think, deserves repeating at some length:

(Quoting Kluber on International Law) Whenever a public treaty shall present a doubtful meaning, it cannot find an authentic interpretation, except by express declaration of the contracting parties or of such arbiters as may have been duly appointed by them. Even the preliminary question as to the doubtfulness of the Treaty can only be decided in the manner just explained.

In the present case, the first question arising is the preliminary one as to the doubtful meaning of the Treaty, notwithstanding Colombia's opinion that the Treaty is perfectly clear, as understood by both Governments up to the present, although the United States have now abandoned their former interpretation.

The Colombian *Chargé d'Affaires* at Washington has recently cabled me that the Senate of the United States approved the Treaty of Panama for the opening of the canal. That Treaty, as I have already expressed it, contains in its first clause the undertaking on the part of the United States to maintain the independence of Panama; that clause suffices by itself as a declaration before the world that Panama cannot maintain its independence except with the military support of your Excellency's Government.

As the said Treaty with Panama is in direct opposition to the Treaty of 1846, supposing—as your Excellency's Government admits, and Colombia's Government denies—that Panama should be a member of the community of nations, the coexistence of the two agreements necessitates the application of the doctrine laid down by Vattel that "no treaties can be made contrary to those which are in force." . . . Should [the United States] reject the justice of the doctrine just mentioned, they would establish the prec-

---

[116] Panamanian lawyers might conceivably have had an additional argument under this heading if the Colombian legislators in 1887 had not expunged the ancient Roman law principle permitting rescission of contracts for grave inequity (see chap. III, p. 17).

edent that a nation, by becoming the judge in matters of its own, may neglect the fulfillment of public treaties by the simple means of entering into new treaties . . . . ; by these means all public treaties, which are the bulwark of law, would be soon brought to an end.[117]

The United States was strong enough to prevent the matter from ever being submitted to the judicial decision that Rico sought,[118] but it was not exactly a victory for international law and order or for the future good name of the Colossus of the North in Latin America.

Subsumed in the general charge of violation of the Treaty of 1846 was the pivotal act of *recognition*, which Rico listed first in his bill of particulars at the beginning of the "Protest." It was premature, he said in effect, to put the gentlest construction on it. By even the most lenient comparison with prevailing doctrine and practice, it surely was. Hardly anyone would say that Panama on November 6, 1903 met the ordinary criteria generally applied by the United States Government for *de facto* recognition of a new state.[119]

This was obviously not the time and place for applying ordinary criteria. Recognition was a condition precedent for a

treaty with Panama, so recognition had to come, ready or not. An even more urgent reason was to discourage Colombia from taking military measures to recapture the straying "province." Pragmatically compelling, but not very helpful as a counter to the Colombian point of law that recognition constituted a violation of the Treaty of 1846.

According to Rico's summary of exculpatory arguments advanced by the State Department:

> The Government of the United States has declared that in recognizing the independence of Panama it acted against a general rule of not acknowledging a new State as independent until it should have demonstrated that it is capable of maintaining its independence, and that that rule arises from the principle of non-intervention; but it holds that its proceeding is justified by three reasons, which are: (1) the rights which they (the U.S.) enjoy under their treaties; (2) their national interests and their own security; and (3) the collective interest of civilization.[120]

He then proceeded to demolish the three reasons like the straw men which they perhaps were, in a sense, but for which the State Department surely supplied some of the straws.

A somewhat more credible effort was made to counter the point by attempting to show that Panama was already independent, in legal theory, and therefore only the slightest overt action was needed to justify recognition. To follow this line of argument it is necessary to advert to the intriguing history of Panamanian separatism (see note 65, supra) and Hay's rather off-hand assertion that the people of Panama had merely "resumed their independence." But whereas Hay had seemed to rely mainly on the Panamanian independence (from Spain) proclamation of 1821, a more recent and in some ways stronger piece of evidence was also put forward.

In 1861 the State of Panama, nominally tied to Bogota but virtually independent for nearly all practical purposes,[121] voluntarily entered into an agreement

---

[117] *Protest of Colombia*, pp. 43-44.

[118] "Colombia protested, and has repeatedly protested, but in vain. The violation of the treaty of 1846, whereby the United States guaranteed the sovereignty of New Granada over the Isthmus of Panama, the flouting of the ordinary rules of international law in recognizing the independence of Panama within a few days of its declaration, the prevention by American marines of all attempts on the part of the Colombian Government to reassert its authority, were affronts of a nature which could not have been dared against a strong nation. Colombia, a weak power, had not alone to submit, but was forced to see its humiliation increased by a peremptory refusal to treat with its envoys or to submit the pending questions to arbitration." Phanor James Eder, *Colombia* (London: T. Fisher Unwin, 1913), p. 51.

[119] ". . . ever since the American Revolution entrance upon diplomatic intercourse with foreign states has been *de facto*, dependent upon the existence of three conditions of fact; the control of the administrative machinery of the state; the general acquiescence of its people; and the ability and willingness of their government to discharge international and conventional obligations." *Foreign Relations of the United States*, 1913, p. 100.

[120] *Protest of Colombia*, p. 27.

[121] The year before, as we have seen (chap III, p. 17) Panama, acting entirely on its own, had adopted the Bello Civil Code which eventually became the law of the Canal Zone.

. . . in view of the circumstances under which the territory of the late Granadine Confederation finds itself at present, and considering the necessity of putting an end to the anomalous condition of this State, . . .

whereby it incorporated itself into

the new national entity called United States of New Granada, and consequently becomes one of the sovereign federal states composing the aforesaid confederation . . .

with reservations preserving a great deal of local autonomy, including that

The Government of the United States [of New Granada] shall have no power to militarily occupy any point of the territory of the State without the express consent of the governor thereof, provided the State itself maintains the necessary force for the protection of the transit of either ocean . . .[122]

In 1863, when peace had been sufficiently restored to make such an undertaking feasible, the above Agreement of 1861 was formalized in a new constitution of the United States of New Granada.

In 1885, following another civil war, the country was reorganized as the Republic of Colombia with a completely different constitution, enacted by military force, in which all the reserved autonomy of Panama was ignored. E.g.,

ARTICLE 201

The Department of Panama shall be subject to the direct authority of the Government and shall be administered in accordance with special laws.

Based on the above set of facts, the counterpoint was formulated by Secretary of State Elihu Root in 1906 as follows:

We assert that the ancient State of Panama, independent in its origin and by nature and history a separate political community, was federated with the other States of Colombia upon terms which preserved and continued its separate sovereignty; that it never surrendered that sovereignty; that in the year 1885 the pact which bound it to the other States of Colombia was broken and terminated by Colombia, and the Isthmus was subjugated by force; that it was held under

foreign domination to which it had never consented; that it was justly entitled to assert its sovereignty and demand its independence from a rule which was unlawful, oppressive and tyrannical.[123]

In more strictly legal terms, the argument stresses that the constitution of 1885 was void or voidable because it changed the constitution of 1863 without following the amendment procedure set forth therein.[124] But anyone with the most rudimentary knowledge of American history must be uneasily reminded by this argument of the fragility of glass houses. The Constitutional Convention of 1787 showed no more regard for the method of amendment prescribed by the Articles of Confederation. Moreover, as Rico was not loath to point out, the claim "that Panama was amply justified in separating from Colombia, is in itself an act of intervention in the internal affairs of another state; . . ."[125]

Subsumed also in the general charge of violation of the Treaty of 1846 was the consequent *unlawful taking of Colombia's vested property rights in the canal works and the Panama Railroad.* Besides the expected income therefrom, there was the interesting question of Colombia's reversionary interest. By Article XXII of the Hay/Bunau-Varilla Treaty, Panama generously renounced and granted to the United States all such property rights "to which it might be entitled." It was not made clear at the time or later how it became entitled to one hundred percent of the rights previously acknowledged to belong to Colombia. Colombia was willing to concede to Panama at most only a pro rata share.

The Colombian position that the Wyse concession was still in force, and therefore the New Panama Canal Company was forbidden by its terms to sell the canal works to the United States, was reiterated in a note from Rico to the United States Minister in Bogota on April 14, 1904.[126] Of course,

---

[122] *Foreign Relations of the United States,* 1903, pp. 325–26.

[123] Senate Document 474, 63d Cong., 2d sess., p. 584.

[124] This was the burden of such treatises as that of Willard H. Schoff, *Why the Colombian Treaty is not Justified by Facts* (publisher unknown, 1914).

[125] *Protest of Colombia,* p. 34.

[126] "I have to inform your honor that at the beginning of November of last year the Government of Colombia, through its agent in France, informed the New Panama Canal Company that, according to article 21 of the con-

as we now know, the sale was consummated anyway, and Colombia was "made whole" by the Thomson-Urrutia convention in 1922 (over the bitter opposition of Theodore Roosevelt and others).[127]

By paying Colombia the monetary compensation of $25,000,000 provided for in the Thomson-Urrutia Treaty, the United States tacitly, grudgingly, finally (after eighteen years) conceded violation of the Treaty of 1846, but still carefully avoided any express admission of wrongdoing.[128]

How differently another treaty violation was handled. The Panama Canal Act of August 24, 1912 exempted vessels in American coastwise trade from payment of tolls, in contravention of the Hay-Pauncefote Treaty of 1901 with Great Britain.[129] In 1914 President Wilson requested repeal of the provision (and it was repealed) in an

address to Congress containing the following language:

> . . . We consented to the treaty; its language we accepted, if we did not originate it; and we are too big, too powerful, too self-respecting a nation to interpet with too strained or refined a reading the words of our own promises just because we have power enough to give us leave to read them as we please. The large thing to do is the only thing we can afford to do, a voluntary withdrawal from a position everywhere questioned and misunderstood.[130]

Substitute the Treaty of 1846 with New Granada for the Treaty of 1901 with Great Britain, and how do the words sound?

(It is hard to fault the spirit of Wilson's words, and the executive branch, at least, of the United States Government since 1964 shows no inclination to wish to do so with respect to the Hay/Bunau-Varilla Treaty. The trouble is that too much water has run through the locks for everything to be put to rights by a simple "voluntary withdrawal from a position everywhere questioned and misunderstood." A complete undoing of everything that has been done "just because we have power enough" might require not only giving the Canal Zone back to Panama but also giving Panama back to Colombia. Such unrestrained atonement would be equally questioned and misunderstood, in some quarters, if not everywhere. What can be done is a voluntary withdrawal (by a new treaty) from most of the area of the present Zone and, as to the remainder, from the Zone concept.)

(c) Unconstitutionality.

This charge does not seem to have been advanced with the same conviction as (a) and (b), but it is interesting enough to mention, and may have enough substance to darken the "cloud" already hovering over the "title." It depends, in the first instance, on the proposition that the constitutional law of Colombia, like the private law (as admitted), continued in force in Panama until duly abrogated. As we have seen, the Hay-Herrán Treaty—and so, a fortiori, the Hay/Bunau-Varilla Treaty—was held to be in contravention of Colombian constitu-

---

tract celebrated in Bogota on March 20, 1878, between said company and the Colombian Government, it was absolutely prohibited from ceding any of its rights to a foreign nation or government. Therefore the Government of Colombia does not accept the transfer which may be made in violation of that article. This ministry would be pleased if your honor would inform the Government of the United States as soon as possible that Colombia has not given its consent to the transfer of these rights, and firmly insists on the fulfilling of said article of the treaty of 1878." *Foreign Relations of the United States,* 1904, p. 225.

[127] One of the others who actively opposed any form of reparation to Colombia was the same J. S. Foraker who had sponsored legislation authorizing a civil government for Puerto Rico after the Spanish-American War (see chap. II, p. 6). Perhaps the best of the tracts in support of ratification of the Thomson-Urrutia Treaty was that of Joseph C. Freehoff, *America and the Canal Title* (published by the author, 1916).

[128] The Senate deleted Article 1 which contained an expression of "sincere regret that anything should have occurred to interrupt or to mar the relations of cordial friendship that had so long subsisted between the two nations."

[129] Before the position of the President had been made known in the matter, the question was ably debated during a meeting of the American Society of International Law. See *Proceedings of the American Society of International Law at its Seventh Annual Meeting held at Washington, D.C. April 24-26, 1913,* pp. 93-126. See also Latane, "The Panama Canal Act and the British Protest," vol. VII *American Journal of International Law* (1913), pp. 17-25.

[130] 5 Hackworth, p. 164.

tional law because it alienated, in practical effect, part of the national territory.

Nevertheless, the Hay/Bunau-Varilla Treaty was signed by the Panamanian plenipotentiary on November 18, 1903, and ratified by the junta on December 2, 1903.[131] The new constitution of Panama was not promulgated until February 16, 1904.

Though clearly invalid as internal law, views differ on the effect of an unconstitutional treaty in international law. Professor Bishop has culled some pertinent quotations from spokesmen representing opposite extremes, from those who would give such treaties no effect to those who would hold contracting states completely bound on the hypothesis that "national law, including constitutions, and international law operate in separate and distinct spheres, with international law superior in the 'international forum.'" From the first group he offers the following:

> From the evidence of American and South American practice we are entirely justified in saying that upon the American and South American continents constitutional limitations are deemed to be fully operative in international law. A treaty which is constitutionally invalid is internationally null and void . . .[132]

Examining the reasoning behind the views of the second group, Bishop finds it based to a considerable extent on the practical grounds that a state is entitled to rely on the representations of a duly constituted organ of another state and should not be expected to look for hidden contradictions in the domestic law thereof. But that reasoning rapidly loses force as the unconstitutionality is patent and known to the other state. "Thus it is probably true that the more 'notorious' and clear-cut the constitutional provision, the quicker we would be to feel that its violation ought to result in a void treaty."[133]

Nothing could have been more "notori-

ous" and clear-cut to Hay than that the treaty he signed with Bunau-Varilla was unconstitutional in Panama—if we accept the above proposition. If we do not accept it, what was the constitutional law of Panama from November 3, 1903 to February 16, 1904?

At the beginning of this chapter I indulged in memories of French Morocco. In closing, certain memories of French Algeria, perhaps a little more apropos, come to mind. Nationalism in Algeria, beginning to stir during the upheavals of World War II, started from a much weaker base. There was no Algerian "nation" when the French came; and the French, after all, had been there since 1830. Some French friends that I made, sensing the coming struggle, explained that they had never known any other home and showed me the graves of their grandparents. "How can anyone say," they asked, "that this is not our country?" Only after a searing crisis of the soul, which almost tore France apart, was the question answered.

There are Americans in the Canal Zone today who can show you the graves of their grandparents. Though not so conscious of "sovereignty" as the Panamanians, they are no less emotional about whose "country" it is. Who wrested this place from the malarial jungle and built it into a tropical American suburbia? Even those whose roots do not go back so far tend to acquire this "Zonian" mentality [134] after a few years and some now back in the states hold power in the Government and are, like Representative Daniel Flood of Pennsylvania,[135] nostalgi-

---

[131] The ratification itself raises a secondary constitutional question as the Junta legally had only such powers as given by the Panama City Municipal Council, which by no theory of law in any civilized state could have had any authority to ratify treaties, much less delegate such authority.

[132] Bishop, "Unconstitutional Treaties," 42 *Minnesota Law Review* (1958), p. 779.

[133] Ibid., p. 801.

[134] Some would call it more than a mentality; almost a "quasi-nationality" if there were such a thing.

[135] According to his own statements, Mr. Flood's extraordinary interest in preserving the American presence and power in the Canal Zone goes back to his childhood when President Theodore Roosevelt was a great friend of his grandfather's and used to visit in his home. He apparently believes that he is fighting the good fight to preserve what Theodore Roosevelt started.

Unfortunately, Mr. Flood has a tendency at times to go further than necessary in making his case and to give vent to remarks which must

cally, more "Zonian" than ever. Probably most Americans, who have never either been there or given much thought to the matter, would not distinguish between the Zone and the Canal, regarding both as United States property.

That is why the end of the Zone will not come easily despite commitments made and the advanced stage of new treaty negotiations. On March 4, 1975 thirty-seven senators, three more than the number necessary to block a treaty ratification, signed S.R. 97 which expresses the sense of the Senate that the United States not surrender its "sovereign rights and jurisdiction" over the Canal (two more signed later, making a total of thirty-nine on the record as of Oct. 1, 1976).

The problem is all the more difficult for the fair-minded and informed person because he knows in his heart that it is not a simple choice between good and evil or right and wrong. Most "Zonians" sincerely believe not only in their right to stay and hold what they have, but that the continued existence of the Zone is actually beneficial to the majority of the Panamanian people—in the spillover of medical and social services, economically, and many other ways.[136] It is a fact that the "Zonians" have often been very generous in charitable contributions to needy Panamanians and to victims of na-

tural disasters, and it is also a fact that Panamanian workers are better off in the Zone than they would be in their own economy and would be better off still but for restrictions imposed on their participation in the Zone economy at the insistence of the influential Panamanian merchant class.[137]

Nevertheless, the fair-minded and informed person concludes that the Zone must go. We cannot say to Panama, "The Zone stays because it is good for you," even if it is.[138] Whatever the international status of Panama in 1903, it is something else now and the Zone has become impossible. How long this impossible situation can last I am not prepared to guess; Panamanian politics in the past, both internal and external, have demonstrated a high tolerance of the impossible. The signs are clear, however, that such tolerance, in this case, is approaching its elastic limit.[139] And when the Zone disappears the exiled Civil Law will be awaiting restoration.

So much for the *ambiente* of the Civil Law return. The main purpose of this chapter has been to revisit the *ambiente* of the Common Law arrival. After so many years memories of this fairly subtle and almost unobserved phenomenon grow dim;

---

appear to Panamanians as gratuitous slurs on the whole nation, as, for example, the following from his testimony before the House Committee on Merchant Marine and Fisheries (House Hearings, "Serial no. 92-30," p. 162):

So we gave them sanitation. Now, they want the canal. They want the zone. They could not collect their own garbage in Panama City, and Colon, and the Panamanians raised the roof about it, and asked us to come back and, will you please, pick up our garbage. They are not even garbage collectors.

Such intemperate—and, one might add, irrelevant—remarks are somewhat reminiscent of predictions freely made at one time that the Egyptians would never have the competence to operate the Suez Canal.

[136] Item from the *Washington Post* of February 25, 1964:

"Balboa, Panama [Canal Zone]—An American medical team from the Panama Canal Zone is fighting an outbreak of yellow fever in a jungle area in eastern Panama. . . ."

[137] As early as 1913 Edwards (*Panama*, pp. 91-93) observed: "The hostility to the Gringos is industriously fostered by the merchants of the Republic, few of whom are native-born Panamanians" . . . and . . . "A small clique, probably not more than one hundred people, including relatives, is succeeding in blinding the entire city to [the advantages to the people of economic cooperation with the Zone] by their ardent anti-Gringo patriotism."

[138] The idea of making a case that Panamanians should be forced to continue tolerating the Zone because it is good for them may sound fanciful or facetious. In fact it is neither. For example, in an article published in the August 1976 issue of Sea Power (pp. 23-31) by Virginia Prewett, the well-known syndicated columnist on Latin American affairs, that very point is strongly implied and buttressed by a whole page of facts and statistics demonstrating how fortunate the Panamanians are to have the Canal Zone in their midst.

[139] As of late September 1976 Panama was experiencing the most serious internal disturbances since the military dictatorship took power in 1968. While the troubles appeared to be arising from primarily domestic issues, such as the cost of living, the Canal Zone problem

even in the midst of many rhetorical, and sometimes physical, clashes over sovereignty little is said directly about the Common Law corollary. The revisitation reminds us that the reception occurred, without much deliberate aforethought, under the umbrella of that very "sovereignty" as bestowed by the Frenchman Bunau-Varilla. It reminds us of the juridical defects in the umbrella. And it helps us to understand why the umbrella is being removed and what that means to everything sheltered under it.

---

is always just below the surface whenever there is trouble, no matter how it starts, and there was some speculation that the end result might be the return to power of Arnulfo Arias accompanied by a softening, or even withdrawal, of Panamanian pressure on the canal issue.

Though unlikely, I would not rule out the possibility of such a development; but I would predict that, if it did happen, such renewed elasticity would be relatively short-lived as the underlying revulsion of most Panamanians to the Zone concept reasserts itself.

CHAPTER V

THE ISTHMIAN CANAL COMMISSION

If the cloak of legitimacy sheltering the Common Law reception was the "sovereignty" granted in Article III of the Hay/Bunau-Varilla Treaty, the instrument of power which set the stage for it was the Isthmian Canal Commission (I.C.C.).

The I.C.C. was quite possibly the most unusual, versatile, productive, omnipotent, and at the same time ineffectual (as a collective), agency ever created by the Congress of the United States to carry out specified functions. In this case the specified functions, in the words of the Spooner Act,[1] were: to "cause to be excavated, constructed, and completed, . . . a ship canal from the Caribbean Sea to the Pacific Ocean." Surely a big enough order all by itself. No one was even certain it could be done.

---

[1] The Spooner Act, to which many references have already been made in other connections, might be considered the first organic law of the Canal Zone (but see note 9, infra). (The second and third were, respectively, the Panama Canal Act of 1912 and the Canal Zone Code Act of 1934.) All the President's powers in the Canal Zone up to 1912, most of which he delegated to the I.C.C., were derived ultimately from the Spooner Act, as supplemented by the Act of April 28, 1904, and the Executive Order of May 9, 1904.

But before the I.C.C. was through—its responsibilities further swollen by additional legislation and executive orders—it had not only built a ship canal but also eradicated malaria and yellow fever, run a railroad, paved and sanitized two cities, operated hotels and businesses, and set up a civil government complete with courts and laws. (Courts and laws were placed at the end of that sentence deliberately because that is probably where they stood on the I.C.C.'s "order of importance" list insofar as it consciously had one.) A full account of the activities carried out by or under the direction of the I.C.C. would (and does) fill several volumes and many cubic feet of archival space. It was required by the Spooner Act to make annual reports to the President, and additional special reports to the President or the Congress upon request: these reports comprise the mother lode of primary source material used by all researchers in Canal history.

As this is not a general history, only incidental reference will be made to the broad range of activities of the I.C.C. and to its basic mission as Canal builder. There would be, in fact, little reason for mentioning the I.C.C. at all except for its role as Lawgiver and supervisor of justice. But in this role it was crucial, and none the less so because

the engineers and military men who comprised it, for the most part, were a far cry from classical solons.

Not unlike a latter-day viceroy, the I.C.C. was the fount and embodiment of all authority in the Canal Zone, answerable only to the President through the Secretary of War, even as the viceroy was answerable only to the king through the Council of the Indies; also as the viceroy, it sometimes legislated with the delegated power of the sovereign and sometimes acted as a conduit, with enforcement powers, for the pronouncements of the sovereign. Many of the early laws of the Canal Zone, including some that might be thought of as constitutional in nature, were enactments of the Isthmian Canal Commission. (Act No. 1, for example, established the Judiciary and Act No. 8 the Executive Branch; Act No. 14 promulgated the penal code, Act No. 15 the code of criminal procedure.)

The purpose of the foregoing introduction has been to explain the relevance of the I.C.C. to the Common Law reception. I realize, however, that, without some further explanation, it may only add to the confusion of non-specialists who have an impression, from general history, of the I.C.C. in another context. Historians have referred to the "first," "second," and "third" "Isthmian Canal Commissions" in a carelessly overlapping and deceptive manner. Thus, the "second Walker Commission" is sometimes called the "first Isthmian Canal Commission" (which is technically correct because it was the first to bear that title), while the different Isthmian Canal Commission created by the Spooner Act also came to be called "first" (then "second" and "third" as it underwent personnel and organizational changes), and this second "first" was also known as the "third Walker Commission" because it was the third to be chaired by Admiral Walker. In order to get out of this terminological and numerical morass, there will be a brief pause for commission identification.

What differentiates the pre-Spooner Act commissions and other bodies—regardless of name, number, or chairmanship—is that they were all concerned only with the problem of site selection and had nothing to do with either building a canal or governing a territory.

The chronology, in broad outline, goes like this:

(a) In 1869 President Grant, who had crossed the Isthmus as an Army captain seventeen years earlier, ordered the Navy to survey possible canal routes. On March 15, 1872 he appointed an *Interoceanic Canal Commission* to appraise the survey reports. The decision of that commission, announced on February 7, 1876, was unanimously in favor of a Nicaragua route. A privately financed American company started construction in June 1890 but was forced to stop work when financing dried up in the panic of 1893.[2]

(b) President Cleveland then appointed a *United States Nicaragua Canal Board* (popularly known as the Ludlow Commission) which made an inspection of the route in May and June 1895. The Board recommended a re-examination.

(c) On July 29, 1897 President McKinley appointed a *Nicaragua Canal Commission* (headed by Rear Admiral John G. Walker and known as the "first Walker Commission") which completed surveys of various routes in March 1899.

(d) On June 10, 1899 President McKinley appointed an *Isthmian Canal Commission* (also headed by Walker and known as the "second Walker Commission") to decide which of several possible canal routes would be most feasible. This commission turned in a 535-page report in 1901[3] which recommended Nicaragua over Panama mainly because of the cost factor (the New Panama Canal Company was asking $109,-141,500 for its property), a recommendation which was later reversed in a "final" report of January 18, 1902 after the asking figure was reduced to $40,000,000.

It was this "final" report of the last of the investigatory commissions which cleared the way for the Panama-oriented Spooner Act of June 28, 1902. And it was Section 7 of the Spooner Act which created the new Isthmian Canal Commission which built the

---

[2] The French canal company in Panama had given up, for all practical purposes, in 1888; thus leaving the American entrepreneurs, as they thought, a clear field. In addition to building a considerable amount of infrastructure, they actually excavated about three quarters of a mile of canal.

[3] Senate Document No. 54, 57th Cong., 1st sess.

Canal and ushered in the Common Law.[4] Constituted with completely different objectives, as we have seen, this Commission had almost nothing in common with the previous one of the same name except the name itself and the chairman. The first was possibly a mistake because of the misleading terminology, and the second was certainly a mistake because of the character of Admiral Walker.

The members of the first post-Spooner Act Isthmian Canal Commission were confirmed by the Senate on March 3, 1904, only five days after exchange of ratifications of the Hay/Bunau-Varilla Treaty. They were: Rear Admiral John G. Walker, the chairman; Major-General George W. Davis, Governor of the Canal Zone;[5] William H. Burr, a professor of civil engineering in Colombia; William B. Parsons, a civil engineer who had just completed the New

York subway; and civil engineers Benjamin M. Harrod, Carl E. Grunsky, and Frank T. Hecker. Section 7 had stipulated a Commission of seven persons, of whom at least four would be engineers, at least one would be an officer of the United States Army, and at least one would be a member of the United States Navy. Compliance with the Act was perfect. The Act forgot to stipulate, however, that at least one member, preferably the chairman, would be a person with executive ability; it also forgot to stipulate an efficient decision-making process.

There were other defects. Neither of the two men who were actually directing the vital phases of the work—John F. Wallace, the chief engineer, and Colonel William C. Gorgas, the chief sanitary officer—was a member of the Commission, from which they were forced to take orders and suffer rebuffs. The members themselves, with the exception of General Davis, made one quick trip to the Isthmus and then returned to Washington where they stayed. Absentee management on top of diffuse and misplaced responsibility was a prescription for stalemate.[6]

As if to further ensure that little progress would be made on the canal, there was the additional mistake of appointing the durable Walker to a "third term." He was a carryover from one era to another who had outlived his usefulness.[7] Fortunately, these

---

[4] Adverting to the principal theme of Chapter II, the indebtedness of this legislation to the immediately preceding experience with the Philippine Commission, created on March 16, 1900, will be obvious. (An earlier "Philippine Commission," the so-called "Schuman Commission," like the earlier form of I.C.C., was not a true predecessor and had nothing to do with governance of the territory.) Moreover, it may be noted that both the Philippine Commission and the Isthmian Canal Commission exercised delegated Presidental powers through the Secretary of War, both were given legislative authority to establish a judiciary and promulgate positive law, and both were enjoined to follow the twin policies of (a) continuance of existing private law (b) insofar as such law did not conflict with "certain great principles of government." Nor is the fact that the Isthmian Canal Commission at first followed, *mutatis mutandis,* the forms of the Philippine owing solely to precedents on paper. There was an even more tangible connection. By the time the I.C.C. started operating, the chair of Secretary of War was filled (both literally and figuratively) by William Howard Taft, who had been the first president of the Philippine Commission. The connection is further underscored by the fact that Taft had been one of President Roosevelt's principal legal advisers in the steps leading to acquisition of the Canal Zone and he accepted the position of Secretary of War because it would put him in a position to continue to make his influence felt in both territories.

[5] Before coming to the Canal Zone, General Davis had held policy-making positions, both military and civil, in the temporary governments of Puerto Rico, Cuba, and the Philippines.

[6] "The commissioners wastefully duplicated and often nullified each other's activities. . . . Every detail of procedure had to be submitted to Washington, passed upon by each commissioner, and approved only after long and exasperating delay, if at all. Wallace, Gorgas, and the other officials on the isthmus, struggling with titanic problems demanding prompt solutions, had far too little authority." Mack, *Land Divided,* pp. 487-88.

[7] "Much of the futility of the first commission must be ascribed to the curious personality of the chairman. Admiral Walker, whom Gorgas irreverently called 'the old man of the sea,' had served his country well in the preliminary negotiations for the purchase of the canal, but neither by training nor by temperament was he equipped to direct the construction of the great waterway. His 'very appearance—his erect figure, his be-whiskered face, his air of command—fairly suggested the past generation to which he belonged . . . The fear that something like French wastefulness and peculation would stain the American achievement haunted him night and day . . . Economy, rather than construction, therefore became his byword . . .

initial shortcomings in organization and personnel did not cripple the I.C.C. beyond repair, and repairs would soon be undertaken by master carpenter Roosevelt.

Meanwhile, another significant piece of legislation had bolstered the legal underpinnings of the embryonic Zone government. The Spooner Act, as noted, had provided a rudimentary organic law; but the subsequent fruition of the Hay/Bunau-Varilla Treaty called for further and more explicit enabling provisions. Congress came through with "An Act to provide for the temporary government of the Canal Zone at Panama, . . ." of April 28, 1904.[8]

Section 2 of this Act fleshed out Section 7 of the Spooner Act by saying that:

. . . all the military, civil, and judicial powers as well as the power to make all rules and regulations necessary for the government of the Canal Zone . . . shall be vested in such person or persons [the I.C.C.] and shall be exercised in such manner as the President shall direct. . . .

The President's directions were forthcoming in executive orders dated March 8, 1904, the discretionary spirit of which may be summed up in the following excepts:

. . . As to the details of the work itself I have but little to say. . . . The methods for achieving the results must be yours. What this nation will insist upon is that the results be achieved. . . .

and May 9, 1904 defining the jurisdiction and functions of the I.C.C.[9]

It is one of the more intriguing facets of the Canal Zone's fascinating legal history that the above vested powers of the I.C.C., though virtually unlimited as to scope, were strictly limited as to time, and were exercised during most of the next ten years without congressional authorization after the time had run out. The quoted operative language of Section 2 was preceded by the qualifying phrase: ". . . until the expiration of the Fifty-eighth Congress, . . ." An Act of Session III of the Fifty-eighth Congress in 1905 provided that "the Commission is hereby revived and continued until the beginning of the next session of Congress."[10] The next session of Congress took no action to restore the Commission's authority, nor did any other session until the Panama Canal Act of August 24, 1912 (q.v., p. 68, infra). The first act in the next Congress relating to the Panama Canal (59 Stat. 5, Dec. 21, 1905) simply provided, without mentioning the I.C.C., for continuance of the construction of the canal and of the government of the Canal Zone by the President and persons appointed or employed by him.[11] This left the I.C.C. in a curious legal limbo—thereafter it issued "ordinances" instead of "acts"—but did not in practice place any effective restraints on its exercise of power in the Zone.[12]

A clear conception of this situation at the outset is necessary for a proper understanding of why there was built up in the Canal Zone a system of control which has been styled variously "paternalism," "modified socialism," and "benevolent despotism." . . . [The Fifty-eighth] Congress went out of existence without taking

---

The Admiral had such an aversion to spending money, even . . . for indispensable work, that at times he would not even open communications.'" Mack, Land Divided, p. 488.

[8] 33 Stat. 429. Incidentally, this Act contained the sentence: "The said zone is hereinafter referred to as 'the Canal Zone.'" Before the Act (and in some cases after) the acquired territory was often referred to, even in official documents, as "the canal strip" and in various other ways.

[9] The Supreme Court of the Canal Zone, in Canal Zone v. Coulson (1907) (see chap. VI p. 87, infra), referred to Executive Order of May 9, 1904 as the organic law of the Canal Zone; but this would seem to be a mistaking of the hindmost part for the whole. I think it more accurate to say that the first organic law consisted of the Spooner Act of June 28, 1902, the supplementary Act of April 28, 1904, and the Executive Order of May 9, 1904. For brevity, the Spooner Act is here called the first organic law, but it should be understood to include the other two promulgations.

[10] 33 Stat. 1246.

[11] "The I.C.C. exercised legislative powers under the Act of April 28, 1904, till the expiration of the Fifty-eighth Congress, on March 4, 1905, when, according to the terms of that Act, it ceased to possess such powers. After March 4, 1905, the Canal Zone government was administered in accordance with laws already enacted and through executive orders down to the completion of the work." Joseph Bucklin Bishop (Secretary of the I.C.C.), The Panama Gateway (New York: Charles Scribner's Sons, 1913), pp. 153-54.

[12] The "ordinances" were considered to have as much legal force as the "acts" though in general they dealt with subjects of somewhat lesser gravity.

further action in the matter, thus leaving the President without congressional authority to continue the exercise of those powers which it had conferred in the act of 1904, and under which he had established a form of government in the Canal Zone, using the canal commission as a legislative body. As he was directed to construct the canal, as the maintenance of a government in the Canal Zone was essential to such construction [not proved but obviously accepted as an article of faith by the canal builders], and as there was an existing government bound by existing laws which continued in effect, though the power to make or amend them had ceased, the President decided that it was his duty, under his constitutional obligation, to see to it that the laws were enforced and that the established government carried out its functions as limited by legislative acts. . . . [Consequently] rule by executive order, rather than through legislative action by Congress or by the canal commission, was established. . . .[13]

(Nevertheless, the collected legislation of the I.C.C. was published in 1922 in a volume entitled "Laws of the Canal Zone, Isthmus of Panama, Enacted by the Isthmian Canal Commission, August 16, 1904 to March 31, 1914," and including both "acts" and "ordinances.")

Then Governor Magoon, testifying in 1906 before the Senate Committee on Interoceanic Canals, strongly urged that Congress renew the provisions of Section 2 of the Act of April 28, 1904, after which the following exchange took place:

> Senator Morgan: Do you think that legislative approval is necessary [to validate] the acts of the Commission in pursuance of their supposed authority under that act?
>
> Mr. Magoon: No: I would not think so because I think that they were all well within the authority which was conferred. But it would save any possible question which might hereafter arise when the time shall come when we will have the action of our courts, for instance, reviewed by the Supreme Court of the United States.[14]

The question that troubled Magoon about the legitimacy of the Canal Zone courts had already been raised in the case of Oli Nifou

and would be raised again in the case of Coulson (see chap. VI). Fortunately for the Canal Zone courts, and indirectly for the progress of reception, the Supreme Court refused to review in both cases on jurisdictional grounds.

The ineptitude of the first Commission, though almost fatal to the Canal, was not a serious impediment to the march of jurisprudence—already hearing a different (Common Law) drummer—in the Zone. This was because none of its members were lawyers and so they prudently left what they did not understand to qualified counsel who drafted and issued jurisprudential enactments in their name. It was not, in any event, a matter with which they were overly preoccupied. After all, if the law is slowly changing, or even if it should be and isn't, nobody will notice; but if the Canal is not getting built, everybody will—and soon did.

But while the legal system could be transformed without noticeable reaction, the trodding on Panamanian economic interests could not. Though not entirely of the I.C.C.'s making, the strains which soon developed over application of the Dingley tariff, inconsiderate postal regulations, and other economic inequities, were more aggravated than alleviated by I.C.C. attitudes. The situation was saved, for the time being, by Secretary Taft who came to the Isthmus in late 1904 and stayed for about ten days.[15] On December 3, 1904, he issued an executive order in the name of the President which greatly reduced the level of Panamanian complaints. The one provision of that order relevant to this book, considered of relatively minor importance at the time, indirectly reaffirmed the noncessionary

[15] Secretary and Mrs. Taft were the guests of chief engineer Wallace who lived in the heart of old Panama City in a house which had previously been occupied by the managing director of the French canal company.[*] His choice of residence, eschewing the Zone, as well as the "genial personality of the rotund Secretary," undoubtedly helped to make a good impression. He was accompanied by Cromwell who later took a good deal of the credit for the success of the mission.

[*] Ira E. Bennett, History of the Panama Canal, (Washington, D. C.: Historical Publishing Company), 1915), pp. 195-96.

[13] Bishop, Panama Gateway, pp. 259-60.
[14] Senate Document No. 401, 59th Cong., 2d sess., p. 910.

status of the Zone by recognizing that Panamanian residents thereof retained full Panamanian citizenship.[16]

It seems to have been primarily Wallace, the frustrated chief engineer, who convinced Roosevelt that the unwieldy seven-headed I.C.C. would have to be reorganized. Roosevelt asked Congress for an amendment to the Spooner Act reducing the membership to five, or preferably three. The House acted but the Senate did not. Determined to proceed, with or without legislation, Roosevelt called for the resignation of all the commissioners and appointed a second commission, at the same time changing the ground rules so that all important decisions would be taken by an "executive committee" of three, two of whom must reside on the Isthmus.[17]

The second I.C.C., effective April 1, 1905, consisted of the following members: Theodore Perry Shonts, the chairman; Charles E. Magoon, newly appointed Governor of the Canal Zone;[18] John F. Wallace,

chief engineer; Rear Admiral Mordecai T. Endicott, a member of the Ludlow Commission of 1895; Brigadier General Peter C. Hains, who had served on the first two Walker Commissions; Colonel Oswald H. Ernst, who had served on the second Walker Commission; and Benjamin M. Harrod, the only member of the first I.C.C. to be reappointed. The first three composed the "executive committee";[19] the others were there to comply with the unamended Spooner Act which specified a membership of seven.

Shonts was a dynamic railroad man with a reputation for getting things done. Though a little on the pompous side, with a good opinion of himself which he troubled little to conceal, he did, during his two years in office, get the gigantic project organized at last and ready to start moving at full speed. In executive ability he was a vast

---

[16] "Sec. 9. Citizens of the Republic of Panama at any time residing in the Canal Zone shall have, so far as concerns the United States, entire freedom of voting at elections held in the Republic of Panama and its provinces or municipalities at such places outside of the Canal Zone as may be fixed by the Republic, and under such conditions as the Republic may determine; but nothing herein is to be construed as intending to limit the power of the Republic to exclude or restrict the right of such citizens to vote as it may deem judicious."

[17] As Edwards commented in 1913: "It was as satisfactory an arrangement as could be made without the new legislation which the Senate had refused to grant. Various bills, legalizing this distortion of the existing law, have been continually before Congress and none of them have been passed. The canal is being built by administrative evasion. It could not be done otherwise. Which is a rather distressing commentary on the brains of our law-makers." Edwards, *Panama*, p. 481.

[18] Effective in August 1905, Magoon also assumed the post of Minister to Panama. Reference has already been made (chap. II, note 4) to the fact that he is the only person ever to hold both positions simultaneously. Obviously, such a concentration of power posed a grave danger to the fledgling Republic of Panama, carrying with it the inference that the United States looked upon Panama as simply an appendage to the Canal Zone. Which is exactly the way most Canal Zone officials saw it, and the result was constant conflict with the Legation and the State Department. The

inside story of how the problem was resolved by Magoon's dual role is told by Sands (see bibliography). With Magoon's departure the built-in strains between the Canal Zone Government (under the Secretary of the Army) and the U.S. diplomatic mission in Panama City (under the Secretary of State) re-emerged and have still not entirely disappeared, being an extension, to a certain extent, of disagreements in Washington between the Department of State and the Pentagon. For example, Hanson W. Baldwin, in the *New York Times* of Aug. 13, 1960 (p. 16L), wrote:

In the past there have often been major differences between the United States Ambassador to Panama and the governor of the Canal Zone and between Pentagon and State about canal methods and policies. . . .

Maj. Gen. William E. Potter, who had been governor of the Canal Zone for the last four years . . . was firm during his regime in upholding United States rights to the exercise of sovereignty over the zone. He and the former United States Ambassador to Panama, Julian F. Harrington, had often disagreed.

Harrington's successor, Joseph S. Farland (1960-1963), also had well advertised differences with Zone officials, and his policies were very unpopular with "Zonians" in general.

[19] The tyranny of terminology again leads to potential confusion. The first commission also had an "executive committee"—composed of Walker, Parsons, and Grunsky—but it was just an internal working group with none of the concentration of authority which characterized the "executive committee" of the second commission.

improvement over the penny-pinching Walker. His own conception of himself as nation-builder, however, carried him into extremes of rhetoric which implied pretensions even more offensive to Panamanians, if they had taken any notice, than the Zone concept. He was fond of claiming to have carved a "state" out of the tropical jungle.[20]

The histories make little of it, and one almost has to read between the lines to find it, but the conclusion seems inescapable that Magoon was the primary, perhaps near exclusive, architect of the legal structure of the formative Canal Zone Government. Not only was he the only lawyer on the second Commission, but he had served during the first Commission (on which there was no lawyer) as general counsel in the Washington Office. And before that he had been the United States Government's leading expert on legal problems of Cuba, Puerto Rico, and the Philippines (see chap. II, note 4). "Both Shonts and Magoon were 'practical' men with the limitations as well as the virtues of their kind, but in manner 'they were quite unlike—Mr. Shonts aggressive, tactless, gruff, and domineering; Mr. Magoon polite, likable, and charming.' "[21]

Wallace, to all surface appearances, was now sitting on top of the world. The I.C.C. had been reorganized to his liking. He was not only a commissioner but also a member of the "executive committee." Yet, after achieving his goals in Washington and returning to the Isthmus on May 24, 1905, he cabled Taft on June 5 for permission to again visit the United States on urgent private business. Versions differ as to his motivation—Magoon thought he might be trying to get Shonts' job—but in any case, in a stormy meeting in New York on June

25, Taft demanded and received his resignation.

The second engineer, appointed almost immediately, was John F. Stevens, another railroad man and apparently a more personable manager than Wallace. He was faced, however, with the same inherent difficulties of working within the Commission framework as then constituted. For some reason he was not appointed to Wallace's old seat on the Commission and so was technically subordinate to the I.C.C., but he exacted a kind of "gentlemen's agreement" that he would have a free hand.[22]

In November 1906 President Roosevelt visited the Isthmus himself (being the first time an American President had ever left United States soil while in office) and while there signed an executive order (November 17) reorganizing the second Commission. The most significant changes were: (a) the "executive committee" was abolished, the duties of the commission were divided among "departments," and all department heads would be appointed by and responsible to the Chairman,[23] (b) the operation of the Panama Railroad was placed under the chief engineer, (c) the office of Governor of the Canal Zone was abolished and the administration of civil government (including

[20] For example: "The present Commission, during its first visit to the Isthmus in July, 1905, decided that a considerable period must be devoted to preparation before the actual work of canal construction could be carried forward. A form of government must be devised and put into operation in order to maintain law and order. In other words, we had to create a State. . . . That, gentlemen, is the record of things done. We have created a State. . . ." *Speech of the Hon. Theodore P. Shonts, Chairman of the Isthmian Canal Commission, before the Knife-and-fork Club, Kansas City, on the evening of January 24, 1907* (Washington, D. C.: Government Printing Office, 1907), pp. 4, 22.

[21] Mack, *Land Divided*, p. 492.

[22] "In work of this kind Mr. Stevens had had large experience in the far Western section of the United States and was an acknowledged expert of the first rank. Mr. Shonts, who was to work with him on the isthmus, was a practical railway man but not an engineer, and while he was nominally Mr. Stevens' superior officer he was actually his intelligent coadjutor and prompt agent in executing the comprehensive and masterly plans which the fertile and trained mind of Mr. Stevens evolved." Bishop, *Panama Gateway*, p. 162.

[23] In a chapter contributed to the Bennett history several years after the event, Stevens claimed most of the credit for elimination of the committee idea. In a letter to President Roosevelt dated August 5, 1906, he had written: ". . . I believe that the power and responsibility should be concentrated, not divided; that the commission, constituted in whatever way it may be, must practically be a unit, and as such, must resolve itself into what will amount to a one-man proposition. . . . While the canal may be paid for by the eighty odd millions of the people of the United States, the construction of it can be successfully carried on only under the supervision of a very limited number of them." Bennett, *History*, p. 222.

the Judiciary) was placed under the general counsel. This last development, with which we are most concerned, was precipitated by the departure of Governor Magoon who had been reassigned to Cuba as provisional governor in October 1906.[24]

Though not mentioned in the executive order, another problem coming to a head was the growing disagreement between Shonts and Stevens. In a clash on a major question of policy—Shonts wanted to open the canal job to private bidders and Stevens wanted to keep it under Government control—Stevens' views prevailed. Shonts felt that his usefulness was at an end and reminded Roosevelt in January 1907 that he had only promised to stay during the preparatory phase. On March 4, 1907 he resigned to become president of the Interborough-Metropolitan Company of New York.

Meanwhile, Stevens had belatedly been appointed to Wallace's old seat on the Commission, and Lt. Colonel George W. Goethals, in February 1907, had been designated "chief engineer under the direction of Mr. Stevens." Upon Shonts' resignation, Stevens was moved up to chairman and Goethals was appointed to the seat on the Commission vacated by Stevens. As Stevens still held the prior title of chief engineer, a precedent was thus set for combining the two key offices in one person—an arrangement which proved to be the key to the final solution. But the person would be Goethals, not Stevens.

Meanwhile, also, another episode must be noted in the strange half-life of the I.C.C. as a plenary legislative body. As we have seen, its legislative authority expired on March 4, 1905, yet it had of necessity made certain amendments to its own legislation since that date. Secretary Taft made it legal by a sleight-of-hand executive order dated February 28, 1907:

All acts and resolutions of the Isthmian Canal Commission passed since March 4, 1905, in so far as they effect changes in the "Laws of the Canal Zone" or other enactments of the Commission relative to the Government of the Canal Zone prior to March 4, 1905, are hereby approved.

An executive order of March 13, 1907, primarily concerned with dividing the Canal Zone into administrative districts, contained the following paragraph firming up the I.C.C.'s authority as a kind of municipal legislative body:

7. Ordinances regulating police, sanitation, and taxation, and any other matters now regulated by ordinance, may be enacted, and existing ordinances may be repealed, by the Isthmian Canal Commission, with the approval of the Secretary of War. . . .

With respect to the chief engineer's job, history repeated itself with a vengeance. After less than a month in the presumably coveted dual role, Stevens resigned. Whatever his reasons, and again versions differ, it was the last straw for Roosevelt. Enough of these fickle civilians. He made up his mind to turn to the Army. In any case, the I.C.C. had fallen apart and would have to be reconstituted. In addition to the loss of Magoon, Shonts and Stevens, Ernst had previously resigned in June 1906, and on March 16, 1907 the other three members resigned.

The two most important specific accomplishments of the second Commission, both owing largely to the initiative of Stevens, had been (a) the recruiting and organization of the labor force (of which more will be said later), and (b) the decision to build a lock canal. With respect to the latter, it may seem surprising in retrospect, but as late as February 1906, two years after the Hay/Bunau-Varilla Treaty, the United States Government still had not decided whether it was building a lock canal or a sea-level canal. In making the decision the I.C.C. overrode the majority opinion of a distinguished international consulting board.[25] The lock canal plan was enacted into law by Congress in June 1906.[26]

---

[24] Magoon left the Isthmus on September 25, 1906. Between that date and November 17 the former duties of the office of the Governor devolved upon the executive secretary.

[25] Bunau-Varilla was back in the action with a complicated scheme for a temporary lock canal which would be progressively lowered, without interruption of traffic, until it reached sea level and then would be called the "Straits of Panama."

[26] As late as May 5, 1909 *The Canal Record* (see p. 66, infra) carried an article subheaded "Relative Merits of Sea-level and Lock Canals" which began: "Although the type of canal at Panama is probably definitely settled in favor of the lock system, there continues to be more or less agitation and discussion of the subject. . . ."

Effective April 1, 1907, Roosevelt appointed the third and last Commission, composed of four Army officers, one Navy officer, and two civilians. The first three years of the I.C.C. had been a time of preparation; the next seven would see the Canal finished, the substantial advancement of the Common Law reception, and the end of the I.C.C. form of government.

The members of the third Commission were: Lt. Colonel George W. Goethals, the chairman (and chief engineer); Colonel William C. Gorgas, chief sanitary officer since 1904 now seated on the Commission for the first time; Major David Du Bose Gaillard; Major William Luther Sibert; Rear Admiral Harry Harwood Rousseau; Joseph C. S. Blackburn, a former senator from Kentucky; and Jackson Smith, head of the division of labor and quarters under the second Commission. All but the two civilians stayed until the end or almost the end of the construction period. Smith resigned in September 1908 and was replaced by an Army officer, Lt. Colonel Harry Foote Hodges. Blackburn retired in December 1909 and was replaced by Maurice Hudson Thatcher, a Kentucky lawyer, who stayed until nearly the end of the Commission's existence (being replaced for the last few months by Richard L. Metcalfe).[27]

The appointment of the third Commission was immediately followed, on April 2, 1907, by the following executive order:

By direction of the President it is ordered: That until otherwise directed, the authority of the Governor or Chief Executive of the Canal Zone, under existing laws, resolutions and executive orders, shall be vested in and exercised by the Chairman of the Isthmian Canal Commission.

That put an end to the partial independence of the civil government which had obtained under Magoon, and also put an end to the office of governor until it was revived with the installation of a permanent form of government in 1914. In addition to now being de facto "Governor" of the Zone, Goethals was chairman of the I.C.C., chief engineer, and president of the Panama Railroad. Thereafter the other commissioners also lived on the Isthmus and became working members, under the chairman, as heads of departments. While definitely not a council of equals, as intended by the Spooner Act, they were no longer mere figureheads to fill up the table of organization.

After a trial run of about nine months with the third Commission, Roosevelt decided he had the right formula at last and the only thing lacking was more of the same. On January 6, 1908 he issued an order entitled POWERS OF THE ISTHMIAN CANAL COMMISSION AND ITS CHAIRMAN NEWLY DEFINED which modified the executive order of November 17, 1906 in such a way as to strengthen the authority of the chairman in the I.C.C. to such an extent as to virtually abolish the latter as an executive body (though it continued to be such in form). Goethals became an absolute dictator.[28] In the euphemistically understated words of the annual report:

The executive order of January 6, 1908, combined several existing orders and defined the duties of the commission more clearly, transferring to the chairman certain details which the order that it superseded had delegated to the commission.[29]

As I have postulated in Chapter I that the Common Law reception was not imposed by conquest, it is at least a legitimate question to ask whether the Zone was not ruled from 1907 to 1914 (the end of the

---

[27] Though they all worked hard and effectively in their respective assignments, the names of only three—besides the chairman—are household words today: Gorgas, whose name is attached to one of the finest hospitals south of the Rio Grande, to which patients are sometimes flown from as far away as Argentina; Gaillard, memorialized in the Gaillard (Culebra) Cut and the Gaillard Highway; and Thatcher for the magnificent bridge of the same name which spans the Canal at Panama City.

[28] This result was not reached without some resistance. The initial attitude of some of the other commissioners has been compared to that of the other members of the First Consulate before they became fully familiar with the character of Napoleon. After the shakedown of January 1908, the situation was described by Edwards (Panama, p. 507): "The other six Commissioners are subordinates, most of them cordial, all of them docile. Certainly modern times have never seen one-man rule pushed to such an extreme. The Colonel, with his immense capacity for work and the restricted area of his domain . . . succeeds in the role of autocrat after a fashion which must cause no little envy to Nicholas II."

[29] Report of the Isthmian Canal Commission, 1908, p. 1.

I.C.C.), during which a large measure of the reception occurred, by a diluted form of military occupation. It is undeniable that the Commission was heavily weighted with the military (four West Point graduates and one naval officer), that Goethals himself had the quintessential military mind, if there is such a thing, and that method and organization followed the military model.[30] And, of course, the direct rule of the President over the I.C.C. was exercised through the Secretary of War. On the other hand, Goethals seemed to go out of his way to reassure all concerned that, however paternalistic and despotic his administration, the Army, as such, was not in control,[31] and the adoption of Army methods was simply a matter of efficiency. It is said that he was never seen on the Isthmus in uniform. So far as having any effect on the evolution of private law, any suspicion of imposition by military occupation seems without foundation.

The order of January 6, 1908, which consummated the trend toward centralization of authority in the chairman, also made some adjustments in what were now called the "departments." With respect to the civil government, what it actually did was give presidential sanction to an adjustment that had already been made by Goethals. Effective May 9, 1907, he had ordained a Department of Civil Administration and placed at the head of it Commissioner Blackburn, the former Kentucky senator. As this proved to be a satisfactory arrangement, it was perpetuated and remained substantially un-

changed, under Blackburn and his successors Thatcher and Metcalfe, for the rest of the construction period.[32]

In the annual report of his department for 1907 Blackburn made some introductory observations which help explain both the organization as it had developed to that point and the philosophical assumptions which made the Common Law reception inevitable:

This department was first organized by the Canal Commission in September, 1904, as "the government of the Canal Zone." Its functions were to exercise the *judicial* [emphasis supplied] and executive rights of government in the Canal Zone acquired by the United States under the treaty with Panama.[33]

Although the department has undergone several changes since its original organization, it still remains in fact what it was then in name. . . . It is only by recognizing the fact that we are building here a government for all time, and, as the President said in his letter of instruction of May 9, 1904, building it upon principles "which have been made the basis of our existence as a nation," [the Bill of Rights of the United States Constitution], that we can hope to make the government one that will command the confidence and respect not only of our *own people* [emphasis supplied], but also of the world at large. . . .

The department as now organized includes the executive office, the courts of the Canal Zone, the office of the prosecuting attorney, the divisions of rev-

---

[30] Mack (*Land Divided*, pp. 501-15) entitled his chapter dealing with the government of this period: "Army Regime."

[31] "Soon after his arrival, at a reception which was given to him, he said: 'I will say that I expect to be the chief of the division of engineers, while the heads of the various departments are going to be the colonels, the foremen are going to be the captains, and the men who do the labor are going to be the privates. There will be no more militarism in the future than there has been in the past. I am no longer a commander in the United States Army. I now consider that I am commanding the Army of Panama, and that the enemy we are going to combat is the Culebra Cut and the locks and dams at both ends of the canal. Every man who does his duty will never have any cause to complain on account of militarism.' He carried out this assurance to the letter." Bishop, *Panama Gateway*, p. 178.

[32] To retrace the succession after Magoon left the Isthmus on September 25, 1906: (a) the functions of the government of the Canal Zone fell to the executive secretary of the I.C.C., (b) by Executive Order of November 17, 1906 they were transferred to the general counsel of the I.C.C., (c) on November 25, 1906 the general counsel left the Isthmus and the functions reverted to the executive secretary, (d) under the Executive Order of April 2, 1907, the functions were assigned to the chairman but the record indicates they were routinely performed by the general counsel, (e) by the chairman's order of May 9, 1907, the functions were delegated, under the chairman, to a Department of Civil Administration headed by Blackburn, (f) by the modifying Executive Order of January 6, 1908 the above disposition was given presidential approval.

[33] As I pointed out in Chapter IV, the treaty with Panama did not expressly grant any judicial rights; they have to be inferred from the "sovereignty" clause.

enues, posts, customs, lands, administration of estates, police, education, fire protection, and public works. . . .[34]

(At the risk of being repetitious, I will call attention to the last paragraph above as a reminder that the whole Judiciary (which will be examined in the next chapter), however much it may appear to be copied after that in the United States, was (and still is, in part) in fact just another "bureau" in the executive structure, not a coequal branch of government created by a constitution.) [35]

It is not clear whether the course of reception was influenced to any extent by the policy line of Blackburn and his successors. Rather than consciously setting or following any directions, it seems more likely that both they and the judges were simply taking for granted that American law would supplant the indigenous "with all deliberate speed" consonant with the presidential admonition of gradualism to reduce the social shock. According to Mack, (Land Divided, p. 511), Blackburn exercised little authority, for Goethals decided all questions of major importance, and his principal function was to deliver flowery speeches, thereby relieving Goethals of many of the ceremonial chores which he detested.[36] One writer,[37]

however, credits the Executive Order of February 6, 1908, extending the Common Law right of trial by jury to the Canal Zone for the first time, to the personal intervention of Blackburn who "regarded it as repugnant to American ideas of justice to deny to Americans on the Isthmus the right to be tried for felonious offenses by juries of their Peers." [38]

After 1908 the structure of the I.C.C. remained stabilized, with Goethals the chief stabilizer. In the next few years the only change worth mentioning, for purposes of this book, was the creation in 1910 of a Department of Law. In a way this was merely a kind of upgrading of what had previously been designated as the office of general counsel, headed by Richard Reid Rogers, but at the same time it raised the prestige of the legal adviser and was a recognition of the growing importance of the subject (to a large extent, it must be admitted, because of multiplying disputes over land titles). Thereafter the annual report of the Department of Law was linked to, and on the same level with, the Department of Civil Administration. It was headed by Judge Frank Feuille, an erudite and dedicated jurist, whose studies and recommendations greatly influenced the development of Canal Zone law and the organization of the Judiciary.[39]

One activity of a judicial stripe on which he had no influence, however, was the so-called Sunday Morning Grievance Court of Colonel Goethals. Unreported in any record of judicial proceedings, the Colonel's decisions appear to have left no permanent imprint on the law; but, according to all accounts—and there are many as most historians found the spectacle an irresistible topic—they had an enormous and immediate impact on the actual behavior of people.

Sunday mornings a scene took place that was strangely reminiscent of the caliphs of Bagdad a thousand years ago. For Sunday morning, at eight o'clock, in his private office at Culebra, the colonel held court. Not a court with a judge and jury; not, indeed, such a court as there was

[34] Report of the Isthmian Canal Commission, 1907, pp. 144-45.
[35] As the Canal Zone Supreme Court said in Canal Zone v. Mena (2 Canal Zone Reports 170 (1912), at 172): "It is true that the political situation in the Canal Zone is unique . . . . the President has . . . promulgated a system of laws . . . and has instituted courts and appointed judges clothed with full power and authority to administer equal justice unfettered by any limitations except their own judicial consciences and a due regard for a proper interpretation and application of the law. . . . The President is undoubtedly invested with larger right, authority, and power here than in any other territory controlled by the United States."
[36] Also: "In addition to directing the government of the Zone, the head of the department of civil administration was the titular representative of the Canal Commission in all matters in which the commission and the Republic of Panama had a mutual interest. However, in practice, the Panamanian Government looked directly to the chairman and chief engineer on all important matters." Frederick J. Haskin, The Panama Canal (New York: Doubleday, Page & Company, 1913), p. 257.
[37] Ibid., p. 258.

[38] The Coulson case (see chap. VI, p. 87, infra). Coulson was a Barbadian Negro but the rationale of the decision would have applied equally to an American citizen.
[39] Feuille had previously served as Attorney General of Puerto Rico and often reasoned by analogy from Puerto Rican precedents.

anywhere in all North or South America, but a court of justice nevertheless. There anyone who had a complaint—man or woman, black or white, young or old, each was free to come with his grievances and ask justice of the colonel. His was the last word, and when he rendered a decision they could appeal only to the President of the United States.[40]

There seems to be no evidence that any such appeal was ever taken.

One admits that the picture does have a certain romantic attraction. Granting only a little leeway to the imagination, it is not impossible to visualize—given enough time and an official reporter—the birth of a court of neo-equity, bursting the restraints of the still surviving conventional forms of action, based on the "Chairman's foot." On the other hand, a close look at some of the decisions most admired by the history writers raises even stronger images of Judge Roy Bean's "law west of the Pecos." Two examples of the colonel's adjudications in the field of labor law:

At one time there was a waiters' strike at the Tivoli Hotel. Colonel Goethals promptly issued an order publishing the names of the strikers and forbidding their employment in any capacity at any future time by the canal commission.[41]

and

When strikes were threatened, Colonel Goethals said: "Gentlemen, decide for yourselves. Quit work if you want to. That is your right and privilege. But if you do so, remember that under no circumstances will you be reemployed." After the boiler-makers strike of 1910, ... the jobs were filled and the strikers were told that the isthmus had no more work for them. There never was another strike among the Americans there.[42]

Nor was Goethals deterred by his lack of qualifications as a comparativist from making decisions involving alleged differences between the English and American branches of Common Law:

The first callers were a negro couple from Jamaica. They had a difference of opinion as to the ownership of thirty-five dollars which the wife had earned by washing. Colonel Goethals listened gravely until the fact was established that she had earned it, then ordered the man to return it. He started to protest something about a husband's property rights under the English law. "All right," the Colonel said, decisively. "Say the word, and I'll deport you. You can get all the English law you want in Jamaica." [43]

When Goethals threatened to deport the male chauvinist Jamaican, he wasn't kidding. Executive Order of May 9, 1904 authorized the I.C.C. to exclude or deport from

the canal zone and other places on the isthmus, over which the United States has jurisdiction, persons of the following classes who were not actually domiciled within the zone on the 26th day of February, 1904, viz.: Idiots, the insane, epileptics, paupers, criminals, professional beggars, persons afflicted with loathsome or dangerous contagious diseases; those who have been convicted of felony, anarchists, those whose purpose it is to incite insurrection and others whose presence it is believed would tend to create public disorder, endanger the public health, or in any manner impede the prosecution of the work of opening the canal . . .

This authority had at first been assigned by the I.C.C. to the Governor of the Canal Zone, then distributed in other ways, but from and after April 24, 1907 it had come to rest, as had most other authority, with the chairman. Some might quibble over whether the Jamaican's seizure of his wife's wash money was likely to incite insurrection, or create public disorder, or endanger the public health; but it really didn't matter which count was relied on as the colonel did not have to explain his decision.

To the international lawyer the really interesting point was the exclusion from the Order of persons "actually domiciled within the Zone on the 26th day of February, 1904." This would seem to have been an

---

[40] Howard Fast, *Goethals and the Panama Canal* (New York: Julian Messner, Inc., 1942), pp. 176-77.

[41] *Bennett, History*, p. 139.

[42] Ibid., p. 162. It is not difficult to see that Goethals' handling of strikers met with the approval of this particular historian. Bennett's personal predilection on race relations is even more transparent: "The British [West Indian] negro is deeply religious and most respectful. He has no dreams of equality. He is polite and deferential and is generally liked. He reminds one of the good old-time 'darky' of the South." Ibid., p. 163.

[43] Edwards, *Panama*, p. 503.

act of voluntary restraint; for if the President (through his representatives on the Isthmus) could deport persons who entered (or were born in?) the Zone after February 26, 1904, why could he not do the same to prior residents? There was nothing in the Treaty to prevent it, nor was citizenship (either United States or Panamanian) any protection.

Deportations were in fact carried out regularly and in fairly large numbers, once the practice got started.[44] The most common reason, it seems (though I have not assembled any statistics) was chronic illness.[45] In any event, and for whatever rea-

son or combination of reasons, deportation was found to be a useful adjunct to the "exercise" of sovereignty and was perpetuated in the Zone after the permanent form

---

to live in the "bush" rather than in Commission quarters, only reporting for work when they run out of money. "The home-making instinct is proving, therefore, to be detrimental to the effectiveness of the labor force, and it is only in appearance that it makes for stability. . . . In order to lessen this class of desertion the recruiting agent in Barbados has been directed not to accept laborers who have ever before been on the Isthmus."

Before calling down an anathema on the I.C.C. for its treatment of labor, however, the times and contemporary world standards must be kept in mind, and in that context the policies of the I.C.C. were, on the whole and in the circumstances, progressive and enlightened. No public or private employer on anything like such a massive scale had ever before gone to such lengths to provide for the health and welfare of its employees. With respect to employees injured on the job, the condition of American citizens during the first half of the construction period was not much better than that of foreign workers. Much of the impetus for the landmark legislation that changed that condition—for all government employees— came from the I.C.C. *The Canal Record* of February 19, 1908 printed an extract from President Theodore Roosevelt's special message to Congress urging passage of a government employees compensation act in which the President specifically alluded to a yardmaster in the Zone who was injured nearly two years before and had since been helpless to support his family. Said Roosevelt: "It is a matter of humiliation to this nation that there should not be on our statute books provision to meet and partially to atone for cruel misfortune when it comes upon a man through no fault of his own while faithfully serving the public." Congress reacted by passing "An Act Granting to certain employees of the United States the right to receive from it compensation for injuries sustained in the course of their employment" of May 30, 1908 (35 Stat. 556). This pioneering Act specifically included employees "in hazardous employment under the Isthmian Canal Commission." * Coverage of canal employees was further extended in "An Act Relating to injured employees on the Isthmian Canal" of February 24, 1909 (35 Stat. 645).

[44] It did not catch on immediately. The I.C.C. in its first annual report said: "So far there has been no occasion to exercise the authority delegated to the Commission by the President in his instructions to the Secretary of War of May 9, 1904, conferring upon them the power to expel from the Canal Zone certain criminal, vicious, or undesirable characters."

[45] Although in law the deportation power of the I.C.C. authorized by Executive Order of May 9, 1904 was not limited by nationality, in fact all or nearly all of the persons deported for being sick were, I believe, imported laborers, nationals of some country other than the United States or Panama. A second point of fact is that apparently no attempt at all was made to distinguish and alleviate cases where the illness might have been contracted owing to conditions of employment. On the contrary, available evidence suggests that the health hazards of working on the Isthmus were discounted in advance by management, and the custom of treating laborers exposed to such hazards as expendable was long established. As Edwards (*Panama*, p. 28), relates, in a chapter entitled "A Cargo of Black Ivory," he heard Canal labor recruiters on Barbados in 1909 telling applicants that no man who had previously worked on the Canal would be taken again. "I do not know why this rule was made, but they enforced it with considerable care." If he had read a little further in his own book, he might have found a hint in the practices established during the railroad-building days. "The railroad company are so far conscious of the debility engendered by a residence on the Isthmus, that they refuse to employ those laborers who . . . return to seek employment. It is found that such are unprofitable servants, and yield at once to the enervating and sickening climate." (Edwards, *Panama*, p. 421.) On the other hand, another reason for the rule is revealed in an article in *The Canal Record* of April 28, 1909 which reports on the problem of laborers who prefer

* Employees of the Panama Railroad were covered separately a few days earlier in "An Act Relating to the liability of common carriers by railroad to their employees in certain cases" of April 22, 1908 (35 Stat. 65) which specifically included railroads in the Panama Canal Zone.

of government was established in 1914.[46] (There has been a certain ambivalence in the attitude of the Republic of Panama about it. On numerous occasions the losers in internal struggles for power have fled into the Zone as a safe haven from which to plot the counterrevolution. The reaction of the government in power has usually been to demand the deportation by Zone authorities of the Panamanian citizens involved.) [47]

There were several small villages within the Zone boundaries when the United States assumed jurisdiction and the first idea of the I.C.C. was to preserve, to the extent feasible, the existing structure of local government.[48] Act No. 7 of September 1904, accordingly, divided the Zone into five municipal districts, each of which would be recognized as a municipal corporation. While the officials thereof would be appointed by the Governor of the Zone— instead of selected by the Government of Colombia as formerly—it was hoped that they could be chosen from the communities which would be largely self-governing and gradually become more like American municipalities.

The tender plant of grass roots democracy failed to flourish for reasons which were explained in the Annual Report for 1907 (pp. 158-59). It seems that there was a dearth

[46] Senator Morgan of Alabama, questioning Governor Davis before the Senate Committee on Interoceanic Canals in 1906, brought out the unique features of the deportation power exercised by the Governor of the Canal Zone:
"*Senator Morgan:* Now, we may assume, for there will be no disputation about the point at all, that there is no State or Territory in the Union, on the continent here or under our control, where the governor of such State or Territory, or any other power of the United States, has the right of banishment.
"*General Davis:* No sir.
"*Senator Morgan:* This is the only case in which it exists?
"*Governor Davis:* The only one that I know of.
"*Senator Morgan:* Is that an important power to be exercised there?
"*General Davis:* I think it ought to be retained by all means." * One of Senator Morgan's purposes, in pursuing this point and throughout the hearings, was to demonstrate that the Canal Zone "belonged" to the United States, that effective control was inconsistent with the existence of a civil government, and therefore the entire Zone (and perhaps most of the Republic of Panama as well) should be turned into a military reservation. (See chap. VI, note 36, infra).
[47] The last such occasion of which I have a personal recollection occurred in 1968 when President Arnulfo Arias and his entourage crossed over in the wake of the military coup which brought the government of General Omar Torrijos to power. Arias was deported (or persuaded to leave "voluntarily" under threat of deportation). The practice by Panamanian dissidents of using the Canal Zone as a sanctuary is apparently continuing as this book goes to press. According to a story in *The Washington Post* of September 18, 1976, page A12: "A Panamanian source in Washington said that in recent weeks opponents of the government of strongman Omar Torrijos had taken refuge in the U.S.-run Canal Zone."
* Senate Document No. 401, 59th Cong., 2d sess., p. 2262. See also chap VI, note 40.

[48] The Act providing for the organization of municipal governments was drawn up by Magoon who explained in his covering report to the I.C.C. that he had examined the previous municipal laws of Porto Rico * and the Philippine Islands. "The conditions prevailing in the Canal Zone, Isthmus of Panama, the tractability of the inhabitants, their friendliness to the United States and their willingness to adopt our ways and measures, render the task of pursuing this policy in the Canal Zone much easier than it was in the Philippine Islands." Records of the Panama Canal, Washington National Records Center, Archives Branch, Record Group No. 185, Entry No. 94L.4.
The municipal government found in existence consisted of an *alcalde* (mayor), appointed by the prefect; a municipal judge, chosen by the municipal council; inspectors of police; a treasurer; and a secretary. The Government of Panama ceased to assume any responsibility for municipal government in the Zone after June 16, 1904. In some cases the incumbent municipal officers stayed on for a while under I.C.C. orders; in others "trustworthy members of the police force were designated to administer the government, and to this end some of the powers of the *alcaldes* were conferred upon them." *First Annual Report of the Isthmian Canal Commission,* p. 80.
* The anglicized spelling frequently used after the change of sovereignty in 1898. The Island officially regained its proper name in Public Resolution No. 20, 72nd Cong., May 17, 1932.

of the "more intelligent citizens of Panama . . . outside the cities of Panama and Colon" while the more intelligent citizens of other nationalities residing on the Isthmus were nearly all employed by the I.C.C. and barred by law from holding any political office. So "there developed the practice of appointing Americans to municipal positions and sending them into the various municipalities to perform their duties." As this left little of the original spirit of self-government, the municipalities were abolished in favor of centralized efficiency by Executive Order of March 13, 1907, which redivided the Zone into four administrative districts (Ancon, Emperador, Gorgona, and Cristobal). The I.C.C. was given authority to enact ordinances on subjects on which the municipal councils had legislated.

Some mention should be made of taxes under the I.C.C. rule. The municipalities established by Act No. 7 had been empowered to levy and collect a variety of taxes, including an *ad valorem* real estate tax, to support local services.[49] Under the new organization, pursuant to Executive Order of March 13, 1907, a district "tax collector" took over the duties of the former municipal treasurer and board of assessors. As the visible officials in both cases were Americans, it did not make much difference to the villagers who seem, on the whole, to have resented the taxes less after the Americans came than before because they could at least see the money being spent in the village rather than sent off to Bogotá. But they had to look fast. Both the real property tax and the landowner who paid it would soon be extinct.[50]

Mention should also be made of another rich source of Canal Zone history material. As indicated earlier in this chapter, some data on almost everything of major importance which happened during the I.C.C. regime can be found in the Annual Reports. Those in search of more detail, immediacy, or local color—who want to mine the capillaries and not just the veins—can be thankful that one of Colonel Goethals' first acts was to establish a weekly publication called *The Canal Record* which he intended as a kind of morale booster and a way of keeping all the far-flung divisions of the enterprise informed of what was going on in the other divisions. Besides carrying directories and current statistics, it had a gossipy, small town newspaper flavor about it, and moreover it long outlasted both the I.C.C. and Goethals himself. It ran as a weekly from 1907 to 1933, then as a monthly from 1933 to 1941, and is now bound in thirty-four volumes.[51]

---

[49] The municipal taxation authorized by Act No. 7 was only a pale imitation, however, of the revenue dragnet wielded by municipal councils under the governments of Colombia and (briefly) Panama. According to the *First Annual Report of the Isthmian Canal Commission*, p. 80, here it is, believe it or not: "Foreign productions of all kinds brought into the municipality for consumption from abroad or from a neighboring town, cattle brought into the municipality from anywhere, fish caught in or outside the municipality, bakeries, commutation or money payment of sentences of imprisonment, peddlers, personal labors, billiards, public amusements, charcoal burning, cane-grinding mills, lotteries, games of hazard, building permits *ad valorem*, traveling musicians, sealing of weights and measures, soda-water dealers, direct taxes, transfer of domestic cattle, auction sales, public assemblies at which admission is charged, estray animals, raffles, hotels and taverns, distillery of spirits, retail liquor trade, property tax, cockpits, public halls, slaughterhouses, rental of municipal property, rental of vacant property, escheated estates, permits to clear forest, income tax."

[50] Although Act No. 7 authorized municipalities to levy a real estate tax, it appears that no such taxes were ever assessed or collected until after the promulgation of the Executive Order of March 13, 1907, and then only until 1912. As to the practice prevailing under the laws of Colombia, some confusion and error of fact crept into later decisional law which has not to my knowledge been put right. In the otherwise thoroughly researched and praiseworthy decision in Playa de Flor Land and Development Co. v. United States (1945) (see chap. I, note 8), the United States District Court for the Canal Zone said: "Prior to the Treaty between the United States of America and the Republic of Panama, there was, so far as this record and available evidence shows, no land tax in the State of Panama." But Magoon's report of 1904 (see note 48, supra) had found: "Under the existing law of Panama, taxes on real estate are collected by the treasurer of the province. The tax is levied by the national government [Bogotá] and apportioned among the provinces." And the First Annual Report of the Isthmian Canal Commission, p. 81, said: "A land tax was one of the general sources of revenue of the State."

[51] After a lapse of nine years, a successor periodical called the *Panama Canal Review* was initiated in May 1950 and is still being published. It appears seim-annually in both English and Spanish editions. Less inward-

Bishop, who might be considered the quasi-official historian of the I.C.C., had this to say about it:

> It increased the efficiency of the force, welded it into a single body, and made it more contented. By giving space also to the social life and activities of the Canal Zone, this beneficial influence was augmented. The paper was distributed free to all employees on the isthmus . . .[52]

Actually, it was not distributed free to all employees literally, but only to employees on the "gold" payroll.[53]

Toward the end of the I.C.C. regime, corresponding to the end of the construction period, certain momentous steps were taken which, though primarily intended only to ensure long-range governmental stability, had the secondary effect of completing the transformation of the Zone into a Common Law enclave. The hallmarks of the transformation—such as the drastic reorganization of the judiciary, integrating it into the federal court system of the United States, and the beginning of serious work on a Common Law civil code—will be discussed in context in Chapters VI and VII. We are concerned here with the basic sociopolitical questions calling for solution.

So long as the gigantic construction project was going on—the *raison d'être* of the I.C.C.—law and government could be

thought of as merely an improvised supporting mechanism (indeed, much of the legislation was specifically justified by the assertion that "an emergency exists"); but with the completion of the canal imminent, attention began to focus on the development of ongoing structures and policies. With most of the thousands of transient workers departing, it was obvious that the future of the Zone would be largely shaped by the policies adopted on two more or less related subjects, land tenure and population.

As the United States Government had scrupulously tried to observe the prior rights of private landowners, and as many of such rights were based on adverse possession (prescription) under Spanish law or alleged royal grants unsupported by documentation, and as boundaries were often vague, the problem of land titles was enormously time- and energy-consuming from the beginning, and became increasingly more so as the Panama Railroad tracks had to be relocated around the artificially created Gatun Lake. Many cases were settled "out of court" by simply buying off the claimants, even those with very shaky legal cases, and helping them to resettle outside the Zone.

The problem was not finally resolved, for better or for worse, until the draconian decision of 1912 to eliminate all private land titles. As late as 1911 Mr. Thatcher, head of the Department of Civil Administration, speculated at some length on what policy the Congress and the President might ultimately adopt with respect to land ownership and population. As one possibility he suggested that the public land might be thrown open to homesteading, by American citizens only.

> If a civil population should be deemed desirable, I believe that a policy of the character just outlined will do more to open up and render valuable the jungles of the Zone than any other that might be projected; and a civil population thus secured and maintained would, because of its loyal and sympathetic interest, be of both moral and police value to the interests of the United States Government and the canal.[54]

---

looking and parochial than *The Canal Record,* it carries articles about Panama and helps to bridge the cultural gap between "Zonian" and Panamanian employees.

[52] Bishop, *Panama Gateway,* pp. 182-83.

[53] The existence of "gold" and "silver" payrolls was a way of segregating employees without any open admission of racism or nationality prejudice. It could be explained as a distinction between skilled and unskilled; but the "gold" employees were nearly all white and mostly American, while the "silver" employees were nearly all non-American and mostly non-white. Like Jim Crowism in the American South, it had its little ironies. Author Harry Alverson Franck,* describing his experiences as a census-taker in 1912, tells of interviewing a Spanish laborer (obviously on the "silver" roll) who had a well-kept library of "Hegel, Fichte, Spencer, Huxley, [et al.], all dog-eared with much reading," in his tiny quarters and wondering what the Spaniard must have thought of some of his semi-literate "gold" roll betters.

* Harry Alverson Franck, *Zone Policeman 88* (New York: The Century Co., 1913), p. 63.

---

[54] *Annual Report of the Isthmian Canal Commission,* 1911, pp. 418-19. Thatcher had apparently forgotten already, or was ignorant of, the assurances of President Roosevelt in 1906 that the United States had not the slightest intention of establishing an independent colony

Before the end of 1911 the Congress and the President were tilting away from Mr. Thatcher's dream and toward the empty land, "urban," Americanized, "communistic," [55] society of a tenant bourgeoisie which has come to pass. In order to determine how many people would be affected by a depopulation (i.e., getting the indigenes off the land) policy, Executive Order of January 12, 1912 provided for taking a census. The census, taken as of February 1, 1912, showed a population of 62,810, of whom 1,521 were Colombians and 7,363 were Panamanians.[56] Thus approximately 8,884 persons (presumably not employed by the I.C.C.) would have to be resettled in Panama, while most of the remainder would be repatriated to their countries of origin.[57]

The figure of 62,810 comes from official I.C.C. reports, but I am indebted to Franck, the census-taker (Zone Policeman, p. 131) for the information that about 25,000 were British subjects (almost all West Indian Negroes) [58] and 5,228 were Americans on

the "gold" role. These statistics will be referred to again in Chapter VII, in connection with the pertinence of the changing population mix to the Common Law reception.

Meanwhile, Mr. Feuille, as head of the Department of Law, was already urging that Canal Zone laws be broadly revised and brought under one complete correlated system—finally achieved (see chap. VII) in 1934—but, as he wrote in his Annual Report for the fiscal year ending June 30, 1912, "until the attitude of Congress toward the canal and the Canal Zone is definitely known through the enactment of a fundamental law this work cannot be safely undertaken."

He did not have much longer to wait for such a fundamental law. The Panama Canal Act of August 24, 1912,[59] the most important legislation on the subject since 1904, made the attitude of Congress definitely known and fixed the form of government which has basically prevailed ever since; thus in effect replacing the Spooner Act as the organic law of the Canal and the Canal Zone.

Section 4 provided

That when in the judgment of the President the construction of the Panama Canal shall be sufficiently advanced toward completion to render the further services of the Isthmian Canal Commission unnecessary the President is authorized by Executive order to discontinue the Isthmian Canal Commission, which, together with the present organization, shall then cease to exist; and the President is authorized thereafter to complete, govern, and operate the Panama Canal and govern the Canal Zone, or cause them to be completed, governed, and operated, through a governor of the Panama Canal and such other persons as he may deem competent to discharge the various duties connected with the completion, care, maintenance, sanitation, operation, government, and protection of the canal and the Canal Zone. . . .

---

in the middle of the State of Panama (see chap. IV, note 92, supra).

[55] It is a common joke among sophisticated Panamanians that the Americans, in the Canal Zone, have already beat the Russians to communism. Juridically, of course, this could hardly be more incorrect, but in terms of the economic system, it is pretty hard to refute. Even in 1911, before the trend had fully developed, Edwards (Panama, p. 562) could write: "The more one stays here, the more one realizes that the Isthmian Canal Commission has gone further towards Socialism than any other branch of our Government—further probably than any government has ever gone."

[56] Those counted as Colombians were evidently die-hards who never recognized the Revolution of 1903. As Franck (Zone Policeman, pp. 47-48) related, occasionally while taking the census he would "burst unexpectedly into the ancestral home of some educated native family who had withstood all the tides of time and change [and who were sociable] when addressed in their own tongue until [angered] at the question whether they were Panamanians. Distinctly not! They were Colombians! There is no such country as Panama."

[57] Hardly any native Panamanians worked on the Canal. The laborers came from almost every other part of the world with the British West Indies contributing the largest share. Spaniards, of whom 8,222 were brought to the Isthmus under contract in the years 1906-8, were said to have been the best workers.

[58] Two or three writers have told anecdotes about how the West Indian Negro, displaying

a touching faith in international law, would sometimes raise himself up with great dignity and say: "You can't address me in that manner, sah. I am a British object." Bishop, Panama Gateway, p. 300.

[59] Full title: "An Act To provide for the opening, maintenance, protection and operation of the Panama Canal, and the sanitation and government of the Canal Zone." 37 Stat. 560.

With legal authority for operation of the finished canal, and continuity of the civil order in the Zone, assured, the I.C.C. could begin phasing out.

Specifically with respect to the civil order, Section 7 provided

That the governor of the Panama Canal shall, in connection with the operation of such canal, have official control and jurisdiction over the Canal Zone and shall perform all duties in connection with the civil government of the Canal Zone, *which is to be held, treated, and governed as an adjunct of such Panama Canal* [emphasis supplied]. Unless in this Act otherwise provided all existing laws of the Canal Zone referring to the civil governor or the civil administration of the Canal Zone shall be applicable to the governor of the Panama Canal, who shall perform all such executive and administrative duties required by existing law. . . .

It will be noticed that the office of Governor, abolished as such when Magoon left the Isthmus in 1906 and Goethals became dictator, has in this Act been restored. But an inquisitorial reading of the above sections discloses that a funny thing happened on the way to the restoration. Whereas Davis and Magoon had been Governor of the Canal Zone, the incumbent under the Act of 1912 would be Governor of the Panama Canal—and only incidentally responsible for government in the Zone (as an adjunct). Congress was careful to ensure that nothing substantive in the way of civil authority was lost in the change of nomenclature, but the "adjunct" took on the connotation of a burdensome but unavoidable baggage rather than something of value in itself.[60]

(It must be remembered, of course, that this legislation came at a time when the Zone was being "depopulated" and all eyes were on the Canal about to be opened. It was not a time for emphasizing the civil government side of the Governor's dual role, or of raising hard questions about the future status of the hinterland. Under the reorganization legislation of 1950, by which time there was no blinking the fact that a permanent and thoroughly Americanized "Zonian" community existed, seemingly without end, the executive was again given the title Governor of the Canal Zone.)[61]

While the 1912 Act was digging the grave of the I.C.C. it was also breathing retroactive legitimacy into its past life. Reference has been heretofore made (see pp. 55-56, supra) to the questionable legality of all the I.C.C.'s actions after March 4, 1905. To take care of that troublesome matter, section 2 provided

That all laws, orders, regulations, and ordinances adopted and promulgated in the Canal Zone by order of the President for the government and sanitation of the Canal Zone and the construction of the Panama Canal are hereby ratified and confirmed as valid and binding until Congress shall otherwise provide. The existing courts established in the Canal Zone by Executive Order are recognized and confirmed to continue in operation until the courts provided for in this Act shall be established.[62]

---

[60] "It was determined that the Canal Zone should be used for the operation of the canal, rather than for a habitation for such settlers as might choose to go there. . . . The permanent Government of the Canal Zone will be, in the main, merely a miniature of the government during the construction period. The law providing for the operation of the canal makes this Government entirely subsidiary to the main purpose for which the canal was built." Haskin, *Panama Canal*, pp. 258, 266.

[61] Under the 1950 legislation, subsequently incorporated into the 1962 edition of the Canal Zone Code, the operation of the civil government and of the Canal were placed on a par. The Canal Zone Government and the Panama Canal Company were created as independent agencies functioning as an integrated enterprise. The latter operates the Canal (and the railroad) and is managed by a board of directors of which the Governor of the Canal Zone is a member (and ex officio President) but not necessarily the dominant member. (On paper the Secretary of the Army is the dominant member, but the actuality of relative influence has varied from time to time depending on the personalities of the incumbents and other factors.) The Canal Zone Government has become a political entity with its own reasons for being, no longer an "adjunct."

[62] As Mr. Feuille, head of the Department of Law, said: "The effect of this provision is to set at rest whatever doubts may have existed as to the authority of the President to enact laws for the government of the Canal Zone since the expiration of the Fifty-eighth Congress." *Annual Report of the Isthmian Canal Commission*, 1913, p. 514. (But see also chap. VI, note 42, infra.)

Lastly, I will direct attention to what might be called the "depopulation" provision or, from another point of view, the "ultimate solution" of the land title problem. Section 3 provided

> That the President is authorized to declare by Executive Order that all land and land under water within the limits of the Canal Zone is necessary for the construction, maintenance, operation, sanitation, or protection of the Panama Canal, and to extinguish, by agreement when advisable, all claims and titles of adverse claimants and occupants.

(The lengthy and weighty dispositions of the Act respecting the Canal Zone Judiciary will be adverted to in Chapter VI. The even lengthier and perhaps weightier dispositions respecting maintenance and operation of the Canal will not be adverted to in any chapter on account of insufficient relevance to the subject of this book.)

Section 3 was implemented separately and in advance of the rest of the Act by Executive Order of December 5, 1912, in which the President did declare, in almost the identical language of the Act, all land in the Canal Zone subject to seizure under the legal fiction of being necessary for the "construction, maintenance, operation, protection and sanitation of the Panama Canal," and the chairman of the I.C.C. was directed to take possession of said land. The work of clearing the Zone of its indigenous population was commenced early in 1913. A joint commission consisting of two Americans and two Panamanians adjusted the claims of the dispossessed persons.[63] As Haskin (*Panama Canal*, p. 260) rather romantically described it:

> These natives, usually almost full-blooded Indians, were treated as kindly as conditions would allow. They were willing to "fold their tents" like the Arabs, and leave their homes behind as they went out to conquer new ones in the jungles where the needs of a gigantic waterway could not encroach upon them.

The broad purpose of the Act, "To Establish a Permanent Organization for the Panama Canal," was carried out by Executive Order of January 27, 1914, the final section of which abolished the I.C.C. as of April 1, 1914. The first steam vessel to pass completely through the Canal under its own power, a crane boat belonging to the dredging fleet, had reached the Pacific entrance about three weeks before and this was evidently taken as symbolic that the waterway was "sufficiently advanced toward completion to render the further services of the Isthmian Canal Commission unnecessary." The Canal was actually opened for commerce on August 15, 1914.[64]

The appointment of George Washington Goethals as first Governor of the Panama Canal under the "permanent government" was confirmed by the Senate on February 4[65] and the new structure went into operation as of April 1, 1914. All the functions previously performed by the Departments of Civil Administration and Law, including the courts and the office of district attorney, were placed in an Executive Department of the Canal Zone Government under Mr. C. A. McIlvaine.

If 1913 was the year of "depopulation," 1914 was the year of "repatriation," the latter referring to the exodus of the common laborers who had built the Canal. In

---

[63] Such a commission was provided for in Article VI of the Hay/Bunau-Varilla Treaty but it had gone out of operation after all the land really necessary for construction of the Canal had been acquired. Executive Order of December 5, 1912 necessitated in effect a revivification of the commission.

[64] World War I had just started in Europe and in the general excitement everybody overlooked the last sentence of Section 4 of the Panama Canal Act: "That upon the completion of the Panama Canal the President shall cause the same to be officially and formally opened for use and operation." The opening was belatedly made official and formal by a Proclamation of President Wilson dated July 12, 1920.

[65] As builder and first Governor of the Panama Canal, surely no one had a greater personal stake and vested interest in asserting the maximum sustainable rights of the United States; yet Goethals himself said in explaining the government of the Canal Zone in a Lecture in 1915:

> It must be remembered that we have, after all is said and done, only a right of way for a canal; . . .

George W. Goethals, *Government of the Canal Zone* (Princeton: Princeton University Press, 1915), p. 85. Goethals was not a lawyer, but eleven years later the eminent international law authority Dr. L. H. Woolsey came to the same conclusion in almost exactly the same words. See chap. IV, p. 42.

sixteen months the net emigration from the Isthmus was 20,400, of whom more than 16,000 were actual workers on the Canal.[66] Many thousands of the West Indian Negroes, however, remained on the Isthmus to work on the banana plantations of the United Fruit Company or subsist in other ways. Some of their descendants are now employed in the Canal Zone and others are scattered throughout the Republic but mostly in the cities. Wherever encountered they are instantly distinguishable by their speech patterns from other English-speaking Negroes, as well as from the Spanish-speaking Negroes, descendants of slaves brought to the Isthmus during the colonial days.

---

[66] Bennett, *History*, p. 182.

CHAPTER VI

THE CANAL ZONE JUDICIARY

The Judiciary of the Canal Zone established by Act No. 1 of the Isthmian Canal Commission, dated August 1, 1904, consisted of a Supreme Court, Circuit Courts, and Municipal Courts. In the table of organization, so to speak, of the Canal Zone government it came to rest, as we have seen, in the Department of Civil Administration.

The First Annual Report of the Isthmian Canal Commission, dated December 1, 1904, describes the government for the Canal Zone as "divided into three branches, to wit, legislative, judicial, and executive." But in the famous words of former Attorney General John Mitchell, "Look at what we do, not what we say." And what the I.C.C. did was place the courts effectively in the executive branch,[1] which, as it happened,

was also the legislative. In short, the American ideal of separation of powers, deriving from a constitution, was simply not transferable in the circumstances, however strong the impulse to cling to it. (On the other hand, there is no evidence that the courts were in any way constricted, by the lack of separation, in the exercise of their judicial functions; nor was any conflict with the other "branches" conceivable. The Canal Zone Supreme Court would never have dreamed of asserting a right of judicial review.)

The internal structure of the court system over the years has undergone some permutations. Hardly anyone today, even in the Canal Zone, remembers either the Supreme Court or inferior courts of the above names. Yet the fundamental orientation and juridical status of the system, in the framework of the overall judicial power of the United States Government, have not changed—and hence can be described in terms which embrace the present.

The successor to the defunct Supreme

---

[1] "The Executive Department was responsible for the administration of Canal Zone Courts [under the I.C.C. regime]. It still is, in part. The magistrate's courts which are situated in each town operate under the direction of the Executive Department." Norman J. Padelford, *The Panama Canal in Peace and War* (New York: The MacMillan Company, 1942), p. 187.

The *Panama Canal Databook*, prepared by the Executive Planning Staff of the combined Panama Canal Company/Canal Zone Government and current as of 1976, explains that (p. 71):

"The two *Magistrates' Courts* are judicial units of the Canal Zone Government with duties and functions prescribed by law, and under the administrative supervision of the Executive."

Court, the United States District Court for the District of the Canal Zone, stands in the same peculiar position as the former within the overall framework. It is a legislative, not a constitutional, court; it is a territorial court apparently, though different from any other territorial court ever established; and it is not for all purposes, despite its name, a United States District Court. Before going into the history of the Canal Zone Judiciary, therefore, it would seem desirable to say a few words about these particularities of its very nature.

The constitutional courts are the Supreme Court of the United States, established by the Constitution itself, and all other courts created by Congress pursuant to its power under Article III. Other articles, however, also invest Congress with the power to create federal tribunals, and these are the legislative courts. According to Moore,[2] the following have in the past been classified by the Supreme Court as legislative courts: (a) Territorial Courts, (b) Court of Customs and Patent Appeals, (c) Customs Court, and (d) Court of Claims. At one time it was considered well settled also that the courts of the District of Columbia were legislative courts.[3] But Mr. Justice Sutherland for the majority (Chief Justice Hughes and Justices Van Devanter and Cardozo dissenting) held in *O'Donoghue* v. *United States*[4] that the higher courts of the District of Columbia are Article III courts (though he had stated in 1912, when a senator, that they were legislative courts) which, however, may also exercise the judicial power conferred by Congress pursuant to Article I, #8, cl. 17.

One of the hallmarks of a constitutional court is that the judges thereof hold office during good behavior.[5] Yet similar tenure has been accorded by Congress to the judges of most of the specialized courts created outside of Article III; and, moreover, Congress has attempted by specific legislation to classify (b), (c), and (d) above as con-

stitutional courts for certain purposes.[6] For these and other reasons almost all the legislative courts, except the territorial, are now sometimes called hybrid courts. In very early American history some territorial courts were created with judges holding office during good behavior, but at the present time all judges "in the territories and insular possessions" are appointed for fixed terms.[7]

The classic distinction between constitutional and legislative courts was drawn by Chief Justice Marshall in *American Insurance Company* v. *Canter*.[8] Marshall said in *Canter* that the courts constituted by an act of the legislative council of the territory of Florida (ceded by Spain in 1819) were legislative courts "created in virtue of the general right of sovereignty which exists in the government, or in virtue of that clause which enables Congress to make all needful rules and regulations, respecting the territory belonging to the United States." The territorial court thus delineated by Marshall was the only kind of legislative court which existed to that date and remains the only kind which has retained its purity.

Subsequent decisions have varied the language of Marshall's definition somewhat but hardly at all the meaning. The right to create territorial courts is not derived from Article III but is a concomitant of the right of Congress to govern territory which in turn is "implied in the right to acquire it."[9]

---

[6] In Glidden Company v. Zdanok, 370 U.S. 530 (1962), the Supreme Court, extending the reasoning of O'Donoghue, declared the Court of Claims and the Court of Customs and Patent Appeals to be constitutional courts.

[7] Katz, *Legislative*, pp. 897-898. Katz does not mention the Canal Zone, but inferentially, and in accordance with prevailing custom, includes it in "territories and insular possessions." Indeed, the Canal Zone is Chapter 6 in Title 48 (Territories and Insular Possessions) of the *United States Code* and so it absorbs by association a categorization not justified even by the 1903 treaty.

[8] 1 Pet. 511 (1828).

[9] Dorr v. United States, 195 U.S. 138 (1904), at 149. It is interesting that this case arrived at the Supreme Court of the United States on error to the Supreme Court of the Philippine Islands, a territorial court under the temporary government established for the Philippines pursuant to the Spooner (the same Spooner) Resolution of March 2, 1901, and involving an enactment of the Philippine Commission (see chap. V, note 4).

---

[2] 1 *Moore's Federal Practice* (1974), 0.4[3], p. 63.

[3] Katz, "Federal Legislative Courts," 43 *Harvard Law Review* 894 (1930) at 895 and 902.

[4] 289 U.S. 516 (1932).

[5] Another distinction is that legislative courts are permitted to exercise certain functions which the Supreme Court has held to be outside the competency of constitutional courts (Katz, *Legislative*, p. 895).

All of which works out very well for territory which is truly "acquired"—Florida, the Philippines, Virgin Islands, Puerto Rico, Guam, et al. The strain begins to show when we try to match the United States District Court for the District of the Canal Zone against the criteria of "the general right of sovereignty" or "territory belonging to the United States."

Moore explicitly lists the District Court of the Canal Zone as a "territorial, and hence legislative" court.[10] But he defines "territories" as geographic areas either incorporated into the United States or "belonging to the United States." [11] *Balzac v. Porto Rico*,[12] putting Porto Rico into the latter category, quoted with approval the decision in *Dorr* (see note 9, supra) that the power to govern territory is implied in the right to acquire it, "given to Congress in the Constitution in Article IV, #3. . . ." Clause 2 of Article IV, #3 is "that clause" which Marshall cited in *Canter*, but the full pertinent language of "that clause" is ". . . respecting the Territory or other Property belonging to the United States; . . ." and there is no way to stretch it to cover the Canal Zone.

Another awkward thing about the relationship between the Canal Zone and territorial courts is that the former is presumed, by treaty and by a powerful body of opinion, to be perpetual; whereas the latter, by consistent decisions and definition, are presumed to be temporary. The rationale for not giving life tenure to judges of territorial courts is that such courts are not expected to endure. In *O'Donoghue* (see note 4, supra) the court was at pains to contrast the permanence of the government of the District of Columbia with the impermanence of the governments of the territories. As many decisions make clear, the territories are expected to be eventually incorporated into the United States [13] or released from United States control. (With respect to the Canal Zone, I do not believe that serious thought is being given any more to the former alternative, although it was once considered.)

It does not seem to make any difference in the essential qualities of a territorial ("and hence legislative") court whether it is created directly by Congress or through an instrumentality so long as its powers are derived ultimately from parts of the Constitution other than Article III. By an act of 1823 Congress authorized the legislative council of the territory of Florida to establish courts, and it was one of the courts so established whose status was defined in *Canter*. The Isthmian Canal Commission, which might be considered the equivalent of a legislative council, likewise established the courts of the Canal Zone (before 1914), though without the benefit of any such specific authorization. Congress itself, in the Panama Canal Act of 1912, established the present District Court of the Canal Zone, but it is neither more nor less a territorial court than its predecessor.

That the United States District Court for the District of the Canal Zone is not, after all, a District Court of the United States was decided by the judge thereof, the Honorable Guthrie Crowe, in *Doyle* v. *Fleming*.[14] This was an action brought by the plaintiff, one Gerald A. Doyle, against "Robert J. Fleming, Jr., Governor of the Canal Zone Government and Cyrus R. Vance, Secretary of the Army in his supervisory capacity for the administration of the Canal Zone Government, Defendants," praying for an injunction to restrain the defendants from flying the flag of Panama at certain places in the Canal Zone at an equal height with that of the United States (in accordance with an agreement between the two governments reached on January 10, 1963), and from certain other actions, which "would place the sovereignty of the United States in the Canal Zone in jeopardy."

Judge Crowe dismissed the complaint on the grounds that the pertinent statute—28 U.S.C. #1391(e)—is limited to actions brought "in any judicial district" and that judicial districts are defined, as used in Title 28 (28 U.S.C. #451), to mean "the districts enumerated in Chapter 5 of this title." The

---

[10] 1 Moore 0.4[3], p. 65.

[11] 1 Moore, 0.4[3-1], pp. 22-23.

[12] 258 U.S. 298 (1922).

[13] As we are making some comparisons here between the territory of Florida and the Canal Zone, it might not be too irrelevant to observe that the treaty of cession of Florida expressly stipulated that the inhabitants were to be "incorporated in the Union of the United States"; whereas the treaty with Panama, silent on the subject, clearly contemplated that the citizenship of the inhabitants would be left undis-

turbed. (See chap. IV, note 109, supra, and chap V, note 16, supra.)

[14] 219 F. Supp. 277 (1963).

districts so enumerated (Secs. 81-131) do not include the Canal Zone.[15] In denying the injunction for lack of jurisdiction, Judge Crowe did not go very far into the merits, but could not refrain from showing his personal feeling of sympathy for the plaintiff's view.[16]

Having now disposed of (or left in total confusion) the genus of the beast, let us return to 1904 and approach the Judiciary from an historical point of view. As all attentive readers are by now aware, legal

authority (if it were sovereign) over the Zone passed to the United States on February 26 with the exchange of ratifications of the Hay/Bunau-Varilla Treaty. On May 4, 1904, with the turning over of the French canal company properties, the United States Government physically took possession. On June 16, 1904 the Republic of Panama ordered all its judicial officers in the Zone to cease functioning.

"From the 16th of June until the 2nd of September, when the new legislation of the Canal Commission [Act No. 1 establishing the Judiciary] went into effect, there was no court that could hear and determine a case ordinarily falling within the jurisdiction of a circuit judge."[17] On the municipal level during this interregnum justice continued to be administered by former Panamanian officials serving under I.C.C. direction (see chap. V, note 48, supra).

The flavor of the judicial dilemma in which the Zone immediately found itself is best conveyed by the case of M. Murati, the Frenchman in charge of the Cristobal/Colón installations of the former French canal company. Just before departing for France near the end of June 1904, M. Murati committed assault and battery on another Frenchman inside the Zone, then fled into the Republic whence he was "informally" extradited. With the fugitive in custody the real trouble began. The Governor wrote to the chairman of the I.C.C. on June 24:

> It is impossible for me to arraign the offender in this case before any court, for none exists, and while I can appoint a judge he cannot enter upon his duties without confirmation by the Commission. Again, if he could enter upon his duties, the procedure must be in accordance with the laws of Panama, and yet the Bill of Rights made applicable to the Zone by the President's Order of May 9, 1904, has practically destroyed the Code of Criminal Procedure under the local laws. It is simply a matter of impossibility to conduct a trial in the Zone under the local laws and also in conformity with the Bill of Rights. Before a judge can hold his first trial a new Code of Criminal Procedure must be prepared.[18]

---

[15] With reference to application of the Federal Rules of Civil Procedure, the Canal Zone Code of 1962 (Title Five, Part 1, chap. 1, #1) provided: "The term 'district court' includes the United States District Court for the District of the Canal Zone."

[16] "The flying of two national flags side by side in a disputed territory for an undeclared purpose is a position of weakness that can lead but to further misunderstanding.

"The people living in the Canal Zone are entitled to police protection, adequate courts, orderly government, health programs, and all the things that stem from the sovereign. When the sovereign is uncertain and in doubt these fundamental rights are of necessity weakened and may be lost."

Less than a year after Doyle v. Fleming the bloody rioting of January 1964 was sparked by the refusal of militant "Zonians" to permit the raising of the Panamanian flag, at an equal height with that of the American, at the Balboa High School in the Zone.

The last previous serious riots had occurred on November 3, 1959—with the flag issue as one of its main causes—and had been followed by President Eisenhower's order that the flag of Panama be displayed on Shaler Triangle as visual evidence of the Republic's "titular sovereignty." Hanrahan (chap. IV, note 98, supra) quoted the *N. Y. Times* of Feb. 4, 1960: "Recognition of titular sovereignty appeared to be an insignificant price to pay for restoration of Panamanian confidence. President Eisenhower expressed disappointment with the attitude of some Americans who viewed such recognition as an abdication of American sovereignty in the Canal Zone."

Commenting on the Doyle v. Fleming decision, Hanrahan (p. 78) said: "For Judge Crowe to suggest that sovereignty in the Zone is uncertain at the present time is, arguably, an admission that the status of United States power in the Canal Zone was always subject to suspicion because of the ambiguous character of the Treaty of 1903."

---

[17] First Annual Report of the Isthmian Canal Commission, p. 83.

[18] Records of the Panama Canal, Washington National Records Center, Archives Branch, Record Group No. 185, Entry No. 94.L.

The record does not disclose whether M. Murati was ever tried.

As has been heretofore remarked, the missing Judiciary was established (or at least authorized) by I.C.C. Act No. 1 of August 16, 1904. (A Penal Code and Code of Criminal Procedure soon followed as Acts No. 14 and 15, respectively, of September 3, 1904.) The salient features of the court system created by Act No. 1 are worth observing in some detail.

The Supreme Court consisted of one Chief Justice and two Associate Justices, appointed by the I.C.C. for staggered six-year terms, with original jurisdiction "to issue writs of Mandamus, Certiorari, Prohibition, Habeas Corpus, Quo Warranto,[19] in cases warranted by the principles and usages of law, and to hear and determine controversies thus brought before it, and in other cases provided by law" and appellate jurisdiction "of all actions and special proceedings properly brought to it from the Circuit Courts and from all other tribunals from whose judgment the law shall specially provide an appeal to the Supreme Court."

There were three Circuit Courts corresponding to: (1) the First Judicial Circuit composed of the municipality of Ancon; (2) the Second Judicial Circuit composed of the municipalities of Emperador and Gorgona; (3) the Third Judicial Circuit composed of the municipalities of Buenavista and Cristobal. The Chief Justice and Associate Justices of the Supreme Court would be assigned to the respective circuits as the Circuit Judge thereof.

The Circuit Courts had the following original jurisdiction:

1. In all actions in which the subject of litigation is not capable of pecuniary estimation;
2. In all civil actions which involve the title to or possession of real property, or any interest therein, or the legality of any tax, impost or assessment, except actions of forcible entry into, and unlawful detainer of lands or buildings, original jurisdiction of which is by this act conferred upon municipal courts;
3. In all cases in which the demand, exclusive of interest, or the value of the property in controversy, amounts to one hundred dollars or more;

4. In all actions in admiralty and maritime jurisdiction, irrespective of the value of the property in controversy or the amount of the demand;
5. In all matters of probate, both of testate and intestate estates, appointments of guardians, trustees, and receivers, and in all actions for annulment of marriage, and in all such special cases and proceedings as are not otherwise provided for;
6. In all cases involving the exercise of eminent domain;
7. In all criminal cases in which a penalty of more than thirty days' imprisonment or a fine exceeding twenty-five dollars ($25.00) may be imposed;
8. Said courts and their judges, or any of them, shall have power to issue writs of injunction, mandamus, certiorari, prohibition, quo warranto, and habeas corpus in their respective circuits and districts in the manner provided by law; and fix, approve and accept bail in criminal cases.

The Circuit Courts had appellate jurisdiction "over all cases arising in the municipal and inferior courts in their respective circuits."

There was a Municipal Court for each of the five municipalities named above. The Municipal Judges, appointed by the Governor of the Canal Zone, had the following original jurisdiction:

A Municipal Judge shall have original jurisdiction for the trial of misdemeanors and offenses arising within the municipality of which he is a judge, in all cases where the sentence might not by law exceed thirty days' imprisonment or a fine of twenty-five dollars, and for the trial of all civil actions properly triable within his municipality and over which exclusive jurisdiction has not herein been given to the Circuit Courts, in all cases in which the demand, exclusive of interest, or the value of the property in controversy, amounts to less than one hundred dollars.

A municipal judge shall also have jurisdiction over actions for forcible entry into, and unlawful detainer of real estate, irrespective of the amount in controversy.

The jurisdiction of the municipal judge in civil actions triable within his municipality, in cases in which the demand, exclusive of interest, or the value of the property in controversy, amounts to twenty dollars or more, shall be concurrent with that of the Circuit Court; provided that the jurisdiction of the municipal judge shall not extend to civil actions in which the subject of litigation is not capable of pecuniary estimation, or to those which involve the title to or posses-

---

[19] In these writs the nose of the Common Law camel may be seen appearing under the tent (see chap. VII, p. 95, infra).

sion of real estate, or an interest therein, or the legality of any tax, impost, or assessment, or to actions in admiralty, or maritime jurisdiction, or to matters of probate, the appointment of guardians, trustees, and receivers, or actions for the annulment of marriage, or eminent domain; but this proviso shall not apply to actions of forcible entry into and unlawful detainer of lands or buildings, original jurisdiction of which is hereby conferred upon municipal courts.

If a felony be committed in the Canal Zone, it shall be the duty of the municipal judge of the municipality in which the offense was committed to investigate the same and cause the arrest of the offender, and to act as an examining magistrate in a preliminary examination; if it shall appear that a felony has been committed and probable cause exists for presuming the accused guilty thereof, the municipal judge shall forthwith remand the accused to the custody of the Marshal, and the papers in the case and the names of the witnesses shall be transmitted to the prosecuting attorney of the Canal Zone for such further action as the due administration of justice may require.

A municipal judge may fix the amount of bail, approve the sureties and form of the undertaking, receive and file the same in any criminal proceeding in his court, and release the prisoner thereon, pursuant to the forms and established usages of law.

Section 41 of the Act provided that unresolved cases at all levels arising in the territory of the Zone and instituted prior to February 26, 1904, could be transferred to the appropriate Canal Zone court with the concurrence of the Panamanian court in which pending.

The Act concluded with:

> Whereas an emergency exists, this act shall be in force and effect from and after its passage.
> Enacted August 16, 1904.

But saying so did not make it so, and in fact it was nearly a year before all its key provisions had been brought into force and effect.[20] Meanwhile, serious doubts would be raised as to whether the Zone really needed such an elaborate judiciary.

The first judge above the municipal level to be appointed and function in the Canal Zone was the Honorable Osceola Kyle of Decatur, Alabama. Kyle lobbied indefatigably for the job, aiming his primary efforts at Taft through an Alabama colleague close to the Secretary.[21] He seems to have secured the endorsement of almost everybody of any consequence in Alabama, including even Booker T. Washington.[22] Taft was persuaded and the next we hear of Kyle he is in Cristobal (probably at the stately old colonial-style Washington Hotel, still standing and recently refurbished) reading a letter dated August 20, 1904 [23] from Admiral Walker, as chairman of the I.C.C. and Acting Governor, enclosing a certified copy of Act No. 1 and asking him to appear in Ancon to take the oath of office. The letter continued:

> The Commission desires that you shall at once proceed to assume and discharge the duties of the Circuit Judge for the Third Judicial Circuit of the Canal Zone, composed of the municipalities of Gatun and Cristobal, and that you will open court and perform such business of said court as requires attention, and that thereafter and until your associates on the Supreme Bench may be appointed that you will open court for the First and Second Judicial Circuits of the Zone at such time and place in said circuits as your discretion shall determine and the public business require.

The letter ended with a somewhat plaintive request for clerical help:

> All of our typewriters are being overworked at present, and therefore I request that you have your secretary make two

---

[20] The date of Sept. 2, 1904 indicated by the I.C.C. as the end of jurisdictional hiatus (see p. 75, supra) evidently marked the nominal organization of the first Circuit Court, but this was only a partial implementation of the Act.

[21] The researcher (at least this researcher) is amazed at how many pies Taft could keep his fingers in simultaneously. While the judges were nominally appointed by the I.C.C., it was Taft who had the last word, and sometimes the first word as well. At the same time he was supervising in equally close detail the affairs of the Philippine Islands, Puerto Rico, and Cuba, and, incidentally, beginning to run for President.

[22] William Howard Taft Papers, Library of Congress, Letter from O. Kyle to WHT dated June 15, 1904.

[23] Records of the Panama Canal, Washington National Records Center, Archives Branch, Record Group No. 185, Entry No. 94.B.

copies of the enclosed law and send them to me for the files of this office.

Kyle replied in a letter dated August 22, 1904: [24]

I shall call on you on the 25th instant and take the oath of office as suggested by you and will begin, at an early date, to prepare rules and regulations for the government of the circuit court, to be submitted to the Canal Commission for their approval.

I note your request that my secretary make two copies of the law that you sent me and send the copies to you to be filed in your office. It will be a pleasure to me to have this done as soon as I can get the paper upon which the laws can be typewritten. . . .

He evidently found the paper somewhere for he wrote Admiral Walker again on August 29, 1904: [25]

In response to your letter of August 20th, 1904, I have the honor to send you herein four copies of an Act entitled "An Act to provide for the organization of a judiciary and the exercise of judicial powers in the Canal Zone, etc."

I also send you herewith two copies of rules of the circuit courts and municipal courts.

Respectfully,
[O. Kyle]
Justice of the Supreme Court [26]

On the same date (August 29, 1904) Judge Kyle addressed another letter [27] to Admiral Walker—Subject: Organization of the Circuit Court at Cristobal—in which he submitted the following specific questions:

1.—In order for the court to be organized, it would be necessary that there would be a marshal and a clerk ready to perform their separate duties. Has a marshal been appointed for each circuit in the Canal

Zone and if not, can one marshal perform the functions of that office within the entire Zone?

2.—Will it be necessary to have an American citizen as marshal and as clerk? On this subject I call to your attention the language of the oath of each officer for the Canal Zone as required by the statute you have enacted, viz: "That I recognize and accept the supreme authority of the United States in said Zone, and will maintain true faith and allegiance thereto."

3.—Can I appoint a temporary clerk of the circuit court, pending Mr. Griffin's return from the United States? He is the only person that I know here, personally, who would likely accept the position who is worthy and competent to serve.

4.—If I appoint a clerk for the 3rd circuit according to the provisions of the statute you have enacted, would it be legal for this clerk to act as circuit clerk within the 1st. and 2nd. circuits and if not, have the clerks for said circuits been appointed?

These ticklish questions were referred to the Governor of the Canal Zone who replied on September 10, 1904 [28] as follows:

1.—Act No. 13, Enactments of the Isthmian Canal Commission makes provision for the temporary performance of the duties of the marshals of the Supreme and Circuit Courts of the Zone, by the Captain of Police of the Zone.

2.—In Porto Rico and in the Philippine Islands there are a large number of government officials, judicial, legislative and executive, who are natives of the Islands. The United States Supreme Court held that the native inhabitants of Porto Rico and the Philippines are not citizens of the United States. This holding has not been considered as establishing the incompetency of the native inhabitants to hold office in the government of the islands. I am of opinion, based upon the precedents thus established,[29] that it is not necessary that the marshals and clerks of the courts of the Zone should be American citizens.[30]

---

[24] Ibid.

[25] Ibid.

[26] Although the early correspondence referred to Kyle as a Justice of the Supreme Court, this seems to have been only an honorary or ex officio title as the record shows that the first appointment to the high bench was not made until the following year. Of course, Act No. 1 provided that Justices of the Supreme Court should be the Judges of the Circuit Courts; so perhaps, conversely, a Judge of the Circuit Courts was ipso facto a Justice of the Supreme Court.

[27] Same as 23.

[28] Same as 23.

[29] See chap. II, passim, on the influence of Puerto Rican and Philippine precedents in the Canal Zone.

[30] Though the question referred only to marshals and clerks, Kyle had raised a point of great importance which could not be restricted to those positions. President Roosevelt settled the matter definitively with an Executive Order of December 8, 1904 waiving the requirement of United States citizenship for employees on

3, 4.—Act No. 13 above referred to, provides for the temporary performance of the clerk's duties by the Judge. The Commission understood that the clerk of the 3rd Circuit Court would return in a few weeks and that if the remaining judges were appointed, they would probably want to appoint the clerks immediately and therefore deemed it inadvisable to make provision for temporary appointments.

The answers evidently sufficed, for the following historic telegram [31] was sent from Colón (Cristobal) to General Davis at Ancon on September 13, 1904:

> Circuit Court was opened here according to law on yesterday.
>
> O. Kyle
> Judge.

[After the formality of opening the Third Circuit Court at Cristobal (it seems probable that no actual case was tried), Judge Kyle apparently proceeded to open Courts for the First and Second Circuits, as directed in the letter of August 20, 1904 from Admiral Walker. *The Canal Record* of April 8, 1914 carried a story about the closing of the old Circuit Courts, in accordance with the Panama Canal Act of 1912, which included some valuable information on the early history of those courts. In what appears to be a minor error of fact, however, the story overlooks the opening at Cristobal and credits the court at Ancon with being the first to open.] [32]

In any case, whether the Third or the First Judicial Circuit was technically the first to open for business did not matter very much. Of more significance was the question whether there would be enough business for three circuit courts anyway, let alone a Supreme Court. (For the few months of his incumbency, Kyle, being the only judge, was truly an old-fashioned circuit rider and judge for all seasons.) On September 14, 1904 General Davis sent the following cablegram [33] to Secretary Taft:

> Have just read law to organize Zone judiciary [I.C.C. Act No. 1]. I believe it sufficient to have one Superior Court. One judge now here has little to do; no more judges should be appointed. When Congress legislates I suggest appeal to some court in United States of America be authorized, following Kittredge bill passed by Senate.[34]

The "Kittredge bill passed by Senate" which Davis referred to must have been S. 5342 (Report No. 1859, 58th Cong., 2d sess.) reported out of committee on April 1, 1904. It is better known to history in its final form as "An Act to provide for the temporary government of the Canal Zone at Panama, [etc.]" of April 28, 1904 (33 Stat. 429), part of the first organic law of the Canal Zone.[35] As amended in the legislative process, however, the bill was greatly condensed and the resultant law contained no provision for appeal.

Sections 16 and 17 of the bill, which were deleted before passage, had provided for a "district court of the United States for the Canal Zone" (much like the one eventually established in the Panama Canal Act of 1912) and for appeal from that court to "the circuit court of appeals for the second judicial circuit of the United States," with

---

the Isthmus "under such regulations as may be provided by the United States Civil Service Commission." A supplementary Order of the President dated January 5, 1905 amended Section VIII of Schedule A of the Civil Service Rules to exclude from citizenship requirements a long list of offices starting with "Chief Justice and Judges of Supreme and Circuit Courts."

[31] Same as 23.

[32] "The first circuit court was established at Ancon [see illustration C], and for a time it transacted all of the circuit court business of the Zone. The first session was held in the old French building, formerly used by the District Court judge, now occupied by the new Magistrate's Court, in the old corral reservation, known in French times, and for a year or so after the Americans came, as 'Ancon Section.' The date of the first session, as indicated by the existing records, was September 16, 1904. Mr.

Osceola Kyle, who was the first circuit court judge, presided, and the first case tried was that of the Government of the Canal Zone vs. Baldomero Cortez, charged with the theft of a quantity of quicksilver from the Pacific Mail steamship *City of Peking*. The court dismissed the case, stating that it was not shown whether the goods alleged to have been taken consisted of 'Quicksilver, or shavings.'"

[33] Same as 23.

[34] Senator Alfred Beard Kittredge of South Dakota was chairman of the Committee on Inter-Oceanic Canals, having succeeded to that position upon the death of Senator Marc Hanna.

[35] See chap. V, p. 55, supra.

a final right of review, in its discretion, by the Supreme Court of the United States.[36]

(An earlier version of the same bill—S. 4513, 58th Cong., 2d sess., introduced on February 23, 1904 but never reported out of committee—had provided for a high court of three judges, appointed by the President with the advice and consent of the Senate, with appeal from decisions of individual judges to the court en banc, and appeal from the court en banc to the Circuit Court of Appeals for the Second Circuit.)

The uncertain future and unsettled status of the Canal Zone Judiciary during its first months of existence can be no better explained than in the words of Secretary Taft himself in the First Annual Report of the Isthmian Canal Commission dated December 1, 1904 (pp. 83-84):

> In the opinion of the undersigned [Taft], there is no necessity for more than one circuit judge and one prosecuting officer. The chief of the Zone police now acts as marshal of the court. So far, there has developed no necessity for the appointment of a marshal.
>
> There is at present no provision for hearing appeals from the decision of the present circuit judge.[37] It does not seem to the undersigned to be necessary or expedient to have appeals from such decisions heard in the Zone. The method that was provided by Senator Kittredge in his bill which passed the Senate, if enacted into law, would provide for an appeal and would serve all requisites in that regard.[38]
>
> It has been urged in dissent to this proposition that an appeal to a court at New Orleans or New York, for example, would be the same as forbidding appeal, for the parties might not have the means

to incur the expense of taking their case so far. There are several Anglo-Saxon colonies of Great Britain where there is but a single judge, and where appeals are taken to England. St. Helena, with a population of about what the Zone has, is one; and Belize, Honduras, with a population of some 40,000, is another; populations like that of the Zone made up largely of negroes.

> The objection to a large judiciary in the Zone is that all judges in excess of one will have nothing to do. These people do not seem to be litigious. So far they have shown themselves to be very tractable. There will probably be more litigation and more criminal charges to be tried after the canal work assumes greater proportions than at present, but it is scarcely possible that the number of persons who may at any time come under the jurisdiction of United States courts will exceed 50,000, and probably not more than 2,500 of them will be Americans of the white race. At present quite half of the inhabitants are foreigners, a proportion that in the future is likely to be largely increased. Surely six municipal judges and one superior judge can attend to the litigation and crimes of the probable maximum number stated.
>
> Another employment has been suggested for the three judges, that of constituting them a land court, such as was created by Act 496 of the acts of the Philippine Commission.[39]
>
> The experience and observation of the writer in the Philippines showed him that the land court of registration served a very useful purpose [in some cases but was not necessary in the Canal Zone as a Joint Commission with such function already existed].

---

[36] On the same day (April 1, 1904) Senator Morgan of Alabama, a bitter opponent of the Spooner Act, introduced a substitute (S. 5342) for the Kittredge bill declaring that the territory acquired under the 1903 treaty "shall constitute a Government reservation of the United States for canal purposes." The Morgan amendment never got out of committee.

[37] The Supreme Court of the Canal Zone provided for in Act No. 1, which would have had appellate jurisdiction, had still not been established; nor had the appeals procedure envisaged in the Kittredge bills been enacted.

[38] Presumably, then, if the appeals procedure in either of the Kittredge bills had become law, there never would have been a Supreme Court of the Canal Zone, regardless of Act No. 1.

Only two cases, both criminal, arising from actions committed during the I.C.C. era, ever reached the United States Supreme Court and both were dismissed, in *per curiam* opinions not reported, on the threshold question of jurisdiction. Katz (p. 903) says that while the constitutional power of the Supreme Court to review the decisions of territorial courts has never been challenged, the basis of this jurisdiction is not entirely clear. The only attempt he can

---

[39] Again showing the recurrent propensity to relate Canal Zone problems to the recent Puerto Rican and Philippine experience.

First United States Court, Ancon, Canal Zone. (*Annual Report of the Isthmian Canal Commission, 1905-06*).

find by the Supreme Court to explain it is in 2 Wall. 160 (1864) at p. 173:

It cannot be disputed that Congress has the exclusive power of legislation in and over the Territories, and, consequently, that the Supreme Court has appellate jurisdiction over the courts established therein.

But his quotation omits the words of the Court immediately following: "under such regulations as Congress may make."

As a practical matter, therefore, it seems that there is no right of appeal absent "such regulations as Congress may make." In the organic laws of Puerto Rico and the Philippines, Congress did expressly provide for appeal to the Supreme Court; but the organic laws of the Canal Zone (prior to the Panama Canal Act of 1912) are silent on the subject.

The first of the aforementioned cases arose on October 14, 1904, hardly more than a month after Judge Kyle had opened Circuit Courts. On that day one Oli Nifou, a Chinese national residing in the Canal Zone, was arrested by order of the prosecuting attorney of the Canal Zone for selling tickets of the Panama Lottery Company— which had been his full-time occupation for the past year and which was perfectly legal under the Panamanian law which had previously prevailed—in defiance of I.C.C. Act No. 3, "Suppression of Lotteries," enacted pursuant to Executive Order of May 9, 1904. On October 17, 1904 Nifou's petition for a writ of habeas corpus was heard and denied in Circuit Court for the Third Judicial Circuit and notice was given by his attorney, Gilbert F. Little, of intention to appeal to the Supreme Court of the Canal Zone. (If appeal had actually been taken to the Supreme Court of the Canal Zone at that time, it would have been from Kyle to Kyle. In taking the case to the Supreme Court of the United States, however, Little pleaded that there was no Supreme Court of the Canal Zone and that the decision of the Circuit Court was a final order from the highest court of record.)

The case *In the Matter of the Application of Oli Nifou for a Writ of Habeas Corpus* came on in the October Term, 1904, and was decided on May 1, 1905: "Motion for leave to file petition for writs of habeas corpus and certiorari denied."[40] The So-

licitor General, opposing, adduced, among other things, that the case should first be tried on the merits, that petitioner could well wait for the constitution of the Supreme Court of the Canal Zone if he wanted to appeal, and that no appeal from the latter court was provided by law.[41]

Ex parte: In the Matter of Oli Nifou, Petitioner. The Records and Briefs in this "Matter" run to a total of 95 pages and the arguments seem almost as vital and alive as if they were written yesterday. It is hard to put down the final "Petition to Reconsider . . ." without a strong feeling of unfinished business.

One of the most interesting agglomerations of memorabilia on the antecedents and the first two years of the Panama Canal and Canal Zone, in four volumes, reposes, seldom disturbed, in the stacks of the Library of Congress under the prosaic title "Investigation of Panama Canal Matters. Hearings before the Committee on Interoceanic Canals of the United States Senate . . . ." (Senate Doc. No. 401, 59th Cong., 2d sess). And in one of the many piquant passages (p. 2270) General (Governor George W.) Davis, under questioning by Senator Morgan, reveals his reaction to the Oli Nifou case—uncomprehending irritation—and the continuing undisturbed autonomy of the Canal Zone judiciary:

Senator Morgan. There was a lottery case that came here [Washington].

General Davis. Yes.

Senator Morgan. Did that originate in one of your courts?

General Davis. Yes; . . . They happened to be Chinamen, I think, and those men were brought before the municipal courts—the lowest court—and remanded to a higher court, and then bonds were given for their appearance and an appeal taken, and finally, in some way or other—I don't know how and I never could quite understand how—they managed to get the case before the Supreme Court of the United States.

Senator Morgan. On a motion for certiorari, I think?

General Davis. Yes.

Senator Morgan. And the Supreme Court declined to take jurisdiction?

General Davis. Yes.

Senator Morgan. And so the judgment of the Zone court stood?

General Davis. Yes.

[40] 198 U.S. 581 (1904). No.   . Original.

[41] The Solicitor General also scored a point on a somewhat lower level by characterizing the petitioner as "[a]n agent of this lottery company, of a race which notoriously is unable to appreciate our code of morals and is especially prone to gambling . . ." and who, therefore, should all the more be brought to trial.

The case of Oli Nifou, despite being an historic first in the legal history of the Canal Zone, is not even mentioned in any published work on the Zone and is, to all intents and purposes, forgotten. It deserves a better fate. Some of the arguments of petitioner (leaving aside, as disposed of by the Insular cases, those based on alleged violations of constitutional rights) raised basic questions of authority and legitimacy which were not persuasively rebutted by the Solicitor General and remain unsettled to this day (at least in the area of international law), as current treaty renegotiations attest. Petitioner asked the Court to declare both the Executive Order of May 9, 1904 and Act No. 3 null and void as a misuse of legislative power; [42] and questioned, in effect,

---

[42] In a memorandum dated January 30, 1909, commenting on an early draft of the bill which eventually became the Panama Canal Act of 1912, Mr. Blackburn, head of the Department of Civil Administration, made this revealing observation: "By the provisions of Section 2, not only is there a ratification of all grants of power, military, civil and judicial, heretofore made by Congress to the President or exercised by him without express authority of Congress, but a very material addition is made thereto. There has been, and still is, grave doubt in the minds of many well-informed men as to the authority of Congress to delegate to the President or anyone else, power given it to enact laws. This authority was assumed by Congress with reference to legislation for the Canal Zone, and with reference to such legislation it has not been judicially determined." * (Is this not the point that was later judicially determined in Panama Refining Co. v. Ryan, 293 U.S. 388 (1934), pp. 414 et seq., and Schechter Corp. v. United States, 295 U.S. 495 (1934), p. 529, when another Congress attempted to grant legislative power to another President Roosevelt? It is difficult to reconcile those decisions with the legislative powers granted in the Act of April 28, 1904 and, retroactively, in the Panama Canal Act of 1912.)

The final postscript, for all practical purposes to the long controversy over the legal status of I.C.C. legislation after March 4, 1905 and the effect thereon of Section 2 of the Panama Canal Act was written by the Supreme Court of the United States in 1923 in the case of McConaughey v. Morrow (263 U.S. 39). In upholding the I.C.C. legislation (without which there could have been no Government

* Records of the Panama Canal, Washington National Records Center, Archives Branch, Record Group No. 185, Entry No. 94.B.7.

the validity of the structure of civil government by alleging that the arrest of Oli Nifou did not involve anything "necessary or convenient" for the erection of the canal as envisaged in the Treaty of 1903.

The case of Oli Nifou and continued failure of Congress to provide any appeal from the Circuit Court to a court in the United States apparently forced a decision, despite all the cold water thrown on the idea by Taft and others, to proceed with the constitution of a Supreme Court in the Zone. The first move, little more than a gesture but an acknowledgement of intent, was made on January 9, 1905 with a "meeting" the minutes of which read as follows:

> Ancon, January 9, 1905.
> This being the second Monday in January of this year, the Supreme Court of the Canal Zone met pursuant to law,[43] the Hon. Osceola Kyle, justice of the Supreme Court being present and presiding. There being no other justice, the Court was adjourned until the further order of the Chief Justice, or until the second Monday in July, 1905. And the Court was duly

---

and no Judiciary in the Zone), the Court cited the Annual Message of the President of December 21, 1911:

> The fact is that today there is no statutory law by authority of which the President is maintaining the government of the Zone. Such authority was given in an amendment to the Spooner Act, which expired by the terms of its own limitation some years ago. Since that time the government has continued, under the advice of the Attorney General that, in the absence of action by Congress, there is necessarily an implied authority on the part of the Executive to maintain a government in a territory in which he has to see that the laws are executed.

The Court then interpreted Section 2 in such a way as to confirm the statutory effect of I.C.C. legislation in general without giving the dignity of law to every minor administrative regulation. This remarkable opinion was not only a legal *tour de force* but a monument to the ubiquity of William Howard Taft. It was written by Taft as Chief Justice; the Annual Message of the President quoted above was written by President Taft; and first-hand knowledge of the history of the subject matter was gained by Taft while Secretary of War in charge of the Zone. (See also note 21, supra.)

[43] Section 6 of Act No. 1 provided that the Supreme Court should hold regular sessions commencing upon the second Monday of January and July of each year.

adjourned upon the day and date above-mentioned.[44]

The very next day—January 10, 1905—the Governor addressed a letter to the chairman of the I.C.C. setting forth serious complaints about the manner in which Judge Kyle had been comporting himself and performing his duties. The main thing that aroused the Governor's ire was his discovery that several cases which had been pending in the territory at change of jurisdiction, and had been transferred to the Zone courts (as provided by Sec. 41 of Act No. 1), had been left unattended for months; and when he demanded an explanation, Judge Kyle said he was unable to dispose of them because of ignorance of the Spanish language and Panamanian law.

The position in which the Government of the Canal Zone is placed by this state of affairs is certainly one that ought not to be continued. It is within my knowledge that Americans acting as judges in countries recently taken over by the United States [Puerto Rico and the Philippines] have not found it impracticable to reach conclusions satisfactory to the people, and to the litigants, the same being heard and determined in accordance with Spanish law, and I am forced to the conclusion that the same should have been done in the cases which have come up in the Canal Zone.

To make matters worse, the letter continued, the Governor had been informed by the American Minister to Panama that Judge Kyle had appeared as a private lawyer in the courts of Panama in opposition to a motion by the American Consul to settle the estate of an American citizen.

If the facts are as stated, it would appear that Judge Kyle, while unable to hear and determine a case that involves documentary evidence and records in the Spanish language, finds himself able to practice before a Spanish court in the neighboring city.

I hope the Commission will deem this matter of sufficient importance to bring it to the attention of the Secretary of War.[45]

It appears that the matter had already been brought to the attention of the Secretary of War. On January 7, 1905, Taft wrote the following letter, typed on plain paper with no letterhead:

My dear Judge Kyle:

After a conference with the President, on my return from Panama, I write this letter.

I learned when I was in Panama that you were not satisfied with the position of Judge there and the conditions which surround it, that you objected to the law under which you were serving [presumably the stipulation that Panamanian law should be applied in the adjudication of private controversies], and that on several occasions you have intimated a desire to resign, especially if you were not to be selected as Chief Justice. I also learned while there that you were not disposed particularly to fit in with the Spanish law, which prevails in the Isthmus and which ought to prevail in the Zone so far as possible, *because it is no purpose of our Government to take from the people of the Zone the laws to which they have been accustomed* [emphasis supplied], except so far as the foundation principles of American government require. You do not know Spanish and you do not seem to have shown yourself adaptable to the situation. My own judgment is, and that too is the judgment of the President, that a knowledge of Spanish is essential to the proper disposal of the business of the court.

These objections, you will understand, Judge, are not to your character or to your integrity, or to your judicial capacity in the United States and among your own people. The objection is founded on your inability, and possibly a lack of desire, to adapt yourself to the new people of the Isthmus. I wish therefore to suggest that you take your leave of absence and that at the end of the leave, you forward your resignation to the Chairman of the Isthmian Canal Commission. Only the President, Admiral Walker and I know of this letter, and you may be sure it will not have any publicity, so that when you forward your resignation it will be entirely voluntary.[46]

Taft and the President and Admiral Walker kept their secret well. The strange disappearance of the first American judge, just when he was apparently in line for the highest seat on the bench, has never before

[44] *The Canal Record* of April 8, 1914, p. 313.

[45] Records of the Panama Canal, Washington National Records Center, Archives Branch, Record Group No. 185, Entry No. 94.B.

[46] William Howard Taft Papers, Library of Congress, Letter from WHT to O. Kyle dated January 7, 1905.

been explained in any published work. He was a fatality of the hazards of dispensing justice according to laws "with which the inhabitants are familiar" when the dispenser was not familiar with either the laws or the language.

On February 24, 1905, while Kyle was on leave, the first appointment to the Supreme Court as such was made. In approving the choice of Hezekiah Alexander Gudger, Taft was clearly determined not to repeat the mistake he had made with Kyle. Gudger had been consul-general in Panama since 1897 and was familiar with both the laws and the language. He was a native of North Carolina and before coming to Panama he had practiced law in that state for many years, as well as serving in both houses of the legislature.

Kyle's resignation was accepted on March 23, 1905 and the Judiciary was back to where it started numerically, though perhaps with some gain in quality.

The second appointment to the Supreme Court, that of the Chief Justice, was made on June 1, 1905 in the person of Dr. Facundo Mutis Durán. Whatever else may have been his failings, he could not be found unfamiliar with the laws and the language. Dr. Mutis was a Panamanian citizen and "an outstanding authority on Spanish, Colombian, and Panamanian Laws." [47] He had also twice served as Governor, "both times without distinction," [48] of the State of Panama while it was still part of Colombia, had been appointed a Justice of the Supreme Court of Panama, and had been employed for several years as an attorney for the Panama Railroad.

No organized biographical data on the first Chief Justice could be found and the specific motivation for his appointment is not known. Putting together glimpses of the man drawn from a variety of books and other documents, certain reasonable inferences can be made, particularly with respect to the question of how a Panamanian citizen in this crucial post could have been entrusted to "recognize and accept the su-

preme authority of the United States" and "maintain true faith and allegiance thereto."

In a recent book by a Colombian historian,[49] Dr. Mutis Durán is described as a lawyer from Santander (Colombia) who through long residence on the Isthmus had lost the true Colombian perspective, or indeed any sense of belonging except to wherever he was prospering; and, moreover, whose affiliation to either Colombia or Panama was further attenuated by long employment with the Panama Railroad and by marriage to an American woman "of great beauty half his age." [50] During his first administration as Governor of the State of Panama, from October 8, 1898 to January 2, 1899, he was in conflict with the chief military officer of the State, General Vásquez Cobo, who expressed doubts as to his loyalty. Dr. Mutis' term ended abruptly, according to the same book, when, feeling threatened by Vásquez, he fled from his home "dressed as a woman" and took refuge in the American Consulate. He served as Governor again from January 3 to September 19, 1903.

In the interim between his two truncated terms as Governor he seems to have been employed in the office of the Panama Railroad in New York City, from which vantage point he participated peripherally in the negotiation of the Hay-Herrán Treaty. There is evidence that both Martínez Silva and Vicente Concha, the Colombian envoys who

---

[47] Quotation from Playa de Flor Land and Improvement Co. v. United States (see chap. I, note 8, supra), at 301.

[48] "En ambas occasiones su actuación careció de brillantez." M. M. Alba C., *Cronología de los Gobernantes de Panamá 1510-1932* (Panamá: Publisher not shown, 1935), pp. 134-35 and 138-39.

[49] Eduardo Lemaitre, *Panamá y Su Separación de Colombia* (Bogotá: Biblioteca Banco Popular, 1971).

[50] ". . . este doctor Mutis Durán, era un abogado santandereano que por su larga residencia en el Istmo, donde venía de tiempo atrás asesorando a la Compañía del Ferrocarril de Panamá, se había panameñizado por completo, e incluso se había casado con una dama norteamericana, de gran belleza, a la que casi doblaba la edad, pues Mutis pertenecía a esa clase de "centranos" que, como el doctor Amador Guerrero y otros tantos, fueron perdiendo poco a poco la perspectiva grande de la nacionalidad y la redujeron a esos estrechos límites parroquiales y utilitaristas que tan cabalmente cifra el adagio latino: 'ubi bene, ibi patria': 'donde te va bien, esa es tu patria'." Lemaitre, *Separación*, pp. 435-36. Lemaitre's account of the Panamanian "separation" is written from the Colombian point of view, but with a scholarly objectivity, and there is no reason to doubt the accuracy of the above assessment.

preceded Herrán and actually did the substantive work on the treaty, went to New York to seek his advice.[51] It is also evident that he impressed upon the envoys the necessity of granting any concession necessary to obtain the commitment of the United States Government to the Panama route.

The Supreme Court (*Corte Suprema de Justicia*) of the new Republic of Panama was constituted effective June 3, 1904, (replacing the *Corte de Justicia*) with Dr. Facundo Mutis Durán as one of its members. However, the record shows that he had been granted leave and his place was taken at the organizational meeting by his alternate.[52] Examination of Panamanian court records for the remainder of the year shows no indication that he ever actually served in that capacity. Nevertheless, it is clear that he was considered qualified for, and was appointed to, the highest court in the Republic, and at the same time was acceptable to the United States Government to be the highest arbiter of justice in the Zone.[53]

Hence, it may be assumed that his ambidexterity was thought to be a virtue at the time, and it probably was.

With the selection of Mutis Durán the Supreme Court was formally organized on the same day and the debate over whether or not to have a Supreme Court was ended. On June 21, 1905 the third justice was appointed, the Honorable Lorin C. Collins, a circuit judge from Chicago, thus completing the organization of the judicial system of the Zone.[54]

Though the Judiciary now had its full complement of three judges, it could not be accused of profligacy with personnel. Each of the three Justices of the Supreme Court also doubled as a judge of one of the Circuit Courts. Whenever a losing litigant appealed to the Supreme Court, he found one-third of that body composed of the same judge from whose decision he was appealing.[55] (Despite this handicap, there were a number of cases in which appellant succeeded in persuading the other two Justices to reverse and remand.) The Marshal authorized by Act No. 1 was never appointed; the function was performed during the entire I.C.C. era by

---

[51] Alba C., *Cronología*, p. 138; Miner, *Fight*, pp. 128, 219.

[52] *REGISTRO JUDICIAL, Organo del Poder Judicial de la República*, Año I—Panamá, 14 de Junio de 1904—Vol. I, No. 19. (In a case before the *Corte Suprema de Justicia* on November 26, 1904, Mutis Durán, together with Pablo Arosemena, appeared as a *jurisconsulto* —i.e., a person versed in the law whose opinion would be treated with respect by the Court. *Registro Judicial*, Vol. II, p. 11 (1905).)

[53] The following exchange took place during the hearings before the Senate Committee on Interoceanic Canals in 1906:

"*Mr. Magoon:* The chief justice is Mutis Durán.

"*Senator Morgan:* Is he a citizen of the United States?

"*Mr. Magoon:* He is not.

. . . . . .

"*Senator Morgan:* How did it ever happen, Judge Magoon, that a man who is not a citizen of the United States became eligible to be the chief justice of the supreme court of any Territory in this Union?

"*Mr. Magoon:* It was based on the precedent of Chief Justice Aribano, of the Philippines. Three out of seven judges of the Philippine supreme court are not citizens of the United States. . . . And in Porto Rico the same thing took place.

"*Senator Morgan:* That precedent aside, do you know of any law of the United States which authorizes the employment of a foreigner, a noncitizen of the United States, as the chief

justice of any judicial court anywhere in the Union?

"*Mr. Magoon:* I do not know that it is expressly provided for; but I do not think there is anything which prohibits it." Senate Document No. 401, 59th Cong., 2d sess., p. 706.

[54] Little else could be learned about Collins except that he was said to be a French scholar, and he was apparently on good terms with Taft as he sent Taft a congratulatory telegram upon the latter's nomination for President in 1908. Mutis Durán was also fluent in French as well as in English and Spanish. On the whole, the original Supreme Court was an assemblage of able and accomplished men. So far as the archival records of the United States Government are concerned, however, they might as well have never existed.

[55] The following exchange took place in the hearings before the Senate Committee on Interoceanic Canals in 1906:

"*Senator Morgan:* These judges try cases also in the courts of first instance?

"*Mr. Magoon:* Yes, sir.

"*Senator Morgan:* When they try cases in the courts below, do they sit in these cases in the Supreme Court?

"*Mr. Magoon:* Yes; they sit, but they do not participate, I think, in the judgment. It would be the other two." Senate Document No. 401, 59th Cong., 2d sess., p. 710.

the Captain of Police (who also served as warden of the penitentiary), while members of the police force acted as bailiffs.

Justice Mutis Durán left the Court upon the expiration of his term in January 1909 and was succeeded as Chief Justice by Gudger who held that position until the Court was abolished in 1914. Thus Gudger was not only the first Justice to be appointed but the only one to serve during the entire life of the Court. The seat vacated by Gudger was taken by Wesley M. Owen. In 1911 Collins and Owen were replaced by William H. Jackson and Thomas E. Brown,[56] who, with Gudger, constituted the Supreme Court at the time of its demise.

J. R. Keedy was Prosecuting Attorney to September 1, 1906, when he was succeeded by G. M. Shontz. Walter Emery was the first Clerk and Reporter; he was succeeded by Elbert M. Goolsby.

The bar, like the bench, was equally open to both American and Panamanian citizens. According to the rules of admission,[57] all attorneys who were permitted to practice their profession within the territory of which the Canal Zone was constituted on or before February 23, 1904 would be entitled to practice before the Canal Zone courts. American residents of the Isthmus who had previously been duly admitted to practice before the highest court of any state or territory of the United States would likewise be entitled to practice in the Zone; but they might be required also to satisfactorily pass an examination upon the codes of law and procedure in force in the Canal Zone. Other persons wishing to practice, besides produc-

ing a certificate of good moral character, would have to pass an examination covering "Real Estate, Personal Property, Equity, Pleading, Contracts, Administrators and Executors, Criminal Law, and the Codes in force in the Canal Zone." All applicants would have to subscribe to an oath accepting the supreme authority of the United States in the Canal Zone.

So far as I could discover there is nowhere in existence a complete list of all lawyers admitted to practice in the Canal Zone during the I.C.C. era, which has to be considered the formative period of the Common Law reception. From the Canal Zone Reports, however, we do have a record of the names of the lawyers who argued before the Supreme Court and the number of cases in which they appeared. And from these data it is possible to make some deductions about the nature of the bar in general, and even, to a certain extent, in particular.

About two-thirds of the names appear to be Anglo-Saxon (hence, presumably trained in the Common Law) and about one-third Spanish. When the number of cases argued by each is added to the calculation, the imbalance in favor of the common lawyer is even greater, more on the order of three or four to one. Moreover, the frequency of Spanish names tends to diminish in the later years. While both groups of lawyers were necessarily making adjustments and adaptations in their habits, the Common Law practices were gaining ascendency, aided by the adoption early on of a Common Law civil procedure code and, even earlier, Common Law criminal codes.

On the other hand, the civil lawyers did have one advantage. As we have remarked before, and will remark again, the Civil Code of Panama remained in force during the entire I.C.C. era (and long after). This was a wasting advantage, however, as the Code was gradually modified by Common Law rules of interpretation and as all the members of the bar became more accomplished comparativists.

Granted that they had to make the greater adjustment—the court system, after all, being undeniably American—those Panamanian lawyers who chose to practice in the Zone apparently encountered no obstacles or discrimination. In some cases argued before the Supreme Court the lawyers on both sides were Panamanians. One who made six appearances was Harmodio

---

[56] Brown was the only member of the high court to come up through the ranks. Prior to his appointment he had served as Acting Prosecuting Attorney and as a District Judge at Cristobal (*The Canal Record*, Vol. I, passim). Brown's appointment was announced by Executive Order of May 16, 1911. By another Executive Order of the same date, and in identical language, one Walter W. Warwick was appointed as Associate Justice of the Supreme Court of the Canal Zone. Whatever happened to him is a mystery to the author of this book. There was no room for him on the Court, which already had its full complement of three, and there is no trace of evidence that he ever served.

[57] Formalized in the new Code of Civil Procedure effective May 1, 1907 and promulgated in Executive Order No. 597½ of March 22, 1907.

Arias (see chap. IV, note 19, supra), who later became President of Panama. That the bar was permitted complete freedom of thought and expression, even as to the controversy over the events through which the Zone was brought into existence, is proved by the example of Oscar Terán, a Panamanian lawyer who appeared in twenty-six cases, making him the fourth most active lawyer in the Zone.

Terán, like Belisario Porras, was one of the few outstanding Isthmians who refused to go along with the Panamanian secession, regarding the whole affair as morally and legally indefensible. Unlike Porras, however, he never left the Isthmus and continued to participate in Panamanian political life without ever recanting his condemnation of the separation and particularly the United States role in it. According to Lemaitre,[58] who described him as a man of integrity, culture, a notable jurist, and a conscientious historian, he was a "sworn enemy of Roosevelt [whom he called a 'Pirate'] and of the United States." During all the time he was practicing in the Zone he was working on a history, which he finally published in 1934, of the Hay-Herrán and Hay/Bunau-Varilla Treaties which was extremely critical of the United States.[59]

The organization of the Judiciary, as set forth in Act No. 1 and finally implemented after the travails described above, remained unchanged through the rest of the I.C.C. era except for some relatively minor modifications at the local level. The first modifications were an incidental result of the Executive Order of March 13, 1907, previously referred to, whose primary purpose was to

abolish the five municipalities and redivide the Zone into four administrative districts (see chap. V, p. 66, supra). Section 4 of that Order provided for the replacement of the former Municipal Courts with District Courts, the Judges of which would exercise in each district the same authority formerly exercised by Municipal Judges (see pp. 76-77, supra. Provision was also made for a senior District Judge for the whole Zone, "who shall sit wherever required of him and who shall once a month preside at and keep minutes of a conference of all the District Judges at which matters of common interest pertaining to their office shall be discussed."

Executive Order No. 731 of January 9, 1908 modified Section 22 of Act No. 1 to make the geographical boundaries of the three Judicial Circuits correspond to the new administrative subdivisions.

In anticipation of the inundation of the Gatun Lake area, an Executive Order was issued on September 12, 1912 by which the administrative district of Gorgona was abolished and its territory added to the district of Empire. In the same Order the number of District Judges was reduced to three and the office of senior District Judge was abolished.

The second of the two cases aforementioned to reach the United States Supreme Court (see p. 80, supra) began in January 1907 when Adolphus Coulson, a Barbadian negro, administered a lethal dose of arsenic to his wife at Gorgona. He was tried in February 1907 in the Second Circuit Court before Judge Gudger and Municipal Judges H. L. Ross and R. B. Myers, of Gorgona and Empire, respectively,[60] found guilty, and sentenced to be hanged. The conviction was appealed to the Supreme Court of the Canal Zone on the sole ground that defendant had been denied the right of trial by jury in contravention of the fifth and sixth amendments of the Constitution. The Supreme Court of the Canal Zone affirmed the lower court decision (1 Canal Zone Reports 50), relying on the doctrine of the Insular cases that the Constitution does not extend

---

[58] Lemaitre, *Separación*, pp. 395, 557.

[59] Oscar Terán, *Del Tratado Herrán-Hay al Tratado Hay-Bunau Varilla* (Panamá: Imprenta de "Motivos Colombianos," 1934). The book was subtitled: "Historia Crítica del Atraco Yanqui Mal Llamado en Colombia 'La Pérdida de Panamá' y en Panamá, 'Nuestra Independencia de Colombia.'" (Translation: "Critical History of the Yankee Highway Robbery misnamed in Colombia 'The Loss of Panama' and in Panama 'Our Independence from Colombia.'") Terán's book—though not pleasant reading for those who would defend the actions of the United States Government in the matter—was carefully researched and authenticated (he spent thirty years on it), and remained the most accurate and complete account of these events until the appearance of the work by Lemaitre in 1971.

[60] Section 171 of the Code of Criminal Procedure provided that "in cases where the penalty of death or imprisonment for life may be imposed, the circuit judge of the court wherein the information is filed or the action is triable shall summon two municipal judges of the judicial circuit to sit with him in the trial of said cause."

of its own force to territories under control of the United States.

On November 9, 1908 the Supreme Court of the United States, in a *per curiam* opinion not reported (212 U.S. 553), dismissed a writ of error to review judgment of the Supreme Court of the Canal Zone for "want of jurisdiction." Unlike *Oli Nifou*, this case had been tried on the merits and had gone through the court of last resort in the jurisdiction; but like *Oli Nifou*, the effort to have the Supreme Court pass on the legality of the civil government and the Judiciary itself had again failed. The story was reported in *The Canal Record* of November 25, 1908 under the headline "Canal Zone Not Under U. S. Constitution."

Even before the *"Matter of Coulson"* had run its full course, the right of trial by jury in capital cases was extended, as a result thereof, to the Canal Zone by Executive Order of February 6, 1908 (see chap. V, p. 62, supra). Hence, the case had a significant effect on the evolution of Canal Zone law (see chap. VII, p. 103, infra. It is also germane to this chapter, however, along with *Oli Nifou*, because it settled, so far as domestic law was concerned, the status of the Canal Zone Judiciary within the overall American legal system.[61] Attempts of counsel for petitioner in the Supreme Court of the United States to distinguish the Canal Zone situation from the kind of territorial government involved in the Insular cases failed.

The petition of Coulson was opposed in the Supreme Court by the same Solicitor General, Henry M. Hoyt, who had obtained the dismissal of Oli Nifou's, and on pretty much the same grounds so far as the issue of constitutional protection was concerned. Petitioner's attack on the Canal Zone Government itself was based more on the legislative lacuna than on excessive delegation of legislative powers. Hoyt argued that the President had authority *ex necessitate* to govern the Zone in view of "legislative omission or failure to provide a new and permanent status," and concluded that "the validity of the Canal Zone Government and of its judicial proceedings . . . can not be successfully challenged." [62]

As a matter of political realism, he seems to have been right. But the Congress was sufficiently uneasy about the provenance of the courts to include the following sentence in Section 2 of the Panama Canal Act of 1912:

> The existing courts established in the Canal Zone by Executive Order are recognized and confirmed to continue in operation until the courts provided for in this Act shall be established.

Actually, the courts in question were not established directly by Executive Order but by legislation of the I.C.C. (Act No. 1) exercising delegated Presidential authority derived from congressional legislation of questionable constitutionality (see note 42, supra).

After much debate and soul-searching, as we have seen, the organizational structure of the Judiciary was completed in June 1905 and did not come under serious re-examination until the Annual Report of the I.C.C. for 1911. In that report Mr. Feuille, Head of the Department of Law, tackled the subject again and came to the conclusion, as had Taft several years before, that "business transacted by the three circuit courts is not sufficient to keep one active judge constantly employed, much less three of them." Specific recommendations for improvement, as he pointed out, must necessarily be conditioned on action, or inaction, by Congress with respect to bills then pending to provide a permanent organization for the Zone.[63]

His recommendation that the three Circuit Courts be reduced to one (thus eliminating, of course, the Supreme Court) was conditioned on the assumption that Congress would authorize appeals to some appellate court in the United States, preferably the Fifth Circuit located in New Orleans. His argument continued:

> That court entertains appeals from the Federal courts in the Gulf States, all of which states are more or less influenced by principles of the civil or Roman law which have passed to them from the

---

[61] Its status in international law was, and is, another matter; which draws our attention back to the Treaty of 1903 upon which its legitimacy, as an exercise of sovereignty (which the President has agreed to renounce), ultimately rests.

[62] U.S. Supreme Court, Records and Briefs,

Vol. 212, Ex Parte in the Matter of Adolphus Coulson, No.   . Original, Brief in Opposition Filed by Leave of Court, pp. 7, 8.

[63] Mr. Feuille was also beginning to work on a revision of the laws (which would be the final phase of the reception process) and there also he was necessarily looking to Congress to provide basic direction (see chap. V, p. 68, supra).

French and Spanish Governments which preceded our own State governments now in existence there. This is especially so in regard to the State of Louisiana, which has a Civil Code substantially the same as that of Panama.[64]

Another part of this plan was that the number of District Judges be reduced from five to three (which was done the following year by Executive Order, as noted above).

Alternatively, assuming that Congress continued to ignore the Judiciary, Feuille recommended the continuance of the three Circuit Courts and the complete elimination of the District Courts. Anticipating the grounds for possible criticism, he argued:

It may be said that tribunals of the dignity of circuit courts should not be required to try ordinary police cases; but an answer to that objection is found in the fact that the United States district courts, whose high character and dignity is universally recognized, have been required to try petty cases under the Federal statutes, and this is especially so in districts including military and other Federal reservations.[65]

The Panama Canal Act of August 24, 1912, providing for a permanent organization for the Canal Zone, settled once and for all, in Sections 7-9, the subsidiary matter of how to organize the Judiciary.[66] Its legitimacy could no longer be questioned; it was duly incorporated, solving the dilemma of appellate jurisdiction, into the hierarchy of the federal court system; the number of superior judges was reduced to one, at long last; and the District Courts were eliminated, leaving only two levels of courts instead of the former three.

Section 7 authorized the President to define the boundaries of subdivisions within the Zone so that there would be one "town" in each subdivision. Continuing:

In each town there shall be a magistrate's court with exclusive original jurisdiction coextensive with the subdivision in which it is situated of all civil cases in which the principal sum claimed does not exceed

three hundred dollars, and all criminal cases wherein the punishment shall not exceed a fine of one hundred dollars, or imprisonment not exceeding thirty days, or both, and all violations of police regulations and ordinances and all actions involving possession or title to personal property or the forcible entry and detainer of real estate. Such magistrates shall also hold preliminary investigations in charges of felony and offenses under section ten of this Act, [security regulations] and commit or bail in bailable cases to the district court. A sufficient number of magistrates and constables, *who must be citizens of the United States,* [emphasis supplied] shall be appointed by the governor of the Panama Canal for terms of four years . . .

Section 8 established in the Canal Zone one (United States) District Court[67] with two divisions, one including Balboa and the other including Cristobal, (thus corresponding to the geographic areas embraced by the jurisdiction of the two magistrates' courts). Continuing:

The said district court shall have original jurisdiction of all felony cases, of offenses arising under section ten of this Act, all cases in equity; admiralty and all cases at law involving principal sums exceeding three hundred dollars and all appeals from judgments rendered in magistrates' courts.

The District Court was also given jurisdiction of all matters and proceedings within the jurisdiction of any of the previously existing Canal Zone courts and not otherwise provided for (i.e., not given to the magistrate's court in Section 7.)

Section 8 also provided for a District Judge, a District Attorney, and a Marshal, all to be appointed by the President for terms of four years. The District Judge would receive "the same salary paid the district judges of the United States" and was authorized to appoint a clerk and one assistant.

The principal subjects dealt with in Section 9 were (a) the transfer of cases pending from the old courts to the new, and (b) appellate procedure from the highest court of the Zone. With respect to (a) it was provided that, immediately upon the organization of the courts created by this Act, all

[64] Annual Report of the I.C.C. for 1911, p. 498.

[65] Ibid., p. 499.

[66] In fact, the dispositions made for the Judiciary have stood the test of time better than those for the rest of the civil government, which was reorganized in 1950 (see chap. V, note 61, supra).

[67] Not to be confused with the previous local courts of the same name.

causes and proceedings whatsoever pending in the old courts should be transferred to the appropriate new court and the old courts should cease to exist; but with the significant exception that the old Supreme Court might continue to function until all the causes and proceedings pending therein were disposed of. With respect to (b) it was provided that appeals could be taken from final judgments and decrees of the District Court of the Canal Zone to the Circuit Court of Appeals of the Fifth Circuit at New Orleans.[68]

Provisions of the Panama Canal Act respecting the Canal Zone Judiciary were implemented by Executive Order No. 1897 of March 12, 1914. For the most part it simply provided the mechanism for carrying out the intent of Sections 7-9 of the Act. The territorial limits of the Balboa and Cristobal divisions of the District Court were explicitly made coterminous with the areas under the jurisdiction of the Balboa and Cristobal Magistrates' Courts. The rules of evidence, practice, and procedure as previously established in the Circuit Courts, so far as "not inconsistent with the provisions of the Panama Canal Act," were extended to the new District Court. The Order was made effective as of April 1, 1914 and on that date the old courts expired, except for the Supreme Court which continued in existence until June 30, 1914.

Both levels of the new courts remained under the administrative supervision of the Executive Department of the Canal Zone Government, and thus indirectly of the War Department; but the District Judge was appointed by the President while the Magistrates were appointed by the Governor of the Zone.

The Annual Report of the I.C.C. for 1914 (p. 514) offered an exegesis on the legislative and executive enactments establishing the new District Court, from which the following may be worth quoting:

Its jurisdiction is similar in some respects to that of the Federal district courts of the United States in that admiralty and equity jurisdiction is conferred upon it,

and this jurisdiction is to be exercised in the same manner and form as is done in the Federal district courts. In consequence, the blended system of practice prevailing in the courts of the Canal Zone heretofore has been abolished, and the dual system of practice of law and equity prevailing in the district courts of the United States substituted for it.

With the transition effected to the court system which still prevails, there is little more to be said about the Canal Zone Judiciary from an organization and management point of view, which is, in general, the orientation of this chapter.

The transition was facilitated by the fact that the first District Judge, William H. Jackson, was one of the three sitting Judges of the old Supreme Court at the time of its demise, and so he only had to change his hat. (In fact, from May 1, when he assumed office, to June 30, 1914, when the Supreme Court went out of business, he was nominally wearing two hats, though he seems to have tried to dissociate himself as much as possible from Supreme Court business during that period.)

Jackson was a son of former Associate Justice Howell E. Jackson of the Supreme Court of the United States, and apparently a bit of an "operator" not reluctant to use his name and connections to further his judicial career. He was endorsed for his original appointment to the Canal Zone Supreme Court by, among others, Senators Luke Lea and John K. Shields of Tennessee and by the chairman of the Republican State Committee of New York. Though somewhat reminiscent in his political tactics of that other "first" judge, Osceola Kyle, he was very unlike Kyle in other ways. He adapted readily to the milieu, becoming proficient in the Spanish language and laws, and popular among the West Indian population as well as the Panamanians to the point that, ironically, his "exoticism" eventually became a political liability.

Jackson undoubtedly liked his job and wanted to keep it but he was not unaware, as his term neared expiration, that he had rubbed some people in the "establishment" the wrong way. He evidently started dropping the countervailing word to his own friends in high places, but to no avail. The bad news came in a letter from the Attorney General dated January 15, 1918:

Justice McReynolds [of the U.S. Supreme Court] has recently discussed with

---

[68] It will be recalled that the Kittredge bill of 1904, which never became law, had designated "the second judicial circuit" at New York. Apparently the argument of Mr. Feuille that appeals from the Canal Zone should be heard by the same court that hears appeals from States of the Union most influenced by the civil law was persuasive.

me your reappointment to the position you now hold, and has made the very proper suggestion that you be informed whether or not your reappointment will be recommended.

I believe your term expires on May 1st next. I have given very careful consideration to the situation and have reached the definite conclusion that a change should be made. I expect to make that recommendation to the President later on. This notice gives you some four months in which to make such business arrangements as you deem proper, and should you feel that you needed a month or two of additional time I could doubtless arrange it to suit your convenience.[69]

Jackson may have been weak in Washington, where it counted, but he was not lacking support on his adopted home grounds. A letter from the Colón Board of Commerce to President Wilson, dated February 25, 1918, strongly urged his reappointment. Some excerpts from that letter:

. . . All of the members of the Canal Zone Bar, *aside, possibly, from some of the government representatives,* [emphasis supplied] are heartily in favor of the reappointment of Judge Jackson on account of his profound knowledge of the law and the fair and impartial manner in which he handles the business of his court. . . .

Since he came to the isthmus Judge Jackson has attained a great popularity among the Panamanians and the inhabitants of the neighboring republics, especially those of Colombia. . . . He has been indorsed for reappointment by the leading Spanish newspapers published in the city of Panama. . . .

A short time ago General Rafael Reyes, former President of [Colombia], made an extended visit to Panama [after which he wrote a series of articles]. . . . He devoted one article to Judge Jackson and his work, and stated therein that Americans of the ability, knowledge and character of the judge could not fail to draw his country and ours into close and amicable relations.[70]

An even stronger letter imploring the President to reappoint Judge Jackson was forwarded on March 11, 1918 from the

Isthmian League of British West Indians, purporting to represent "a large West Indian population resident in the various towns and settlements of the Panama Canal Zone, about 19,000 of whom are on the payrolls of the Panama Canal." This letter emphasized that the majority of litigants appearing before the Canal Zone District Court "for one cause or another" are West Indians and that Judge Jackson had gained their confidence through his "thorough understanding . . . of the peculiar coinage of their provincialisms. . . ." After listing a number of specifics, the letter concluded that "it would be nothing short of a calamity to West Indians generally should your Excellency find it necessary to retire Judge Jackson at this time."[71]

The next document in the archival records of the matter is a Depatrment of Justice MEMORANDUM "In re: WILLIAM H. JACKSON" dated May 31, 1918. Prepared four and a half months after Jackson had been told by the Attorney General that he would not be reappointed, which news apparently stirred up a storm of support for the Judge, it reads as if some subordinate had been told to go through the files and put together enough derogatory information to justify the Attorney General's action for the record. (That may not be the case but the impression is so strong that this completely unbiased author would feel remiss not to mention it.)

The memorandum lists a series of incidents, mostly petty and hardly relevant it would seem; in the only two controversies of any gravity the Judge is clearly shown to have been in the right.[72] In two other cases it appears that Judge Jackson, because of his prestige in the Republic, was asked to mediate internal disputes for the Government of Panama and that he asked for permission to do so which was denied. After

---

[71] Ibid.

[72] One of these developed into a rather long and involved suit * for which a Special District Judge had to be called in because Judge Jackson was himself the plaintiff. Jackson prayed for a writ of mandamus to be issued against the Auditor of the Panama Canal compelling payment of $1,131.76 unlawfully, as Jackson maintained, withheld from his salary. The decision vindicated Jackson's position on all counts.

* Jackson v. Smith, Auditor, 3 Canal Zone Reports 59 (1916).

---

[69] General Records of the Department of Justice, Records Group 60, Box 151, Appointment Clerk Applications and Endorsements 1901-1933.

[70] Ibid.

reciting these "offenses" the memorandum
dribbles away in a concluding paragraph
smacking of non-sequitur:

> The files do not show any serious
> charges against Judge Jackson. As a
> matter of fact, his troubles have been in
> connection with many and childish mat-
> ters. The Judge is undoubtedly a meddler
> and a trouble-breeder. He has continu-
> ally bothered the Department with minor
> matters, requests for opinions, etc. He
> has incurred the ill-will of the great ma-
> jority of the other officials on the Zone.
> There has been no question as to his
> honesty or his character. It is clear from
> the files that he lacks ability and firmness
> of decision.[73]

One last tempest in the area of organization and management needs to be recorded
before taking leave of the Judiciary. That
had to do with the definition of "supervision," which, as has been noted, remained
with the President under the Panama Canal
Act and had been traditionally exercised, on
the whole, through the War Department.
Yet we have just observed the Attorney General playing a decisive role in the appointment of a Judge. So what did supervision
mean? The question had evidently been
raised somewhere along the line because
we find in the Justice Department archives
the following unsigned and somewhat enig-
matic Memorandum dated July 27, 1918:

CANAL ZONE

> Appointment Clerk, Panama Canal
> Commission, says there is no Executive
> Order giving War Department jurisdic-
> tion over appointments of U. S. Judges,
> Attorneys, and Marshals of the Canal
> Zone. Routine is one of practice. It was
> agreed some years ago that the Attorney
> General should make the nominations for
> these places, but in doing so he should
> consult the Secretary of War.[74]

The memorandum does not make clear
exactly when this unwritten agreement was
reached, but evidently it preceded the Panama Canal Act as we find candidates as far
back as Osceola Kyle sending endorsements
both to the Attorney General and to the
Secretary of War. The Secretary of War
seems to have had the predominant influ-

ence on appointments while Taft held that
office; but later, and especially after the
Panama Canal Act, recommendations were
made by the Attorney General and consulta-
tion with the Secretary of War was only
pro forma.

By Executive Order No. 6166 of June 10,
1933 the President finally transferred from
the War Department to the Department of
Justice the function of supervision of the
District Court of the United States for the
Panama Canal Zone (leaving the Magistrates' Courts, however, still under the Executive Department of the Canal Zone Government).[75] The meaning of supervision
thereupon unexpectedly became a burning
issue as it turned out that all the "perquisites, privileges and allowances" to which
the personnel of the court had become accustomed were dependent upon its status as
a ward of the War Department (as was
everything else in the Zone).

A way out of this dilemma was found by
the Attorney General in an Opinion dated
October 26, 1933.[76] The critical section of
the Executive Order read:

> Each agency, all the functions of which
> are transferred to or consolidated with
> another agency, is abolished.

But the reorganization statute (47 Stat.
1517, Section 16), pursuant to which the
executive order was promulgated, compre-
hensively defined the meaning of the term
"executive agency" to include

> any commission, independent establish-
> ment, board, bureau, division, service, or
> office in the executive branch of the gov-
> ernment.

---

[73] Same as 69.

[74] Same as 69.

[75] Executive Order No. 6166 was in the
form of a proclamation reorganizing a number
of executive agencies. Section 6 thereof dealt
with "Insular Courts" and transferred to the
Department of Justice not only the District
Court of the United States for the Panama
Canal Zone, but also the United States Court
for China and the District Court of the Virgin
Islands. The provenance of the Order is interesting in itself. Its statutory basis derived
from Section 16 of an appropriations Act of
March 3, 1933 (the last day of the Hoover
administration) (47 Stat. 1517). The introductory language of Section 16 makes clear
that its underlying purpose was to effect governmental economies to help combat "the
general economic depression. . . ."

[76] 37 Attorneys General Opinions 321.

As Congress had failed to include the term "court" within this definition, the Attorney General opined that the President was given no authority under the reorganization act "to deal with or in any way affect the present status of said court as such."

The President is authorized, however, to transfer functions of one "executive agency" to another. The War Department is an "executive agency" within the meaning of the reorganization statute and now exercises the function of supervision of the said court. Hence, the effect of the above-quoted provisions of Executive Order No. 6166 is to transfer this function to this Department.

So the Department of Justice obtained supervision of the functions of the court, while the personnel thereof were able to keep their "perquisites, privileges and allowances" flowing from the War Department. And on that happy note we close this chronicle of the Canal Zone Judiciary in the period of Common Law reception.

CHAPTER VII

THE EVOLUTION OF CANAL ZONE LAW

The changeover of the Canal Zone from a Civil Law to a Common Law jurisdiction —or in other words the "reception" of the Common Law—was a truly evolutionary, rather than a sudden or revolutionary, process. American policy makers did not consciously and deliberately plan the reception. On the contrary, the record demonstrates intent to disturb existing law as little as possible consistent with the change in political control of the territory. But certain underlying assumptions, based on questionable premises, about the nature of the American "presence," later augmented by a drastic change in the composition of the population, led to the creation of a set of conditions from which the changeover, or reception, inevitably followed.

An important factor in the first stage of the transition was the superior development in the Common Law family of the public law concept, against whose encroachments the Civil Law had but little defense.

As the backdrop for a brief amplification of this point, the circumstances of the birth of the Common Law itself are worth recalling. When the Normans took over England in 1066 they did not bring with them any cohesive body of law to be received (the Romano-Germanic family was still incubating in the universities of northern Italy). Neither was there any cohesive body of law in England to be displaced. In the same spirit which animated Theodore Roosevelt in 1904, the Conqueror expressly proclaimed that existing Anglo-Saxon customary (local) laws would remain in force. (Consequently, even now it is sometimes possible for English lawyers to invoke and apply a rule of law from the Anglo-Saxon period.) [1]

But the Normans had a talent for administration which likewise led to the creation of a set of conditions conducive to a profound, though unplanned, effect on the law. The Royal Courts at Westminster, originally an arm of administration to secure the interests of the Crown in fiscal and land title matters, gradually extended the reach of their cognizance to include some partially or wholly private disputes. So there came into being for the first time a body of law common to the realm and based on some kind of reason rather than on mere custom; that is to say, a Common Law. The stamp of its public purpose origins has remained with the Common Law

---

[1] David and Brierly, *Major Legal Systems,* p. 261.

94

ever since. Though enormously grown over the centuries to embrace all manner of relationships, it is, essentially, a public law, in sharp contrast to the Civil Law which developed originally for the settlement of purely private disputes and has never been really comfortable about mixing the rights and duties of the sovereign with those of the individual citizen.

It should not be surprising, then, to find that in the very first confrontation of legal systems in the Zone, it was the public law component of the Common Law that spearheaded the penetration. In Executive Order of May 9, 1904, heretofore characterized as part of the first organic law of the Canal Zone, (see chap. V, note 9, supra), reception in the public sector is distinctly foreshadowed in the same sentence which implies a disinclination to disturb existing law generally:

> The laws of the land, with which the inhabitants are familiar, and which were in force on February 26, 1904, will continue in force in the canal zone and in other places on the isthmus over which the United States has jurisdiction until altered or annulled by the said commission [the Isthmian Canal Commission], *but there are certain great principles of government which have been made the basis of an existence as a nation which we deem essential to the rule of law and the maintenance of order, and which shall have force in said zone* [emphasis supplied].

The "great principles" thereupon set forth are simply an abridged version of the Bill of Rights, with a conspicuous proviso regarding deportation (see chap. V, pp. 63-64).[2]

Between May 9, 1904 and March 4, 1905, when its authority to legislate expired with the Fifty-eighth Congress, the Isthmian Canal Commission "altered or annulled" the "laws of the land" with twenty-four Acts. The first twenty-three were concerned exclusively with public law matters and the

twenty-fourth had some public law aspects. Acts 14 and 15, respectively, of September 3, 1904, brought the substantive and procedural criminal laws of the Zone into the Common Law family.[3]

Act No. 1 (creating the Judiciary) of August 16, 1904 is of particular relevance in this connection because of its specific evocation of the primordial Writs,[4] than which nothing could be more characteristic of the Common Law. As Plucknett said of Glanvill's twelfth-century treatise:

> He is, in fact, the first exponent of the new common law which in the course of the centuries was to supersede the ancient legal institutions of the land. Already we can see the main features of that common law in Glanvill's book: it is royal, flowing from the King's Court; it is common, for local variations receive very little sympathy; it is strictly procedural, being based upon writs and expressed in the form of a commentary upon them.[5]

Which leads to a consideration of the next distinguishing mark of the Common Law, its extraordinary emphasis on procedure. (As is well known, it almost strangled in procedure before the reforms of the nineteenth century.) At a very early stage in its development the rigidity of procedure led to the growth of a supplementary body of law, confusingly called Equity, as if the Law itself were not equitable, and now generally comprehended within the term Common Law. Both the emphasis on procedure and the very idea of Equity are alien to the ethos of the Civil Law. Consequently, one may legitimately look at the appearance of these phenomena in the Canal Zone law as signposts of accelerating reception.

Evidence of the first is not hard to find; for while the substantive Panamanian civil (as distinguished from criminal) law was allowed to remain in force until 1933, a

---

[2] These Common Law "great principles" thus were a part of Canal Zone law from the very beginning and were never afterward questioned or improved upon. When the first Canal Zone Code was adopted in 1934 (see p. 120, infra) Title 1, "Personal and Civil Rights," was a verbatim reprint of the language of the Executive Order (minus the proviso on deportation).

[3] These criminal codes, modeled after those of California, remained in effect until 1934. Prior to their enactment, as pointed out by the Governor in the case of M. Murati (see chap. VI, p. 75, supra), the "great principles" had practically destroyed the previous Civil Law criminal procedures without providing the mechanics of a Common Law replacement.

[4] See chap. VI, note 19, supra.

[5] Theodore F. T. Plucknett, *A Concise History of the Common Law* (Boston: Little, Brown and Company, 1956), p. 257.

new Common Law Code of Civil Procedure was drafted posthaste and ordered into effect as of May 1, 1907.[6] The Panamanian codes under which justice in the Zone was dispensed until 1907 and 1933, respectively, were translated into English by Frank L. Joannini, under the direction of general counsel Charles E. Magoon, and were published in July 1905 by the Isthmian Canal Commission.

Mr. Joannini's task, of course, was not only a translation of language from Spanish to English but also of legal terminology from Civil Law to Common Law equivalents. The result was an impressive piece of scholarship on both counts. With regard to the latter, it is not taking anything away from his accomplishment to observe once again the essential similarity of many of the basic working concepts in the two families of law. In discussing second instance procedure, for example, Joannini hardly needed hesitate at all to call an "*apelación*," an "appeal" or a "*recurso de hecho*" a "writ of certiorari."

No matter how expertly translated, however, or how many points of kinship to the Common Law might be discovered by legal philosophers, the Panamanian Code remained strange to Common Law practitioners on the nuts and bolts level. That the Civil Code lasted so long was apparently owing to the fact that it was found susceptible to interpretation,[7] plus the complexity of producing a suitable replacement. The Senate Committee considering revision of the Canal Zone laws in 1932 said:

> It never has worked well, and the courts have been obliged to resort to forced interpretations to make it work at all.[8]

With respect to the Code of Civil Procedure, the some Senate Committee said:

> An effort was made from 1904 to 1907 to use the Judicial Code of Panama; but

neither the American judges nor lawyers could adjust themselves to it.[9]

The Common Law Code of Civil Procedure which went into effect in 1907, and thus set the incipient reception irreversibly in train, was also based on that of California,[10] with adaptations as required by the peculiarities of the Canal Zone. Comparison with the superseded Panamanian Code shows many interesting similarities and parallels, as well as variations. To take an example at random, both codes treat "presumptions of law" under Rules of Evidence. Beneath the differences in wording and approach, the lines of reasoning are seen to be much the same, the principal divergence being that the Panamanian Code does not seem to recognize any presumption as conclusive.[11]

But even if we grant that, in a large sense, the differences were more in formulation than in objective, it is nevertheless easy to see why the common lawyers much preferred the new Code from California. The translated Panamanian Code, though concise and logically organized, was heavily encrusted with references to previous codes, innumerable amendments, subrogations, etc., so that it could not really be used efficiently without a considerable knowledge of Colombian legislative history.[12] Moreover, instead of asserting its own importance, as common lawyers would expect a decent procedural code to do, it rather attached itself as a necessary, but distinctly subordinate, appendage to the Civil Code. The very first Article declares that

> The object of a civil action (*juicio civil*) is to decide the controversies arising on rights conferred by the substantive law.

---

[6] Executive Order No. 597½ of March 22, 1907.

[7] The U. S. Supreme Court noted with approval in Panama R. R. Co. v. Bosse (249 U.S. 41, 1919, at p. 45) that "As early as 1910 the Supreme Court of the Canal Zone announced that it would look to the common law in the construction of the Colombian statutes, . . ."

[8] Senate Report No. 941, 72nd Cong., 1st sess., p. 9.

[9] Ibid.

[10] The reason for using California as a model will be discussed later in connection with the adoption of the Civil Code.

[11] E.g., under the Common Law Code the issue of a wife cohabiting with her husband, who is not impotent, is conclusively presumed legitimate if born within a certain time span; whereas under the Panamanian Code, "the presumption is destroyed by the statement of the husband, corroborated by the confession of the wife."

[12] So much was it still, in fact, Colombian law that the word "Panama" does not even appear in it and references to "Colombia" have to be understood as applying, *mutatis mutandis*, to the governmental structure of Panama.

Of course, that is perfectly true of a Common Law civil action as well, but it is hard to imagine a Common Law procedural code, especially at that period, starting off with such a blunt admission.

Refreshingly, the Common Law procedural Code of 1907 does not bother about introductory orientation but comes straight to the point and begins setting out definitions and rules of conduct. It is a replacement, not a successor. The break with Colombian procedural legislation is clean and complete. Yet certain peculiarities of the Canal Zone, as remarked above, had to be taken into account and so there are links with the past, and with the exotic environment, which catch the eye. One or two of these may merit brief notice.

Section 12 stipulates that English will be the only official language of all courts and their records: a striking reminder of the importance of the language factor in Common Law reception anywhere, and not least in the Canal Zone. It is probably no exaggeration, in fact, to call it a *sine qua non*. In Puerto Rico, where Spanish continued to be recognized, along with English, as an official court language, the reception never proceeded to fruition. (In the United States itself the reception of the Common Law after the Revolution was by no means a sure thing—sympathies for a time being more with France and the French Civil Law —and its final triumph owed much to the ability of American lawyers to read Blackstone and their inability to read *Le Code Napoleon*.)

In the 1907 Code there is almost no mention of previous Spanish law, which makes it all the more interesting that one of the rare exceptions should be in the field of family law. It is a truism that family law lies at the very core of any legal system and is the most resistant to reception. Yet for some reason the Canal Zone legislator felt moved to break into this core at one specific point only—the appointment of guardians:

Sec. 587. *Spanish law as to power of family council in guardianship matters repealed.*—All provisions of Spanish law heretofore prevailing in the Canal Zone giving to the family council any authority in the appointment of guardians for minors or other persons, are hereby repealed.

That no intention to derogate further from the prerogatives of the family council was intended may be deduced from the following section which occurs a little further on:

Sec. 632. *Settlement of intestate estates, without legal proceeding, in certain cases.*—Whenever all the heirs of a deceased person are of lawful age and legal capacity, and there are no debts due from the intestate estate, or all the debts have been paid by the heirs, the heirs may, by a family council as known under Panamanian law, or by agreement among themselves, duly executed in writing, apportion and divide the estate among themselves, as they may see fit, without proceedings in court.

A further significant indicator of the way the wind was blowing is found in Section 399 of the new procedural Code under the heading "Duties of the Clerk of the Circuit Court":

He shall also act as exofficio registrar of land titles until relieved by law, and shall keep proper books of record which shall at all reasonable hours be open to the public.[13]

In order to appreciate the importance of this little provision it is necessary to show how it ties in with and complements concurrent developments affecting the status of the Notary Public—a powerful and prestigious official under the previously prevailing Civil Law. In the Common Law system the Notary is a minor, but essential, cog in the judicial machinery. His essentiality is attested by the fact that I.C.C. Act No. 2 of August 17, 1904 (one day after creation of the Judiciary by Act No. 1) provided for the appointment of Notaries Public and defined their duties. Conspicuously absent from the list of duties, however, was that of acting as registrar of land titles, a function performed from time immemorial by Civil Law Notaries.

Consequently, to avert an imminent hiatus, the I.C.C. issued on the same day a companion Act (which was never numbered or published in the Canal Zone Laws but a copy of which exists in the Archives) as follows:

---

[13] Chap. XVI, p. 90.

AN ACT TO ENABLE NOTARIES
PUBLIC TEMPORARILY TO
EXERCISE CERTAIN POWERS
AND PRIVILEGES RESPECTING
THE DRAFTING AND RECORDING
OF INSTRUMENTS AFFECTING
TITLES TO REAL ESTATE

By authority of the President of the United States, be it enacted by the Isthmian Canal Commission:

Section 1. Until the enactment of a new system of registration of land titles providing that notaries public shall no longer be the legal depository of original instruments affecting titles of land, the notarial law of the Republic of Panama, and the law regulating the drafting of instruments subject to record, in force in the territory of the Canal Zone, Isthmus of Panama, on the 26th day of February, 1904, as recognized by the instructions of the President of the United States, set forth in his letter dated May 9, 1904, are continued in force and the Notaries Public appointed under the provisions of this Act [evidently referring to I.C.C. Act No. 2], are hereby authorized to exercise the powers and privileges conferred upon Notaries Public by said laws.

Section 2. Whenever a law shall have been duly enacted and become operative establishing a new system of registration of land titles, it shall be the duty of every Notary Public within the Canal Zone to deposit in the office of the governor of the Zone all registers, files, original documents, protocols and notarial instruments of every kind which are in his possession or custody.

Section 3. Whereas an emergency exists, this act shall be in force and effect on and after its passage.[14]

The "new system of registration of land titles" eliminating the Civil Law role of the Notary Public, was forthcoming in Executive Order of March 12, 1907 (effective April 15, 1907, just fifteen days before the effective date of Section 399 quoted above) "establishing rules for making and recording instruments in writing affecting real property in the Canal Zone." Section 5 thereof provided, however, that

Any document relating to real estate or affecting property or personal relations, executed under the Spanish law prior to

this order may be recorded for the purpose of preservation.

Executive Order of May 12, 1907 was later repealed and replaced by an Executive Order of February 2, 1911 which centralized record keeping in a new office called Registrar of Property of the Canal Zone. This latter Order adds little to the Common Law transformation of the Notary Public already nailed down by the former, and is of interest chiefly for perpetuating the principle, followed in all subsequent actions, that all notarial deeds affecting property in the Zone executed and recorded in accordance with Spanish laws prior to February 26, 1904 would be given full faith and credit.

It will be noted that the marks of reception thus far observed in this chapter were initiated by legislative action (exercised, as were all other powers, by the Executive). During the time period concerned—that is to say, the first two or three years—legislation did in fact lead the way and the ordinal primacy hereinabove given it is compelled by historical honesty, whatever theories may suffer. But in the long run, as everybody knows, Common Law reception can only be made to stick through judicial decisions and the practice of the bar. Reception in this form was also quietly going on from the very first decisions of Osceola Kyle in 1904; after about 1907, and until enactment of the Common Law Civil Code in 1933 (which may be considered the substantial completion of the process), it was the predominant form. The rest of this chapter, therefore, up to the Civil Code, will trace the march of reception mainly through the decisions, with some expatiation on a few topics of special interest.

Just as the receptional significance of the 1907 Code of Civil Procedure is best seen in the light of comparison with the previous Colombian/Panamanian Code, so the trend of decisional law in the Zone after 1904 is best appreciated by comparison with the contemporaneous decisional law of Panama. Though both had their beginnings at about the same time, the Panamanian might properly be considered a continuation of the main trunk, while the Zone went off on a branch line. Fortunately, official collections of both were maintained from the very beginning, in the *Registro Judicial* of Panama and in the Supreme

---

[14] Records of the Canal Zone, Washington National Records Center, Archives Branch, Record Group No. 185, Entry No. 94-A-133.

Court Reports of the Canal Zone. A few days of contemplative and comparative digging in these lodes cannot fail to enrich the legal mind, a bonanza quite in addition to the signposts of reception which will be discovered and the conclusions which will suggest themselves.

The appearance of Equity on the scene, heretofore denominated a signpost, was passed over temporarily in order to permit a full development of the emphasis on procedure, and also in order to separate it from the ramifications of legislative action. It welled up spontaneously from the decisional law in a relatively early case in 1906:

> [The attorney for the plaintiff] recites many cases and decisions made by the courts of the United States to sustain this view, and calls to his aid the application of the rules of equity. Equity is defined by the law writers to be "the correction of that wherein the law by reason of its universality is deficient." In other words, it signifies, used in a broad sense, "natural justice." It is the power conferred on the courts to do equal and exact justice between contending parties when the facts either admitted or proved show that justice cannot be administered under the stern rules of law. Following the English law and the practice in the United States, there could be but little doubt as to the right of the court in certain matters to give equitable relief.[15]

Thereafter, if not before, Equity was part and parcel of Canal Zone Law and there was never even a little doubt about it.

Now what about *stare decisis?* How much effect did this Common Law doctrine have in differentiating the developing decisional law of the Zone from the decisions of the continuing Civil Law system in Panama? The answer is a little complicated and cannot be found by depending entirely on surface appearances. In theory, *stare decisis* is of the very essence of the difference between the Common Law and the Civil Law: essential to the security and certainty of a judge-made law; anathema to a strictly statutory law. In fact, the actual practices of the two families are not so far apart as they seem, and this was

already true at the turn of the century— even more so with respect to Spanish law than to other branches of the Romano-Germanic family.

The role of precedent in Spanish law is expressed in the *doctrina legal* (written into the Code of Civil Procedure of 1881), by which is understood a judicial practice based on several decisions of the Supreme Court which lower courts are then obliged to follow.[16] Colombian Law 153 of 1887 [17] followed the Spanish lead by declaring that three uniform decisions of the Supreme Court sitting as a Court of Cassation would "most probably" constitute *doctrina legal.*

In order to appreciate the resultant effect of judicial precedent on Panamanian law, even after independence, and thus have a realistic basis for comparison with the Common Law doctrine of *stare decisis,* we could do no better than consult a book published in 1921 by Panamanian District Attorney (*Fiscal del Circuito de Colón*) Augusto A. Cervera.[18] Cervera's book is a compilation, "extracted and arranged in alphabetical order," by subject of Panamanian Supreme Court decisions from 1903 to 1920 and is frankly and avowedly intended to help make future decisions more predictable and consistent. In justification for such a book he cannot, of course, invoke the rationale of *stare decisis,* or even the *doctrina legal;* but he comes close to both, and incidentally shows how close they are to each other, even while tiptoeing around the meaning of *la jurisprudencia* [19] in a very interesting foreword (*Advertencia*):

---

[16] Some Spanish jurists have questioned the validity of the *doctrina legal* on the ground that it was not mentioned in the subsequent Civil Code of 1889, but the answer to that is that the Supreme Court (of Spain) does in fact observe it.

[17] See chap. III, p. 17, supra.

[18] Augusto A. Cervera, *Jurisprudencia de la Corte Suprema de Justicia* (Panamá: Tipografía Moderna, 1921).

[19] In purest theory, the Civil Law does not admit that *la jurisprudencia* (decided cases) can be a source of law. (As the Panamanian Court said, ". . . the Court is not a legislator and its legitimate influence on the laws with respect to the matter is very limited. . . .") *
The legal rule on which the decision turns must be found in a statute and can not, as in the Common Law, be found in the decision

---

[15] Perrenoud et al. v. Salas, 1 Canal Zone Reports 24 (1904), at 28.

* *Registro Judicial* vol. VI, No. 142, (1909), at p. 579. Translation by author.

. . . [A]s none of our Codes contain an analogous or similar provision [to Colombian Law 153] and we do not even have the abovementioned Court of Cassation, the opinions of the Court are not binding, although they will deserve, as is logical, the greatest respect.

That said, it is appropriate to observe that the term *Jurisprudencia* which appears in the title of this work has been employed by extension to mean *the most authoritative interpretation of the law and its application in each case and not as a series of uniform decisions or opinions on the same point of law or on the same subject,* inasmuch as the Court lacks the power to establish a *doctrina legal* and so *jurisprudencia* can not be understood in that sense. Nevertheless, the advantage which judges, lawyers, and citizens in general will derive from a work of this nature is indisputable, in which may be found brought together in an orderly manner all the precedents of the Court, some of them of inestimable juridical value, to be consulted and cited in each case and whenever convenient to illustrate debates on controversial points, contributing also to a most noble end: that of giving consistency, uniformity and vigor, wherever possible, to judicial decisions, which should be sure norms in application, guides of the law (*derecho*), of criteria, and, in sum, the best "complement of the law (*ley*)," as so rightly said the compiler Garavito.[20]

In the next few paragraphs Cervera notes that the decisions for the period covered involved interpretation of two different bodies of legislation, as Panama continued to use the Colombian Codes until 1917-18,[21] and thereafter its own. (With respect

to the Civil Code, the Canal Zone followed suit.) He also explains how his extracts may be checked against the full decisions in the *Registro Judicial* and provides information about the procedure and personnel of the Court. But in the final paragraph he returns to *la jurisprudencia* in something like a paean to decisional law:

It must not be forgotten that *Jurisprudence* is also one of the most legitimate sources of positive law (*derecho*). A country which possesses an abundant jurisprudence, on which may be established the bases of new precepts, . . . is a country which has not died and from which much may be expected in the recovery (*reivindicación*) of its own laws (*derechos*).[22]

It is morally certain that respect for precedent, as articulated by Cervera, was very much in the minds of Panamanian judges and lawyers at all times and they were obviously at pains not to fly recklessly in the face of it. But they also respected the theories and principles of law inherited from Justinian. To keep something in mind is one thing; but to go on record with a statement of the reason for an action taken is another. When the judge came to putting down his decision in writing (and this is where appearances begin to be misleading), theory prevailed. Authorities cited in the *Registro Judicial* are the pertinent Code provisions, overwhelmingly in first place, followed far behind, in second and third places respectively, by the doctrinal writers and the compilers.[23]

---

itself. This theory has been subjected by legal writers to many qualifications and is far too complicated a subject to explore further here; nor is it necessary to do so as Cervera is not discussing the legal rule but is simply making a distinction between single cases and *doctrina legal*.

[20] Cervera, *Jurisprudencia*, pp. I, II. Translation by author.

[21] Interpretation by the Panamanian Court of the Colombian Civil Code tended to give it a slightly different meaning from that obtaining at the same time in Colombia itself, though the Panamanian construction undoubtedly differed less than that of the Canal Zone Supreme Court (see note 7, supra). Many examples of interpretation of the Colombian Codes can be found in the *Registro Judicial* but the *auto interlocutorio* in the case against Donaldo Velasco for

rape * will be taken as it can also be used to illustrate other topics a little further on. The defendant Velasco introduced what purported to be a written pardon from the victim (the judge remarked that the handwriting was suspiciously similar to that of the defendant but did not pursue the point), which would have extinguished the action under Art. 188 of Law 153 of 1887. Though Art. 188 appeared to be still in force (*vigente*), the judge ruled that a later provision of the Penal Code of 1890, under which the action was not extinguished, was governing in the case.

[22] Cervera, *Jurisprudencia*, p. III. Translation by author.

[23] In the Velasco case above (see note 21), for example, the judge supports his ruling primarily with a long quotation from "the com-

* *Registro Judicial* vol. II, No. 41, (1904), at pp. 15-16.

Yet deference to precedent even in the written decisions, though hard to find and mostly discovered by reading between the lines, is not totally absent. In the Velasco case (see note 21), the judge conceded that his decision was partly based on concern for its future effect and said he had "come to the conclusion that it is not prudent to admit a precedent which might have a regrettable effect on society. . . ." [24] Again, let us look at the following passage in another decision:

Appellant argues that the Court has set a precedent on the point and cites the ordinary action (*juicio ordinario*) case of Rio Indio Co., v. F. E. King in which various documents not yet recorded had been admitted in evidence. This case is similar but not in all respects the same, the difference being that in an ordinary action case it is not necessary to produce a title whereas in a third-party action case (*tercería*) the documents must be based on a real estate title.[25]

This one is particularly interesting inasmuch as (a) the Court does not question the validity of citing a judicial precedent, but (b) proceeds to distinguish the cited precedent in exactly the same way a Common Law judge would do.

Having laid a basis for comparison, we may now look at *stare decisis* in the Canal Zone Reports and venture an answer to the question posed at the beginning of this passage. And the answer has to be that *stare decisis*—though not so incompatible with Spanish law concepts as sometimes supposed—did have a visibly differentiating effect, which loomed steadily larger and clearer as time went on. It was not forced or hurried—the first citation of judicial precedent does not appear until April 1907 [26]—but what impresses the reader

freshly turned from perusal of the *Registro Judicial* is the naturalness and seeming inevitability with which it begins to come in as soon as appropriate and feasible. While it may well be, as some comparativists would say, that the difference is more in attitude than in effect, the difference is nonetheless striking; judicial precedent is wielded as a cutting edge, not slipped in surreptitiously or apologetically.

A reader of the Canal Zone Reports will notice that in the early years citations to Code provisions, text books, and even law dictionaries, seem to be more frequent than is normal in court decisions in the United States; and citations to previous decisions less frequent. With respect to the ratio of statutory to decisional citations, at least, the impression is supported by statistics: in Canal Zone Reports Vol. 1 (1905-8) there are 29 citations to decided cases and 81 to statutes; in Canal Zone Reports Vol. 2 (1908-14), however, there are 93 citations to decided cases and 56 to statutes. In Canal Zone Reports Vol. 3 (1914-26), after the Supreme Court was converted into a District Court of the United States, the trend continues in the same direction and no longer seems any different in that respect from any other District Court.

It would surely be fallacious to conclude from the above evidence that Canal Zone judges were hesitant at first for any doctrinal reason to invoke *stare decisis* and then gradually became bolder. Two other possible explanations, I suggest, are more credible: first, the nature of the earliest cases, which simply did not lend themselves to much citation of judicial precedent; and second, the nature of the early library available to the Court, which was heavy on statutes and reference books and light on reports.

Another way of recognizing the Common Law influence is in the *form and style* of appellate decisions.[27] By tradition and

---

piler Angarita." Also, note that Cervera, himself a compiler, quotes "the compiler Garavito" (see note 20).

[24] *Registro Judicial* vol. II, No. 41, (1904), at pp. 15-16. Translation by author.

[25] *Registro Judicial* vol. XXII, No. 62, (1924), at p. 599. Translation by author.

[26] In a case decided in August 1906, however, the Canal Zone Supreme Court made clear that it would, should occasion arise, follow the doctrine of *stare decisis* though the courts of Panama did not: "Common law does not exist in the Republic of Panama, nor are judicial decisions within the Republic of any binding force. (See article 17, Colombian Code). This

article and the rule laid down by the same must be understood to apply only to the decisions of the courts of the Republic of Panama and not to decisions made by the Supreme Court of the Canal Zone" Perrenoud et al. v. Salas, 1 Canal Zone Reports 24, at 29.

[27] In this connection, of course, given the small scale of both the Canal Zone and Pan-

training, Common Law judges are more discursive, individualistic, sometimes literary, and less constrained by format than their Civil Law brothers. They tend to explain more and never quite shed the mental habits of advocacy acquired as practicing lawyers. This is a tricky subject to generalize about, however, as the differences, particularly in style, within the Civil Law family (between Germany and France, for example) are in some respects sharper than between a given member of the family and the United States. It seems more profitable, therefore, to simply grant the well-known general differences between appellate decisions of the Anglo-American strain and those of Hispanic law, deriving from their different histories, and go directly to some specific topics which distinguished—or had the potential to distinguish—the style of Canal Zone decisions from those of Panama.

Citation (or not) of judicial precedent.

Already covered in the discussion of *stare decisis.*

Categorization.

Entries in the Canal Zone Reports are not broken down by genre; they are all just cases, headed, in the Common Law manner, "A v. B" or "In Re . . ." or "In the Matter of . . ." Entries in the *Registro Judicial,* on the other hand, fall into distinct clearly identified classes, the main ones being: judgments (*sentencias*); resolutions of the whole Court on a subject (*acuerdos*); interlocutory decisions (*autos*); and public notices (*edictos*).

Factual content.

There is little difference between the Canal Zone and Panamanian decisions in the amount of factual material introduced, but a marked difference in the way it is introduced. The Canal Zone decision, again in the Common Law manner, is expository, sometimes narrative, mixing fact and law as it goes along. It is usually prefaced by the sentence: "The facts appear in the opinion." The Panamanian decision, following a more rigid format, puts all the

factual material at the beginning, prefaced uniformly by the word *"vistos"* (which might be translated freely as "factual data considered"), and then applies the law—usually the pertinent Code provision.

Opinions; identification of author—dissent.

Colombia inherited from Spain the practice of the "secret book"—all decisions of the supreme tribunal were unanimous and internal dissent, if any, was never made public. After independence Colombia, along with the rest of Latin America, began to draw heavily on the constitutional system of the United States and paid special attention to the work of the Supreme Court,[28] with the result that the right of dissent was recognized in Panama from the beginning of that country's independence.[29] Thus, the practice of the Panamanian Supreme Court, as reflected in the *Registro Judicial* during the time period used for comparison (approximately 1904 to 1914), was mixed. All judges who took part in the deliberation were required to sign the decision (as in Spanish practice); there was no way of telling which one wrote it; however, a dissenting judge, who was identified, was allowed to exercise a right of *salvamento de voto* (rarely used) wherein he explained the reasons for his dissent.

Typical of the Common Law individualism, going beyond that which had occurred in the Republic of Panama, and hence a mark of reception, every decision of the Canal Zone Court was signed by the judge who wrote it. (After reading several cases it is sometimes possible to tell which judge wrote a particular decision without even looking at the name.) A dissenting judge was not required to sign the majority opinion, but wrote his own dissenting opinion which—as in the United States Supreme Court—was often as long and as

---

amanian judicial structures, we are dealing only with appellate decisions.

[28] Nadelman, "The Judicial Dissent," vol. 8 *American Journal of Comparative Law* 415 (1959), at 421.

[29] "As far as Cuba and Puerto Rico are concerned, when they were occupied by the United States at the end of the last century [see chap. II, *supra*], one of the first acts of the Military Government was to put an end to the Spanish system of the secret book and to prescribe publication of dissents together with the decision. The reform has been maintained. The same occurred in the Philippines." *Ibid.*

persuasive as the majority opinion.[30] Incidentally, the term "majority opinion" is used herein with some reservations. As will be remembered, the Court consisted of three Judges, who also wore the hats of Circuit Judges, and the cases which came before it (except for those few of original jurisdiction) were appeals from the decision of a Circuit Judge. The latter therefore disqualified himself, leaving only two to hear the case. If both disagreed with his decision (as happened rather frequently) it was overturned. If one agreed, he constituted an affirming majority.

Identification of counsel.

In accordance with traditional Spanish practice, reported cases in the Panamanian Court made no mention of the lawyers representing either litigant. In accordance with American practice, the lawyers for both sides are named in every case in the Canal Zone Reports.

While not necessarily exhaustive, the above recitation of salient features should be sufficient to demonstrate the extent of divergence in form and style of appellate decisions in the Zone, attributable to the reception of Common Law practices, from those obtaining concurrently in the Republic. Next, we will trace briefly, for illustrative purposes, the inroads into the body of the law of certain Common Law principles, selected, hopefully, both for intrinsic legal values and for a modicum of general interest adhering to the circumstances. (Obviously, a meticulous discovery of every Common Law excrescence as it surfaces for the first time in the cases would bore even the most patient reader to extinction, and without really making the point any finer.)

The Common Law right of trial by jury, introduced incrementally beginning in 1908, was surely such an inroad and a memorable contribution to the edifice of reception. Whether or not it belongs here with a discussion of mainly decisional developments is arguable, but, against the logic of inclusion, too frivolous an objection to argue about. The legislation (by Executive action) which put trial by jury into Canal Zone law was precipitated by, and intended to "correct" the results of, a landmark judicial decision which also had other ramifications.

The essential facts of the Coulson case were set forth in the preceding chapter (pp. 87-88). The legislative reaction was Executive Order of February 6, 1908 "establishing jury trials in the Canal Zone." In all honesty it cannot be said that the reception of this particular Common Law principle resulted from the unanimous pressure of Common Law practitioners on the spot. Even though the right of trial by jury established in that Order (wherein the eye of the legislator was myopically fastened on the Coulson case) was strictly limited to criminal prosecutions in which the penalty of death or imprisonment for life might be inflicted, it was accepted with little enthusiasm by the Law Department of the Canal Zone Government. This is what the department said in its annual report for 1911:

> Considerable difficulty has been met in obtaining verdicts of guilty in jury trials on the Zone. These trials are limited to criminal cases in which the punishment imposed may be death or life imprisonment in the penitentiary. The juries are formed from among the American employees and these are very reluctant to find a verdict of guilty, especially against an American, upon the testimony of West Indians and non-Americans.[31] It would be of very doubtful expediency to extend jury trials to all felony cases. The jury system has not given good results in the Canal Zone, and should at least be limited to capital cases, otherwise the due administration of justice would be seriously obstructed. It is earnestly recommended that the system be not extended beyond its present scope.[32]

Inevitably, another case soon arose which strained the rationale of the limitation to

---

[30] See, for example, Canal Zone v. Houston, 2 Canal Zone Reports 239 (1913).

[31] Actually, there was no justification in law for the practice of limiting juries to American citizens. The only existing law on the subject —the Constitution having been ruled inapplicable—was the Executive Order of February 6, 1908, which contained no citizenship requirement. There was such a requirement from and after April 1, 1914, effective date of sec. 8 of the Panama Canal Act.

[32] Annual Report of the I.C.C. for 1911, p. 495.

capital cases.[33] One J. Frank Houston shot to death in front of the Y.M.C.A. in Gatun a man whom he suspected of undue familiarity with his wife. He was charged with murder in the second degree, tried without a jury, convicted, and sentenced. Defendant's attorneys at the trial had filed several demurrers, all of which were overruled, the most important being that the words "malice aforethought" in the information made the charge first degree murder in fact if not in form, and defendant was therefore entitled to trial by jury. The Supreme Court of the Canal Zone affirmed the lower court's decision, citing section 148 of the procedural code then in effect, which reads as follows:

Murder which is perpetrated by means of poisoning, lying in wait, etc. is murder in the first degree, and all other kinds of murder are in the second degree.

In other words, said the Court, ". . . murder which is committed in a certain way and under certain circumstances *with malice aforethought* is murder in the first degree and . . . murder committed in a certain other way and under certain other circumstances *with malice aforethought* is murder in the second degree."

Predictably, the Secretary of War had difficulty with a concept which allowed trial by jury in the one case and not the other and promptly fired off a cable to chairman Goethals suggesting a broader application. The Law Department responded to Goethals' request for advice with a memorandum dated May 12, 1913, which included the following paragraph:

I am not in favor of amending the Executive Order which limits trial by jury to capital cases. I am very much afraid that the provision in the Panama Canal Act [passed on August 24, 1912 but not yet in effect] granting jury trials in the District Court [created in the Panama Canal Act] will prove to be a detriment to the service. Inasmuch as juries are limited to American citizens there will be few in the Canal Zone other than American employees and if they are taken away from their work the administrative services on the zone must necessarily be interfered with. . . .[34]

As a temporary and half-way measure to correct the anomalies of the Houston case, Executive Order of June 30, 1913 (effective July 4, 1913) amended Executive Order of February 6, 1908 to extend the right of trial by jury to all criminal prosecutions for felonies.

With the Law Department still kicking and screaming, the process was completed when the Panama Canal Act went into effect on April 1, 1914. Section 8 provided that "a jury shall be had in any criminal case or civil case at law originating in said court on the demand of either party." In its annual report for 1914 the Law Department made its last effort to reverse the trend:

The effect of the congressional enactment is to broaden very materially the field for jury trials in the Canal Zone. But few demands for a jury trial have been made since the law went into effect. Two jury trials in criminal cases were had . . . Both cases were against American citizens charged with personal violence against British West Indians. The two trials resulted in acquitals.[35] But one demand for a jury has been made in a civil case, and a mistrial resulted . . . The American community, from which jurors must be selected, is small and is naturally affected by bias or prejudice . . . It is my opinion that an amendment to the law, limiting jury trial to capital cases, would be of benefit to the administration of canal affairs, and more substantial justice would be obtained than can be expected under the present system.[36]

But the movement was in the mainstream of reception and irreversible. From 1914 trial by jury was imbedded in Canal Zone law to the same extent as in any Common Law jurisdiction in the United States.

Another example with tell-tale indicators

---

[33] Canal Zone v. Houston, 2 Canal Zone Reports 238 (1913).

[34] Records of the Panama Canal, Washington National Records Center, Archives Branch, Record Group No. 185, Entry No. 94-A-22.

[35] In fairness to the Law Department (i.e, Mr. Frank Feuille), these results tended to support the implied argument in the report for 1911 that American juries could not be relied on to return unbiased verdicts against non-Americans. Giving him the benefit of the doubt with respect to the racist or nationalistic overtones in some of his comments, it thus appears credible that Feuille's opposition to the jury system was based at least in part on a sincere belief that non-Americans would receive "more substantial justice" without it.

[36] Annual Report of the I.C.C. for 1914, pp. 511-12.

of slightly more than run-of-the-mill interest was the case of *Kung Ching Chong* v. *Wing Chong*, decided by the Canal Zone Supreme Court in 1910 (2 Canal Zone Reports 25). The operative facts were simply that Kung Ching Chong, the plaintiff, gave defendant Wing Chong $700 with which to buy certain real estate on his behalf; defendant did so but took title in his own name; plaintiff thereafter made substantial improvements to the property and defendant refused to convey title. Plaintiff prevailed in the Circuit Court in an action to establish a resulting trust, and the Supreme Court affirmed on appeal.

The first error assigned by appellant was that the action was one of revendication and that the Panamanian Civil Code (applicable, as will be remembered, in the Canal Zone), under the titles "Of Revendication" and "Of Possessory Actions," required an allegation in the complaint that the plaintiff had been in the quiet, peaceful, and uninterrupted possession of the premises for a full year. Rejecting appellant's argument that this was a "possessory action, though conceding it was "revendicatory" in nature, the Court found sufficient language in the Code provisions, by choosing and reaching a little, to justify the desired result in Civil Law terms; but made it clear that it preferred to step over the line and call it a resulting trust. A rose by any other name, perhaps, but to the Common Law (Equity branch) way of thinking, that kind of transaction was a resulting trust, and from now on a resulting trust it would be called.

The second error assigned was on the ground that the amount involved exceeded 500 pesos and therefore the mandate should have been in writing, in accordance with pertinent and cited provisions of the Code. In disposing of this argument, the Court construed the Panamanian law as "evidently intended to cover express trusts and not those created by operation of law, under the common law." Any remaining doubt after that as to which system of law should prevail in the matter was dispelled in the following paragraph:

> The court can not hold that the Panamanian Code would require a mandate of this kind to be in writing, it being clearly permitted by the provisions of the code; *but were it not* [emphasis supplied], this court would still be bound to declare

a resulting trust for the reasons already given.

In another part of the decision, in which the Court was forced to deal once again with the ever-troublesome promise of Executive Order of May 9, 1904 to respect the ". . . laws of the land, with which the inhabitants are familiar, . . ." this declaration of juridical independence is found:

> What is a Circuit Court of the Canal Zone? A court limited in its jurisdiction by the substantive law of Panama? Not so. They are courts of equal plenary jurisdiction with the Court of Kings Bench in Great Britain and the Circuit Courts of the States of the Union and the United States.

And, finally, comes the clincher which sums up the underlying "receptionist" philosophy of the decision:

> Transplanting courts of plenary jurisdiction to a land barren in liberal and generous construction can not operate to take from such courts their inherited jurisdiction as enjoyed in the land of origin.
>
> In determining the vested rights of people in the ceded [*sic*] territory of the Canal Zone, this inhibition is upon the courts; but in cases arising after the establishment of said courts, relief on facts subsequently arising, is to be given in harmony and in accordance with the established law of the United States, where life, liberty, and property are involved.
>
> Therefore property here is governed by the inhibition that it shall not be taken away without due process according to the common law of the United States.
>
> As there are no authoritative decisions of the Supreme Courts of Colombia or Panama on the meaning of their statutes [not a proper function, theoretically, of courts in Civil Law jurisdictions] the courts of the Canal Zone are in duty bound to follow the rules of statutory construction of the courts of common law and ascertain by them the meaning and spirit of the codes.

Before leaving this case there is a countercurrent in the decision worth remarking, not because it is unusual but rather because it is typical and important and this seems as good a place as any to make sure it is not overlooked. That was the almost ritual asseveration of the excellence and completeness of Panamanian law, even while departing from it, plus a resourceful determination to show, wherever possible, that

the Common Law-oriented outcome is not, in fact, inconsistent with it. For example, in discussing which contracts have to be in writing—and before declaring that the *Kung Ching Wong* transaction would be a resulting trust regardless of the Panamanian Code—the Court pointed out that the Statute of Frauds has its exact counterpart in Panamanian law. To demonstrate that its decision, though clearly dictated by Common Law reasoning from a position of strength, could be reconciled with Panamanian law, the Court felt constrained to add:

> No greater system of substantive law has been prepared by man than the Spanish Code; but it must always be carried in mind that by reason of its universality it must at times lack in specificity and that into its universality must be breathed the spirit of liberal construction.
> And yet in the case at bar the Spanish law fits the facts even though substantive, . . .

The funny thing is that protestations of this ilk which frequently accompanied encroachments of the Common Law in the decisions were not necessarily disingenuous. The two systems did have much in common and were coming closer all the time in the natural course of events.[37]

On one point of land law, which lies at the core of any legal system, the Civil and Common Law families have differed significantly throughout most of their long histories. The difference was virtually eliminated in Colombia by legislation in the nineteenth century, so that the laws had already come together before the United States takeover of the Canal Zone. The after-effects of the difference continued to be felt, however, and the courts skirmished with the problem through several cases, resulting in a kind of supererogatory reception with a saving clause barring retroactivity.

As has been mentioned (mainly in chap. V, supra), the matter of land titles was extremely important in the early years of the Zone and occupied an inordinate share of the time and energy of the Law Department. In accumulating property from private owners for Canal building, it was sometimes necessary to trace titles back for

centuries and the issue arose as to whether title could have been acquired by prescription as against the government. At Common Law, of course, it could not; but in Spanish law, since the *Fuero Juzgo* of the seventh century,[38] it could. The crucial case in which the Judiciary pronounced that the Common Law tradition prevailed in the Zone for most practical purposes (though not necessarily *because* it was the Common Law) was *United States of America* v. *Andrade,* decided by the Canal Zone Supreme Court in 1907.[39]

The parcel of land involved, which lay in the path of the Canal, had been occupied —and cultivated—by Andrade since 1888. The United States of America claimed to be owner of the parcel (characterized as public land) as successor to the Republic of Panama and its predecessor, the Republic of Colombia. Andrade attempted to set up title to the land by virtue of prescription. The opinion, adverse to Andrade, was written by Chief Justice Mutis Durán, obviously the Court's foremost authority on Colombian law.

Finding that it was in fact public land, Judge Mutis disposed summarily of the prescription claim; though not as he would have under the Common Law, but by citing Colombian Law 48 (Art. 3) of 1882 specifically ending prescription of public lands. Judge Mutis took more seriously the question whether Andrade had a good claim based on "cultivation," which was still admissible against the government, and the opinion leaves the impression that Andrade might have prevailed on that ground but for two weaknesses; (a) he had failed to perfect the title by obtaining an "adjudication" as required by law, and (b) this particular piece of public land had already been set aside for a special use, viz., the French canal.

In the case of *Villalobos et al.* v. *Foleston et al., United States of America, Intervenor,*[40] decided by the Canal Zone Supreme Court in 1910, the question of acquiring title by prescription as against the government was again raised. In its decision the Court quoted from the *Andrade* case—"By prescription public lands can not be acquired"—but also recognized merit in

---

[37] See chap. III, supra, particularly the last paragraph, and chap. VIII, infra.

[38] See chap. III, note 9, supra.
[39] 1 Canal Zone Reports 64.
[40] 2 Canal Zone Reports 34.

the contention that "such is not applicable to the case at bar as claim of the original Villalobos is anterior to the time such opinion was made, . . ." In another part of the decision the Court did not attempt to refute plaintiff's contention "that in 1846 lands so held and declared by the Government could be acquired by prescription." This time the decision went against the landholder, not on the law of prescription, but apparently because of the Court's "interpretation of the evidence." (One may perhaps be forgiven a suspicion that the Canal Zone Supreme Court followed, if not the election returns, the evident determination of the President that nothing should impede the construction of the Canal.)

Meanwhile, after *Andrade* and before *Villalobos*, the United States Supreme Court spoke on the subject. In *Cariño* v. *Insular Government*,[41] Mr. Justice Holmes for the majority delved deeply into the history of Spanish land law for the purpose of settling a dispute in the Philippines. He concluded that:

As prescription, even against crown lands, was recognized by the laws of Spain, [emphasis supplied] we see no sufficient reason for hesitating to admit that it was recognized in the Philippines in regard to lands over which Spain had only a paper sovereignty.

This may have influenced the tacit acceptance of the principle by the Canal Zone Supreme Court in the *Villalobos* case, but it remained misunderstood by most of the practicing common lawyers in the Zone and had to be explained again as late as 1945 by District Judge Bunk Gardner in *Playa de Flor Land & Improvement Co.* v. *United States*,[42] by far the most exhaustive and scholarly study of the entire history of land law in the Zone, from the Spanish conquest to the Civil Code of 1934, ever written by anybody.

Since the Panama Canal Act, wherein all public land was set aside for special use,[43] the subject has been academic, so far as the possibility of any action arising subsequently thereto. Nevertheless, the judicial reception of the Common Law principle, even if only perfunctory and in a sense superfluous, served the salutary purpose of throwing a judicial searchlight on the Spanish *derecho comun* thus aiding the quest for justice in cases with ancient roots.

Finally, under the rubric of reception through decisional law, I have selected a congeries of cases in which are intermingled the following relevant motifs: (a) the Common Law doctrine of *respondeat superior*, (b) the Common Law rule on wrongful death, (c) the ambiguity resulting from the hesitancy of the courts to admit what they were doing, (d) the effect on adjectival law of the insulation of the Canal Zone courts, and (e) the effect of the "population" factor on Executive Order of May 9, 1904.

The first case in point of time, decided by the United States Supreme Court in 1906, was appealed from the United States District Court for Puerto Rico and has nothing to do with the Canal Zone except that it offers a study in contrast in the way it resolved a conflict between Spanish and American adjectival law. The contrasting resolution helps to explain, obversely, the early momentum of reception in the Zone, and also raises doubts about whether it would have occurred had decisions of the court of last resort in the Zone been appealable to the Supreme Court of the United States as they were in Puerto Rico.

In *Pérez* v. *Fernandez*[44] the Supreme Court overturned a decision of the District Court on the ground that the Common Law action of malicious attachment had been brought against the appellant whereas the quite different Civil Law action for false attachment should have been brought. At the beginning of its opinion the Court philosophized:

The case affords a striking illustration of the difficulty of undertaking to establish a common law court and system of jurisprudence in a country hitherto governed by codes having their origin in the civil law, where the bar and the people know little of any other system of jurisprudence.

Progressing from the general to the specific, the Court then observed that:

---

[41] 212 U.S. 449 (1909).

[42] In Playa de Flor reference was made to the Villalobos case (pp. 323-324) and to the Cariño case (p. 345). See also chap. III, note 9, supra.

[43] See chap. V, p. 70, supra.

[44] 202 U.S. 80 (1906).

The action proceeded in all respects in form and substance as it would had it been begun and prosecuted in a common law State.

That was the nub of the problem, and the decision turned essentially on whether the District Court was obligated, as counsel for defendant in error contended, to "follow the principles of common law and equity as established by the courts of the United States, [including] procedures, rules and records [45] . . . , thus overriding antecedent local law of civil procedure. (Again the issue of conflict was clouded by strenuous efforts to show—through numerous citations back to *Las Siete Partidas* and the law of the Twelve Tables—that the Common Law action of malicious attachment was not truly inconsistent with the spirit of Spanish law.)

The Supreme Court ruled clearly and forcefully that it was the intent of section 8 of the Foraker Act [46] to secure to the people of Puerto Rico the continuation of the laws and practices with which they were familiar, and that, moreover, section 34, in establishing the United States District Court for Puerto Rico, gave to it also jurisdiction of all cases cognizant in the Circuit Courts of the United States together with instructions to proceed therein in the same manner as a Circuit Court. The decision cited section 914 of the Revised Statutes of the United States:

> The practice, pleadings, and forms and modes of proceeding in civil cases, other than equity and admiralty cases, in the Circuit and District Courts, shall conform, as near as may be, to the practice, pleadings, and forms and modes of proceeding existing at the time in like causes in the courts of record of the State within which such Circuit or District Courts are held, any rule to the contrary notwithstanding.

The logical conclusion, of course, was that:

> So, in the present case, there being no such common law action enforceable under the Porto Rican procedure, a court of that district would have no jurisdiction to entertain the suit. [47]

And the effect was to compel the United States District Court for Puerto Rico to adopt the (Civil Law) practice of the Puerto Rican courts. [48]

While the reception of Common Law procedure was thus being drastically slowed, if not stayed, in Puerto Rico, it was growing almost unchecked at about the same time in the Canal Zone, even before formal adoption of the Common Law Code of Civil Procedure in 1907. The moral, in case it may have escaped an inattentive reader, is that reception can sometimes be facilitated by neglect, whether salutary or otherwise. The failure of Congress to put the territorial courts of the Canal Zone on the same footing with other territorial courts left them free of any such restraint as was applied by the Supreme Court to Puerto Rico. By the time Congress acted to change that condition the time for restraint had passed, owing to changed circumstances (notably the "population" factor), and Supreme Court decisions tended to accelerate, rather than restrain, reception in the Zone.

The next two cases in point of time, though also laden with most of the other motifs mentioned above, are intended primarily to focus attention on the doctrine of *respondeat superior. Fitzpatrick* v. *The Panama Railroad Company*,[49] decided by the Canal Zone Supreme Court in 1913, came first. The action arose from injuries caused by the alleged negligence of train personnel, and the defense was predicated on the contention that, "under the laws in force in the Canal Zone on February 26, 1904, the master is not responsible for the acts of his servant or agent if it is shown that by the exercise of proper authority and care on the part of the master he could not have prevented the act complained of . . ."

---

[45] The quotation is from Art. IV of General Orders No. 88 establishing a United States Provisional Court for Porto Rico, which counsel contended was applicable to the U.S. District Court as its successor.

[46] See chap. II, p. 6, supra.

[47] Same as 44, at p. 100.

---

[48] Just as a reminder, and recognizing that the analogy is of limited applicability, this decision was 32 years ahead of Erie Railroad Co. v. Tompkins. Another side observation, of perhaps more relevancy, that might be made about this decision is that the Court relied heavily on Señor José María Manresa y Navarro, "said to be a text-writer of the highest authority in Spain," and also cited the American text-writer on Hispanic law, Clifford Stevens Walton (see chap. II, note 16, supra), while placing little or no emphasis on decided cases, thus acting more like a Civil Law than a Common Law tribunal.

[49] 2 Canal Zone Reports 111 (1913).

and that the case is not governed by "the general principles of law relating to master and servant in the United States."

Written by Judge Jackson, the decision flatly rejected that contention and held that the Common Law doctrine should prevail. The supportive reasoning gets a bit tortuous at times but never loses direction. "The laws of the land with which the inhabitants are familiar, etc." receives its usual obeisance, followed by

But we also recognize the fact that the Canal Zone is largely peopled by Americans, and that American ideas, methods, modes of living, and conduct of business, predominate in the Canal Zone, and that, so far as may be reasonably done, the laws here should be given a construction in keeping with those in the States.[50]

Having said that, however, the Court was still reluctant, at this stage, to appear to be resting its decision on the "population" factor and so continued a painstaking examination of the pertinent Code provisions, showing how they—or similar provisions in other Civil Law codes—had been applied in other cases in a manner not inconsistent with the desired Common Law result, concluding:

Therefore, a careful review of the decisions of the Supreme Courts of Panama and Colombia, the courts of the Philippines and Porto Rico, and particularly of the Supreme Court of Louisiana, lead to the conclusion that, at least so far as the empresarios of railroads are concerned, they must, within the Canal Zone, be held liable for the negligent acts of their servants, agents, and employees, by the adoption of the rule of *respondeat superior* as that rule is understood and applied in the States of the Union. Viewed, therefore, both from the standpoint of the provisions of the Civil Code as applicable here, and also from the standpoint of the general rules of negligence under the common law, we hold that the defendant company was liable for the admittedly negligent acts of its agent in causing the injury to Fitzpatrick.

The second of the two cases, though involving the same issue and reaching the same result, must be considered more definitive because it emanated from the United States Supreme Court.[51] In *Panama Railroad Company* v. *Bosse*,[52] decided in 1919, the injury was caused by the Railroad Company's chauffeur's negligent driving of a "motor omnibus" at an excessive rate of speed in a crowded thoroughfare in the Canal Zone. Mr. Justice Holmes, in delivering the opinion of the Court, met the conflict head-on and left no doubt that he intended to settle it once and for all:

The main question in the case is whether the liability of master for servant familiar to the common law can be applied to this accident arising in the Canal Zone.

The defense was the same as in *Fitzpatrick*, with the addition of reinforcing language from the Panama Canal Act, and was summed up by Holmes as follows:

On these facts it is argued that the defendant's liability is governed by the Civil Code alone as it would be construed in countries where the civil law prevails and that so construed the code does not sanction the application of the rule *respondeat superior* to the present case.

Coming to the heart of the decision, it could be said that Holmes followed the pattern of *Fitzpatrick* almost exactly except that his reliance on the changing "population" factor was more forthright and unequivocal and his attempt to reconcile the result with the Civil Law was a little more perfunctory. Thus, with respect to the former:

But there are other facts to be taken into account before a decision can be reached. . . . It is admitted by the plaintiff in error that the Canal Zone at the present time is peopled only by the employees of the Canal, the Panama Railroad, and the steamship lines and oil companies permitted to do business in the Zone under license. If it be true that the Civil Code would have been construed to exclude the defendant's liability in the present case if the Zone had remained within the jurisdiction of Colombia it does not follow that the liability is no greater as things stand now. The President's order continuing the law then in force was merely the embodiment of the rule that a

[50] Ibid., at p. 122.

[51] At the time of the Fitzpatrick decision there was still no way of getting from the Canal Zone Supreme Court to the United States Supreme Court. It was literally true that "you can't get there from here."

[52] 249 U.S. 41 (1919).

change of sovereignty does not put an end to existing private law, and the ratification of that order by the Act of August 12, 1912, [the Panama Canal Act] no more fastened upon the Zone a specific interpretation of the former Civil Code than does a statute adopting the common law fasten upon a territory a specific doctrine of the English Courts.

And with respect to the latter:

It is not necessary to dwell upon the drift toward the common-law doctrine noticeable in some civil-law jurisdictions at least, or to consider how far we should go if the language of the Civil Code were clearer than it is. It is enough that the language is not necessarily inconsistent with the common-law rule.

And so, with the grafting of yet another principle, the reception of the Common Law moved perceptibly onward.

Ironically, it seems that some entrepreneurs may have been lured into the Zone by the explicit assurance of the Law Department—given seven years before the Fitzpatrick decision—that Canal Zone law did *not* embrace the Common Law doctrine of *respondeat superior.* My evidence is a letter dated October 19, 1906 addressed to a Mr. Walston H. Brown, 43 Wall Street, New York and signed by then general counsel Richard Reid Rogers. Mr. Brown apparently represented an association of contractors who were seeking information as to the extent of employers' liability under Canal Zone law.

The Rogers letter called attention to two recent decisions of Judge Lorin C. Collins (apparently in the Circuit Court) on the points with which Mr. Brown was concerned:

You will observe that the result of the first decision is to very greatly curtail the common law doctrine of *respondeat superior.* In effect the Master is not held responsible for the acts of the servant who disobeys his orders, or is guilty of negligence which the Master had no reason to anticipate. If this doctrine were applied in the United States, it would unquestionably cut out by far the greater portion of the negligence cases which in this country ultimately proceed to judgment.

The second decision is equally important, inasmuch as it shows that in the opinion of Judge Collins there exists no legal liability in the Canal Zone for death occasioned by a wrongful act. That is to say that in the absence of further legislation upon the subject, the family or personal representative of a man killed by negligence cannot recover damages for his death.

. . . Indeed when it is considered how greatly circumscribed will be the contractor's liability under the law and conditions above described, and when it is further taken into account that under the contract the contractor is not required to assume responsibility for accidents due to defective machinery furnished him by the Commission, this liability may fairly be said to be almost negligible.[53]

A contemporaneous Note and Comment[54] reviewing the *Panama Railroad Company* v. *Bosse* decision, titled "The 'Source of Law' in the Panama Canal Zone," perspicaciously exposes the one disturbing element in the decision, which is not any disagreement as to the justice of the outcome, but the ambiguity as to the source of the rule of law applied. While obviously not thinking in terms of the panorama of reception in the Zone, the reviewer was acutely aware of the dilemma of the courts in attempting to resolve the conflict of laws in a manner acceptable to the Common Law imperatives yet within the constraints of Executive Order of May 9, 1904. In one sentence ("The courts have apparently had the most difficulty in amalgamating the Roman law and the common law in cases involving delictual liability") he also put his finger on the link, half obscured by more visible issues, between the Puerto Rican case of *Fernández v. Pérez* and the two Panama Railroad cases.

They all involved a delictual liability. It is a well-known fact that the classic Roman law made little distinction between torts and crimes and so—as suggested in an earlier Note and Comment[55] reviewing *Fernández v. Pérez*—this may account for the meagreness of the law of torts in the Spanish Civil Code. It was even argued in *Fernández v. Pérez* that "at the time when the attachment writ complained of in this

---

[53] Location of the original copy of the cited letter could not be determined, but its authenticity is beyond question.

[54] 17 *Michigan Law Rev.* 497 (1918-19). "Contemporaneous exposition is in general the best." Maxims of Jurisprudence, Canal Zone Code of 1934.

[55] 4 *Michigan Law Rev.* 631 (1905-6).

record was issued there was no such thing in Spanish jurisprudence as a civil action sounding in tort." [56] Opposing counsel in that case offered a contrary view:

> The administration of the civil law in Spain and her dependencies in regard to actions for torts, did not at the time of the institution of this suit greatly differ from that administered in other civil law countries, and apart from methods of procedure did not greatly differ from that in vogue in common law countries . . .[57]

But it seems fair to say that this was an understatement of the actual gulf between the Civil and Common Law in that particular area.

Returning to the gravamen of the Note and Comment on the *Bosse* decision, the reviewer questioned the logic—one might almost say the honesty—of construing the phrase "with which the inhabitants are familiar" to mean the present inhabitants instead of the inhabitants at the time the Order was issued in May 1904.[58] Such a construction was obviously at variance with the intent of the legislator but indispensable to the progress of reception.[59] The reviewer somewhat wryly observes both the efforts to reconcile Common Law results with Civil Law principles and the consistency with which the latter does most of the reconciling. He concludes:

> Where the common law has come into conflict with the Spanish-Roman or Dutch-Roman law in the English or American dependencies the principles of the former have generally supplanted that of the latter. The English doctrine of "consideration" has proved superior to the modern Roman law doctrine of "cause" in Louisiana and Cape Colony, South Africa. . . . In the instant case [*Panama Railroad Company* v. *Bosse*] also the com-

mon law principle is victorious, although we are not quite certain whether it has won because it was identical with the civil law principle or because the case was finally determined by our Supreme Court.[60]

We find most of the same motifs again in *Panama Railroad Company* v. *Rock* (266 U.S. 209), decided by the United States Supreme Court in 1924, in which the main issue was the Common Law doctrine on wrongful death. This was an action brought by one James Rock to recover damages for the death of his wife alleged to have resulted from the negligence of the railroad company. The jury verdict in favor of the plaintiff was affirmed by the District Court for the Canal Zone and by the Circuit Court of Appeals. "The sole question presented for our determination," said Mr. Justice Sutherland for the majority, "is whether, under the law of the Canal Zone then in force, there was a cause of action."

The Court took it as "settled" that no private cause of action arises at Common Law from the death of a human being, any such right being dependent wholly on specific legislation. Plaintiff's case rested, therefore, on interpretation of article 2341 of the Panama (and Canal Zone) Civil Code:

> He who shall have been guilty of an offense or fault, which has caused another damage, is obliged to repair it, without prejudice to the principal penalty which the law imposes for the fault or offense committed.

Noting that the provision was adopted from the Code of Chile [61] and the absence of any evidence that it had been construed by the courts of Chile previous thereto or by the courts of Colombia or Panama subsequently, and rejecting as irrelevant the interpretation by the French courts of a similar provision in the *Code Napoleon*, the Court concluded that

> . . . the reach of the statute is to be determined by the application of common law principles, *Panama R. R. Co.* v. *Bosse*, 249 U.S. 41, 45; and, applying these principles, it is clear that the general language of Art. 2341 does not include the right of action here asserted.

If this one small step in the forward march of the Common Law reception

---

[56] Ibid., at p. 633.

[57] Same as 44, at p. 87.

[58] The reviewer gives the date of the Order as March 1904, but this is obviously an error; there is no doubt that he is actually referring to the Order of May 9, 1904.

[59] It might have been argued—though so far as I could discover it never was—that this kind of "updating" construction was consistent with Colombian Law 153 of 1887 (Arts. 8, 13 and 48), which sanctioned the interpretation of the norm "in the light of current social and economic realities so as to solve the actual problem without much regard to what the legislator may have had in mind." Chap. III, p. 18, supra.

---

[60] Same as 54.

[61] See chap. III, pp. 16-18, supra.

strikes the modern mind as an "unsatisfactory" result, so did it no less to four members of the Court whose dissenting opinion was written by Mr. Justice Holmes, author of the precedent upon which it relied. Holmes was more inclined to accept the *Code Napoleon* as the likely germinal source of article 2341, and therefore to be guided by the interpretation of the French courts, and less inclined to accept the applicability of *Panama R. R. Co. v. Bosse* to the instant case.

The common law as to master and servant, whatever may be thought of it, embodied a policy that has not disappeared from life. . . . Without going into the reasons for the notion that an action . . . does not lie for causing the death of a human being, it is enough to say that they have disappeared. The policy that forbade such an action . . . has been shown not to be the policy of present law by statutes of the United States and of most if not all of the States. In such circumstances it seems to me that we should not be astute to deprive the words of the Panama Code of their natural effect.

Nevertheless, the words were deprived of their natural effect, and there was less room for uncertainty, such as the reviewer found in *Bosse,* as to whether the Common Law principle had been victorious "because the case was finally determined by our Supreme Court."

(The above wrongful death case was moved slightly ahead out of chronological order so that the aforementioned congeries may be concluded on what I hold to be, pragmatically, the most relevant motif, the "population" factor. For the fact is that the last line of defense against reception crumbled on that motif in the last two cases to be cited hereinafter.)

In all the appellate decisions affecting Canal Zone law, including both those emanating from the Zone itself and from higher courts in the United States, no words have been quoted more often than these from Executive Order of May 9, 1904:

The laws of the land, with which the inhabitants are familiar and which were in force on February 26, 1904, will continue in force on the Canal Zone, and in other places on the Isthmus over which the United States has jurisdiction, until altered or annulled by the said commission . . .

Excluding questions of overriding public policy, for which specific exception was made, it is clear that the intent of the Order was to leave undisturbed the private law as it was understood and applied prior to the Hay/Bunau-Varilla Treaty. But for how long? No expiration date was specified, but two little verbs, "are" and "were," were set on a collision course. If the first "are" had also been "were," there could never have been any dispute about the plain literal meaning of the provision. (Almost certainly the reception would have come anyway but it would have had to take a different course.) The trouble was that the two clauses qualifying "the laws of the land," though perfectly in harmony on February 27, 1904 and for a short time thereafter, became increasingly irreconcilable as time went on.

By June 30, 1907 the total labor force employed by the I.C.C. in the Zone was 29,446.[62] This number far exceeded the native population—even at that time, before "depopulation"—and a large majority of them came from the British West Indies where the law with which they were familiar, to the extent that they were familiar with any law, was the English Common Law. (Court records show that they also provided the overwhelming majority of "cases"—mostly on "drunk and disorderly" charges.)

The first census, taken as of February 1, 1912 (still before "depopulation"), showed a total population of 62,810, of whom only 8,884 were Panamanian or Colombian citizens.[63] And after 1913, of course, the percentage of the population who could be presumed to be familiar with the laws which were in force on February 26, 1904 was negligible.

In *McGrath* v. *Panama R. R. Co.,*[64] decided by the United States District Court for the Canal Zone in 1922, plaintiff brought an action for injuries received on board defendant's vessel 14 or 15 months prior to filing of the suit. The Court held that plaintiff's suit in admiralty was barred by laches, using as a guide the time period of one year fixed by the Canal Zone procedural code for similar actions at Com-

---

[62] *Report of the Isthmian Canal Commission,* 1907, p. 26.

[63] See chap. V, p. 68, supra.

[64] 3 Canal Zone Reports 410 (1922).

mon Law.[65] Plaintiff had relied upon the three-year limitation statute applicable to admiralty practice in Colombia, quoting once again, with unquenchable optimism, the Executive Order of May 9, 1904.

In one short sentence the decision intoned what amounted to the obituary of that provision of the Order:

When the reason for a law fails the law itself fails.[66]

To make sure that the point was not missed by future potential litigants, the decision continued:

It can hardly be contended that a citizen of the United States, or a corporation formed under the laws of one of the States of the United States, are better acquainted with the Colombian Code than they are with the laws of their own country. It would seem an anomaly to invoke the laws of a foreign jurisdiction in action between citizens of the United States, in a court created by the United States. *Under existing conditions, the occasions when the Executive Order referred to can be invoked must be few, and these few must continue to grow fewer* (emphasis supplied).

In *Domingo Díaz A., et al.* v. *Patterson,*[67] decided by the United States Supreme Court in 1923, the appellants were attempting to maintain an adverse claim to lands which Patterson and his predecessors had held in open, uninterrupted, and notorious possession since 1790. The claim was grounded on Art. 2526 of the Civil Code of Panama (and the Canal Zone):

The acquisitive prescription of real property or of real rights constituted therein does not obtain against a recorded title, except by virtue of another recorded title, nor shall it begin to run but from the date of the record of the second.

Appellants relied upon a sale in 1832 "afterwards set aside," a later simulated sale of the heir of the grantee to herself, and the recording of a "fictitious title" in 1895, "although none of the grantees ever was in possession at any time, or brought any action until 1917 . . ." It was argued that constructive possession follows the record and should be enough to destroy after ten years the previous title completed by the extraordinary prescription of thirty years under Art. 2531. Mr. Justice Holmes delivered the opinion of the Court in favor of Patterson.

The reasoning was brief but potent, and its very brevity bespoke an impatience with any further resistance to the Common Law interpretation and viewpoint:

The effect attributed to Art. 2526 depends in part upon its operation after the Canal Zone was taken over by the United States as the ten years had not run when the Zone was transferred. . . . Taking it simply as a law of the United States we should see no reason for attributing to it the unjust operation contended for. . . . If we recur to the origin of the law we do not believe that a different view would be taken in Panama. But the considerations that have been urged for following local decisions in places like Porto Rico having their own peculiar system, do not apply in the same degree to a code that in its present application governs a predominantly American population and derives its force from Congress and the President.

Here is Holmes again justifying his decision ultimately on the "population" factor, distinguishing the situation from that in Puerto Rico, but this time almost casually as if the proposition no longer needed arguing (and also showing his predilection for arriving at "justice" even at the cost of a little seeming inconsistency with his own previous decisions).[68]

---

[65] Sec. 820 of the Code of Civil Procedure of 1907 fixed a prescription of one year for personal injury actions, which was in conflict with Art. 2358 of the Colombian/Panamanian/Canal Zone Civil Code which fixed a period of three years. Sec. 820 was applied by analogy in the McGrath case. Not until 1933, in Waterman v. Powell, decided by the 5th C.C.A. (66 F.2d 80), was it ruled specifically that sec. 820 repealed Art. 2358.

[66] The last chapter of the Canal Zone Civil Code of 1934 consisted of a list of 34 Maxims of Jurisprudence. The first Maxim: "2832. When the reason of a rule ceases, so should the rule itself." These maxims were taken verbatim from the California Civil Code as enacted by the legislature of that state in 1872 and were doubtless very familiar to Canal Zone jurists who had looked to the laws of that state as a model from the very beginning. (Incidentally, the maxims are still in the California Code today without the change of a word.)

[67] 263 U.S. 399 (1923).

[68] As a kind of postscript to this passage on the role of judicial decisions in the Common Law reception, a peculiar appropriateness

We are now ready to turn our attention to the last step in the Common Law reception—the formal consolidation, as it were —which was subsumed in the enactment of a comprehensive Canal Zone Code.

The term "code," like the term "common law," has been used in several different ways. It does not mean quite the same thing as applied to different stages in the development of law or as used in different legal systems. In its broadest sense, as used

might be observed in the fact that the climactic role was played by Oliver Wendell Holmes, author of the classic work on *The Common Law* published in 1881 long before he could have dreamed it would ever have any applicability to the Isthmus of Panama.

As pointed out earlier in this chapter, the momentum which the reception gained during the I.C.C. era might have been slowed, as it was in Puerto Rico, had not the Canal Zone Judiciary been insulated from the United States Supreme Court. By the time the insulation was removed (in the Panama Canal Act of 1912), the radical alteration in the demographic factor no longer permitted, in Holmes' view, the kind of decision he had applied to Puerto Rico. "Justice" could only be achieved by adjusting the "life of the law" to the dictates of both logic and experience.

On his deathbed in 1935 Holmes explained to his former clerk Thomas G. Corcoran one facet of the philosophy which had guided his judicial behaviour:

"Because [Chief Justice] White had been in the war on one side and I had been in the war on the other side, it was our business to see that there was never a civil war in the United States again.

Now, one of the ways to prevent that is when you handle the hot social issues you never dramatize them. You handle them in such a way that you decide the particular case before you on as narrow ground as possible. You make no big talk about how this great right is being protected.

White and I had a technique. He wrote opinions so long no one could understand, except the result; I wrote opinions so short no one could understand, except the re~ lt. *But we edged the law along* (emphasis supplied). No more Dred Scott decisions." °

While the social issue (reception) in the Díaz case might not have been quite so hot as the one in Dred Scott, it was far from negligible and Holmes undoubtedly edged the law along in precisely the manner described.

° *The Washington Post,* March 12, 1975.

by the historical school of jurists, codification means simply the reduction of customary law to written form. As societies became more advanced, codification called for periodic rewriting with a certain amount of organization and logical arrangement of subject matter. The period of modern codes, in which the goals of completeness, systematization, and order reached the level now generally expected of a code, was inaugurated by the *Code Napoleon* in the early nineteenth century.[69]

Codification in the modern sense was an idea whose time had come and it has now spread far and wide, finally even breaking down the resistance of the Common Law family. One of its earliest and most evangelical advocates in the United States was David Dudley Field of New York. Though unsuccessful in selling it to his home state (except for the procedural part), the "Field Code" was adopted by several other states, one of the first being California in 1872.[70] In the study of comparative law, it would be difficult to exaggerate the significance of the acceptance of codification by Common Law jurisdictions, inasmuch as the "uncodification" of its body of law had been almost a part of the definition of a Common Law system: codification must certainly be viewed as one of the means by which the Common Law and Civil Law systems are coming together (a tendency which should make the reverse reception of the Civil Law in the abolished Canal Zone a shorter trip than was the original reception of the Common Law).

On the other hand, it would be a mistake to assume that the penetration of codification into the Common Law family carried

[69] For a concise historical summary of codification, on which this paragraph is partly based, see the article by Charles Sumner Lobingier, III Encyclopedia of the Social Sciences 606 (1930 ed.).

[70] It is probably more than coincidental that the first prominent jurist in California, later Chief Justice of the California Supreme Court and an Associate Justice of the Supreme Court of the United States, was Stephen J. Field, a brother of Dudley David Field. This information and some of the subsequent factual material in the text relating to the early history of California were gleaned from a Special Feature entitled "The Development of Law in California" which is found in vol. 1 of West's *Annotated California Codes* (1954 ed.), pp. 1-64.

with it all the assumptions and spirit and nuances of codification in the Civil Law family. The civilian concept of a code as all-inclusive law, in and of itself, was not fully embraced in jurisdictions with a Common Law tradition, which preferred to think of a code, in theory at least, as simply the systematization, revision, and promulgation of pre-existing law which, insofar as not covered in the code, continued to exist in full force, and, even if covered in the code, might still have an effect on how the code is applied.[71] (We will see this uneasiness about the idea of a code as original law concretely exemplified in the legislative process by which the Canal Zone Code of 1934 was enacted.) As Schlesinger expressed it:

> For the continental lawyer it is hard to understand that judicial powers and remedies can exist without an express basis in the written law.[72]

For all their inherent family differences, a certain parallel can be seen between the Civil Code of Chile as the progenitor of the Romano-Germanic Civil Code of Colombia/Panama/Canal Zone (until 1933), and the Civil Code of California as the progenitor

---

[71] Obviously, because of our federal form of government (with the great body of private law reserved to the states) as opposed to the unitary form of France, no direct comparison can be made between the U.S. Code and the Code Napoleon. Nevertheless, a look at the cautious approach to codification of national law in the United States can be illustrative of the inbred suspicion in the Common Law tradition of codes as original law. The first edition of the U.S. Code in its present form, that of 1926, contained this express disclaimer in the preface:

"No new law is enacted and no law repealed. It is prima facie the law. It is presumed to be the law. The presumption is rebuttable by production of prior unrepealed Acts of Congress at variance with the Code."

Since then, of course, the "reception" of codification in the Continental sense has come a long way. Several titles have already been enacted, piecemeal, into law and others are being prepared as separate bills for passage by the Congress. As the preface to the 1970 ed. says:

"When this work is completed all the titles of the Code will be legal evidence of the general and permanent law and recourse to the numerous volumes of the Statutes at Large for this purpose will be unnecessary."

[72] Schlesinger, Comparative Law, p. 235.

of the Common Law Civil Code of the Canal Zone which replaced it. The 1855 Code of Chile rested basically on the Code Napoleon but was made viable for the New World by the inspired adaptations of Bello.[73] The 1872 Code of California rested basically on the work of David Dudley Field, drawn to fit the needs of New York, but was adapted to the actualities of a frontier state carved from the territory of Civil-Law Mexico.

The Treaty of Guadalupe-Hidalgo, by which the province of California was ceded to the United States, guaranteed the integrity of private land titles but made no sweeping promises about preserving the laws of the land with which the inhabitants were familiar. Both a drastic change in the composition of the population and a formal reception of the Common Law came swiftly. In 1844 there were probably no more than 100 Americans in California; in 1846 (the year in which occupation of the territory by American troops was completed) there were less than 2,000 resident Americans out of a total population of about 10,000 exclusive of Indians; by mid-1849 the population had risen to about 50,000, mostly American. The California Legislature, at its first session in 1850, enacted that

> The Common Law of England, so far as it is not repugnant to or inconsistent with the Constitution of the United States, or the Constitution or laws of the State of California, shall be the rule of decision in all the Courts of this State.[74]

There are two things to be said about reception by act of the legislature, California-style: first, it filled in the background, thus contributing greatly to the ideal of certainty in the law, but it still had to be implemented by the practice of bench and bar to become effective; second, it offers the opportunity to point out by contrast that no such background of certainty facilitated reception in the Canal Zone but rather the background was painted in—to make it legal, so to speak—after the fact.

During the first few years of the American "presence" in California the practice was erratic, to put the best face on it. The structure of the judiciary set up by the first California Constitution (1849) was almost

---

[73] See chap. III, p. 16, et seq., supra.
[74] California Statutes, 1850, chap. 95, p. 219.

identical, except for the names of the respective courts in the hierachy, to that previously existing under the laws of Mexico. Neither the structure nor the theory had much meaning for most people, however, whose only contact with the law was in the lowest level or local courts.

> Few, if any Alcaldes or justices of the peace [especially in the northern settlements] knew what the Mexican law was; as a result, in some courts the common law was applied; in others, the civil law; and in still others, it was a combination of these two plus the law of the states familiar to the judge or counsel, and only too often the Alcalde or Justice of the Peace made up the law to suit the occasion. . . .[75]

Even the legislative reception of 1850 and the statutes enacted at the first session of the legislature of that year did not create instantaneously a uniformly applied California Common Law.

> "A lawyer in those days was lucky if he had even a dog-eared copy of Blackstone or Kent's Commentaries." . . . Lawyers practiced with whatever few volumes and whatever legal lore and experience they had. The law library of one prominent Sacramento attorney consisted of a single volume titled "The New Jersey Justice." [76]

What they did create, and the importance of this fact far transcends any temporary eccentricities such as those cited above, was a certainty that California was a Common Law jurisdiction, and confirmation by the practice only awaited the printing and distribution of appropriate legal materials.

The underlying weakness of jurisprudence in the Canal Zone from 1904 to 1933-34, which frustrated any normal or healthy growth, was that no one could be sure what the law (derecho) of the jurisdiction was in the most basic sense. In the beginning, by Executive Order of May 9, 1904, it was the Civil Law of Colombia/Panama, except for "certain great principles of government" in the public law sector (amounting substantially, as we have seen, to the Bill of Rights). The next exceptions, also in the area of public law, were the Penal Code and the Code of Criminal Procedure (taken from the respective codes of Cali-

fornia) of September 3, 1904. Then the Colombia/Panama law of civil procedure was replaced by the Common Law Code of Civil Procedure of 1907 (taken from California). This left in force only one of the inherited civilian codes, but it was the most important, the Civil Code, comprising the main body of substantive private law. In theory, as there had been no enactment to the contrary, the Zone was still a Civil Law jurisdiction—with certain reasonably clear exceptions.

The area embraced by the exceptions soon began to grow less and less clear, however, as the courts in one instance after another (as we have seen) nibbled away at the Civil Code by interpretation giving it an increasingly Common Law coloration. Predictability based on the essential nature of the law (derecho) was becoming impossible. Two decisions of the Canal Zone Supreme Court will illustrate the anomaly of the situation. In Meléndez v. Union Oil Company, decided in 1908, the Court reversed a judgment of the lower court for exemplary damages on the ground that such damages are justifiable only in Common Law doctrine and the Common Law does not exist in the Zone:

> For one hundred years and more the territory of which the Canal Zone strip forms a part has been governed by the Napoleonic Code [sic], and such a thing as common law entirely unknown.[77]

Two years later in the case of Kung Ching Chong [78] (confirmed by the Supreme Court of the United States in 1919 in the case of Panama R. R. Co. v. Bosse [79]) the Court declared, nevertheless, that the Civil Code must be interpreted by Common Law principles. Obviously, Kung Ching Chong by itself did not convert the Zone from a Civil Law to a Common Law jurisdiction; but, coming on top of the exceptions already created by legislation, and enlarged by other judicial decisions trending the same way, it left the Civil Law categorization of the Zone little more than an anachronism—certainly nothing a potential litigant could count on.

The first evidence that Congress might be ready for some concrete action to get rid of the anachronism is found in a routine appro-

---

[75] "The Development of Law in California" (see note 70), p. 12.
    [76] Ibid., p. 29.

[77] 1 Canal Zone Reports 106, at 110.
    [78] See p. 105, et seq., supra.
    [79] See p. 109, et seq., supra.

priations act of April 6, 1914 (38 Stat. 330), in which the following paragraph appears:

Authority is hereby given to employ and pay, from appropriations heretofore made, an attorney versed in the Spanish law, and familiar with the conditions on the Isthmus in connection with the acquisition of privately owned lands in the Canal Zone, *and in connection with the codification of the Canal Zone laws* [emphasis supplied], at a salary not exceeding $7,200 per annum.

The attorney employed was Judge Frank Feuille, former head of the Canal Zone Department of Law,[80] but the litigation over land titles took priority and nearly all his time, so that only a start had been made on the codification when he resigned from the position in 1920.[81]

For all practical purposes the legislative history of the Canal Zone Code begins with the Act of May 17, 1928, "An Act To revise and codify the laws of the Canal Zone," (45 Stat. 596), the first Section of which reads:

Be it enacted by the Senate and House of Representatives of the United States of America in Congress assembled, That the President be, and is hereby, authorized to have all the laws now in force in the Canal Zone revised and codified, and when such revision and codification has been completed to report the same to Congress for its approval.

This time the Congress meant business. To carry out the purposes of the Act the President was authorized to employ persons "skilled in the codification of laws," to call on the assistance of the District Judge and District Attorney and members of the Canal Zone bar, and to pay all the necessary expenses incidental to performance of the task.

The President delegated his responsibilities under the Act to the Governor of the Panama Canal Zone. The "skilled" person employed as codifier, supplied by West Publishing Company, was Mr. Paul A. Bentz, a lawyer with eight years experience in such work. To follow subsequent legislative developments it is necessary to keep clearly in mind that revision and codification, while a unity in terms of

overall objective, were treated as separate and distinct stages. The scrupulous care taken to ensure prior enactment of the revisions was surely a manifestation of the innate Common Law aversion to the idea of a code as original or innovative law.

The draft revision was prepared by a committee of three composed of Mr. Bentz, the District Judge J. J. Lenihan, and the District Attorney C. J. Riley.

It was then submitted by the governor to a committee composed of eight men in the canal administration whom he considered best qualified to review it. Six of these men were qualified in the law, one was a naval officer versed in navigation laws and rules, and the eighth was an Army officer familiar with government administration. After this committee of 8 had considered the various projects they were returned to the revision committee of 3, by whom they were reconsidered. The final report of the revision committee of 3 was submitted by the governor to the President, who in turn submitted it to the Secretary of War and the Attorney General. After they had acted upon the revision, the projects embraced therein were sent to the Congress by the President on June 9, 1930.[82]

(During hearings on the revision held December 28, 1929 before the House Committee on Interstate and Foreign Commerce the District Judge for the Canal Zone favored placing the administrative supervision of the courts under the Department of Justice by statute while the Governor argued that it should be done by Executive Order of the President.)[83]

The President's Message to the Congress of June 9, 1930, recommending enactment of the "changes in existing law," transmitted a "Report submitted by the Secretary of War on progress made in the revision and codification of the laws now in force in the Canal Zone."[84] The Report of the Secretary of War, dated June 5, 1930, submitted the work of the aforementioned revision committee in the form of proposed bills revising various laws, together with an explanation that this procedure had been deemed advisable so that the completed Code "could be submitted to Congress by

---

[80] See chap. V, p. 62, supra.
[81] House Report No. 531, 72nd Cong., 1st sess., p. 3.

[82] Ibid., p. 4.
[83] Ibid., p. 5.
[84] Reproduced in House Document No. 460, 71st Cong., 2d sess.

the President as containing all the laws in force in the Canal Zone . . ." [85] Expatiating, the Secretary's Report quotes from a letter of the Governor of the Canal Zone dated October 29, 1929:

It is our understanding that it is planned to submit this revision not concurrently with but ahead of codification. By so doing the proposed amendments may be inserted with the remainder of the laws as codified, whereupon the Code of the Laws of the Canal Zone in complete form can be submitted to the Congress with the assurance that it embodies no change in the then existing laws.[86]

While most of the proposed bills were "revisions" in the strict sense, some dealing with quite minor matters (Proposal No. 5, for example, was "Fire hunting at night, and hunting by means of spring or trap"), Proposal No. 8 was actually the cornerstone new Civil Code and Proposal No. 27 was the only slightly less important new Code of Civil Procedure. Proposal No. 29 is also noteworthy because this bill (amending sections 7-9 of the Panama Canal Act concerning the Judiciary) by deliberate omission left administrative supervision of the District Court of the United States for the Panama Canal Zone with the President.[87] The Secretary's Report explains that Proposal No. 29 reflected a considered decision to effect the transfer of supervision from the War Department by Executive Order rather than legislation in order to retain the flexibility (read unhampered Presidential control) which "has been found to give entire satisfaction during the years which have intervened since a government

for the Canal Zone was first provided." [88]

Fortunately for the legal historian, Proposal No. 8, the longest and most important of the "revisions," was accompanied by a Memorandum well worth attention. The first part of it bespeaks the unmistakable intent of the legislator to eliminate once and for all any lingering confusion as to the basic law (goodby *derecho*) of the jurisdiction:

This proposed Civil Code is a complete restatement of the substantive law of the Canal Zone. . . .

The Civil Code now in force is based upon the continental civil law, as distinguished from the common law; and for that reason alone it would seem particularly unsuitable to be embodied in a codification of the laws of the Canal Zone, the remainder of which were derived from a common-law source. . . . Moreover, the Civil Code of Panama has never proven adaptable or satisfactory in the zone, and has therefore been the cause of considerable uncertainty. The preparation of a new code has been uniformly advocated.

The latter part explains (though only partially, in my opinion) the rationale for looking to California as a source of text:

The Civil Code of California has been made the basis of this proposed code by reason of its completeness and suitability, and for the further reason that the two Criminal Codes and the Code of Civil Procedure were derived from that source. Most of the California Civil Code provisions have been in force for many years, which will afford the zone the benefit of the construction of these provisions by the California courts over a long period of time.[89]

While the matter was still before the House a General Statement elucidating the need for the proposed legislation was included in one of the supporting House documents. As the following paragraph from the Statement will show, the population factor, from having progressively grown

---

[85] As an aside note to any possible future researcher in the field, the Secretary's explanation goes on to say that "Instructions to this effect were embodied in an order of the Secretary of War, by direction of the President, dated September 4, 1920, . . ." A reading of those instructions would be interesting and might throw further light on the then prevailing philosophy of codification. No trace of such an order could be found by this author, however, despite the most diligent search and even after allowing for the possibility that the date might wrong. (It does not seem logical that an order could have been issued in 1920 apparently modifying or implementing an Act of Congress passed in 1928.)

[86] Same as 84, p. 2.

[87] See note 83 above and chap. VI, pp. 92-93, supra.

[88] Same as 84, p. 3. Proposal No. 29 was amended in sec. 7 by the House Committee to require a preliminary hearing in a Magistrate's Court in all cases whereof the original trial jurisdiction is in the District Court, the reason for this safeguard being the lack of any grand jury system in the Canal Zone.

[89] Same as 84, p. 43.

as part of the *ratio decidendi* of judicial decisions, was now being advanced unabashedly as a ground for changing the statutory law:

> Most pronounced of the changing conditions in the Canal Zone was that relating to the population itself. From 1904 to 1912 no less than 20 villages, inhabited largely by Colombians or Panamanians, existed in the Canal Zone, and in the rural sections were hundreds of small farms also occupied by natives. Between 1912 and 1914 all of these were moved from the Canal Zone. Thus the native population which was accustomed to the old laws of civil relations disappeared from the Zone, and there remained only Americans and West Indians, people accustomed to the common-law system.[90]

In due course all the revisions contained in the President's Message of June 9, 1930 were passed by the House of Representatives substantially as proposed.[91] In the Senate hearings were held by the Committee on Interoceanic Canals.[92] Material in the Senate Report adds little to the record on the subject previously written in the House. About the only addition of interest, for purposes of this book, is the following bit from a letter of the Secretary of War, dated January 28, 1932, supporting the new Code of Civil Procedure:

> In addition, the preparation of a new Civil Code, as provided for in another bill, H.R. 7522, also drawn from the California Code, to supplant the present Civil Code of Colombia, makes it desirable to prepare this proposed new Code of Civil Procedure in order to insure completeness and consistency between the substantive and remedial laws.[93]

So, in the end, all the so-called "practice codes" were drawn from the codes of California, which I find eminently sensible; but perhaps for better reasons than simply that A must be drawn from the same source as B because B was drawn from the same source as A.

There is one other point of considerable interest which shows up in both the House and Senate Committee hearings on the proposed separate bills, and that is the surprising but evident fact that the Canal Zone Code Act of 1934 was used to legitimize Presidential abuses of power in the area of civil government committed after the Panama Canal Act of 1912 in the same way that the latter Act was used to cover actions of doubtful legality in the preceding years. To understand the full import of the parallel it is necessary to reread section 2 of the Panama Canal Act (chap. 5, p. 69, supra), and the discussion of its effect found in Chapter VI, note 42, supra. As will be seen, the head of the Department of Civil Administration, writing in 1909, doubted that even a subsequent act of Congress could validate the delegation of legislative authority, and the Supreme Court decision upholding the I.C.C. legislation establishing the Canal Zone Judiciary was written by William Howard Taft who was not exactly a disinterested party. In any event, it was the stated understanding of the Congress that section 2

> . . . ratified the laws then in effect, and placed the legislative power in Congress. At present, therefore, there is no local legislature for the Canal Zone [since the abolition of the I.C.C.], that authority being in Congress only.[94]

For a close-up look at history repeating itself one need only read the Memorandums accompanying the proposed bills. For example, these excerpts:

Proposal No. 5

> This bill is offered for the reason that it is considered that the President was without authority to promulgate the order of January 27, 1914, and it is desired to validate the provisions thereof.

Proposal No. 6

> The bill is offered for the reason that it is considered that the authority of the President to promulgate the Executive Order [of March 6, 1920] is doubted . . .

Proposal No. 11

> This proposed bill is designed to supplant the Executive Order of March 19, 1913 . . . and the ordinance of the canal commission of August 22, 1913 . . . ,

---

[90] Same as 81, p. 3.

[91] A few amendments of no great consequence were made in a further Message of the President of December 4, 1930 (reproduced in House Document No. 675, 71st Cong., 3d sess.).

[92] Reproduced in Senate Report No. 943, 72nd Cong., 1st sess.

[93] Ibid., p. 9.

---

[94] Same as 81, p. 2.

both the Executive order and the ordinance being deemed to have been promulgated without authority of law.

Proposal No. 13

This subject matter is offered for congressional enactment for the reason that it is considered that the President was without authority to define the offense and prescribe the punishment contained in said rules 171 and 172; and it is thought desirable to have a valid enactment on the subject.

All the proposed bills were reported favorably to the Senate with little or no opposition and proceeded in due course to final passage, one at a time, according to plan. Those of particular interest will be noted below for the record.

Proposal No. 29 amending sections 7-9 of the Panama Canal Act was enacted on February 16, 1933.[95]

Proposal No. 1 revising the Penal Code was enacted on February 21, 1933.[96]

Proposal No. 9 revising the Code of Criminal Procedure was enacted on February 21, 1933.[97]

Proposal No. 27 providing a new Code of Civil Procedure for the Canal Zone was enacted on February 27, 1933, to become effective October 1, 1933.[98]

Proposal No. 8 providing a new Civil Code for the Canal Zone was enacted on February 27, 1933, to become effective October 1, 1933.[99]

The final step was the blending of all existing laws, as codified by Mr. Bentz, with all the above-mentioned "revisions" passed as separate laws into a single comprehensive Code of Laws for the Canal Zone which was enacted on June 19, 1934.[100] It was designated the "Canal Zone Code" and was to take effect on the expiration of ninety days.

(Thus, the Canal Zone Code of 1934 is usually cited for simplicity as the beginning of the statutory Common Law era in private legal relations, but actually the last vestige of statutory Civil Law disappeared on the effective date of the new Civil Code in 1933.)

This first comprehensive Canal Zone Code contained seven titles, to wit:

Title 1. Personal and Civil Rights [101]

Title 2. Operation and Maintenance of the Canal and Government of the Canal Zone Generally [102]

Title 3. The Civil Code

Title 4. The Code of Civil Procedure

Title 5. The Criminal Code

Title 6. The Code of Criminal Procedure

Title 7. The Judiciary.

It also included, in an appendix, (a) texts of the most pertinent treaties to that date, commencing with the Clayton-Bulwer Treaty, (b) general laws of the United States applicable to the Canal Zone, and (c) parallel reference tables:

> It is sought in the parallel reference tables to facilitate reference to the former law by showing the origin thereof, whether in act of Congress, Executive order, or act or ordinance of the Isthmian Canal Commission, and, in addition, in the cases of titles 3 to 6, to show the sources of the sections in the California law in order to render more accessible the decisions of the California courts construing those sections.[103]

The California Codes had been in force for more than fifty years and the reference tables made effective the benefit which Proposal No. 8 promised would be derived from using them as a basis for the Canal Zone Code. California was one of the first code states and the benefit of experience and judicial construction was real enough, but there was more than that in the California connection.

At the beginning of this passage on codification a certain functional parallel was noted between the California Codes of 1872 and the Chilean Code of 1855. In closing,

---

[95] 47 Stat. 814 (H.R. 7523).

[96] 47 Stat. 859 (H.R. 7519).

[97] 47 Stat. 880 (H.R. 7520).

[98] 47 Stat. 908 (H.R. 7521).

[99] 47 Stat. 1124 (H.R. 7522).

[100] 48 Stat. 1122.

[101] Title 1 was public law, setting forth the aforementioned "certain great principles of government."

[102] The first part of Title 2, relating to operation and maintenance of the Canal, was the only segment of the Code executing rights clearly intended to be granted in the Hay/Bunau-Varilla Treaty. All the rest grew out of a dubious inference from a shaky assumption; the assumption being that the Treaty was completely valid and binding in international law, and the inference being that the "entire exclusion" clause overrode the "general purpose" clause (see chap. IV, pp. 42-43, supra).

[103] Canal Zone Code, 1934 ed., preface.

a limited comparison of the California experience and the Canal Zone experience might throw some additional light on the particular attraction which the California Codes seemed to hold for Canal Zone law makers. This feeling of affinity was not discovered suddenly when comprehensive codification began in 1928 but was already evidenced, as we have seen, as far back as 1904 with Acts No. 13 and 14 of the I.C.C.

In looking for a model in one of the states of the Union the Canal Zone law makers did not, in fact, have a very wide choice. That of Louisiana was, of course, even older and more tested. It would certainly have been a less radical change, and for that very reason was obviously not seriously considered. The Rubicon had been crossed and the first qualification for a model was that it had to be based on the Common Law. A second useful qualification would be the experience of having replaced a previously existing Spanish system of law. Here there were some similarities and some differences. I suggest that the strongest, and, pragmatically at least, the most persuasive similarities were (a) the population factor, and (b) the common inheritance of a grass roots Spanish-type judiciary in place and a complex land title problem; and the most significant difference was that the California Codes of 1872 were actual codifications of Common Law-based statutes (from both New York and California), while the Canal Zone Code was "born yesterday" so to speak.

As the Canal Zone law makers (both legislative and judicial) began to rely more and more on the nature of the population to justify the displacement of the Spanish law by the Common Law, they could not have been unaware that the same logic had been applied in California:

> In February 1850, the members of the Senate Judiciary Committee appointed during the first session of the California Legislature declared it to be "very certain" that
>
> ". . . the Common Law controls most of the business transactions of the country. The American people . . . have taken the Common Law, the only system with which they were acquainted, as their guide. Their bargains have been made in pursuance of it—their contracts, deeds, and wills have been drawn up and executed with its usual formalities—their courts have

taken its rules to govern their adjudications—their marriages have been solemnized under it—and, after death, their property has been distributed as it prescribes. . . . The first settlers of the United States brought with them from the mother country the Common Law, and established it in an uninhabited region. The emigrants to California have brought with them the same system, and have established it in a country almost equally unoccupied." [104]

As in the Canal Zone, the "emigrants" to California found *alcaldes* administering Civil Law justice, after a fashion, at the local level; they also found themselves committed by higher authority to preserve the integrity of land titles, which were often vague and enormously difficult to reconcile with the Common Law of real property. These circumstances, too, gave the Canal Zone law makers something of a feeling of *déjà vu*.

The thing that made the Canal Zone Code different from the Codes of California, or of any other Common Law state, is that it had no familial reservoir of tradition to draw on. Sections 4 and 5 of Title 3 (Canal Zone Civil Code) were copied from the California Civil Code of 1872 as nearly verbatim as circumstances permitted. This is what they said:

> 4. Rules of construction.—The rule of the common law, that statutes in derogation thereof are to be strictly construed, has no application to this title. The title establishes the law of the Canal Zone respecting the subjects to which it relates, and its provisions are to be liberally construed with a view to effect its objects and to promote justice.
>
> 5. Provisions similar to existing laws,

---

[104] From a Special Feature entitled "The California Civil Code" in vol. 6 of West's *Annotated California Codes* (1954 ed.), p. 3. While the California reasoning served in principle in the Canal Zone, the facts were substantially different in degree. The practical application of Spanish-Mexican law in California, even before the arrival of the Americans, was attenuated almost to the point of non-existence and the number of inhabitants governed by that law was infinitesimal. As to the latter point, attention is invited to chap. II, note 19, supra.

how construed.—The provisions of this title, so far as they are substantially the same as existing statutes, must be construed as continuations thereof, and not as new enactments.

But the corresponding Section 5 of the California Civil Code had said:

> 5. Continuation of similar existing law *or common law* [emphasis supplied] provisions similar to existing laws, how construed.—The provisions of this Code, so far as they are substantially the same as existing statutes *or the common law* [emphasis supplied], must be construed as continuations thereof, and not as new enactments.

The emphasized words, desirable as they would have been for adding certainty and completeness to the law, had to be omitted because they were not grounded in reality, as clearly recognized and enunciated by the Canal Zone Supreme Court in 1908.[105]

In contrast, the Supreme Court of California could say in 1889, despite the identical provisions of Section 4 above of the California Civil Code:

> The common law underlies all our legislation, and furnishes the rule of decision except in so far as the statutes have changed the common law. When the common law is departed from by a provision of the code, effect is to be given to the provision to the extent—and only to the extent—of the departure.[106]

The Canal Zone Code might start with a clean slate and tacitly disavow any Continental heritage, but it could not completely escape the consequences of having no heritage of its own. The law, like nature, abhors a vacuum. It is a continuum and must constantly be interpreted in some manner. A critical analysis of all interpretations applied by the Common Law courts since 1934 would show that the influence of the Civil Law, *ex necessitate,* never entirely disappeared.

---

[105] See note 77, supra.

[106] From the same Special Feature (p. 32) cited in n. 104 supra.

CHAPTER VIII

THE GHOST OF RECEPTION FUTURE

I said something in the Foreword, not very original, about the past being prologue, then followed up the thought in Chapter I with an overview of one event that happened in the past, i.e., the reception of the Common Law in the Panama Canal Zone. The purpose of this chapter is to invite attention to the obverse of that little aphorism and suggest that some thought be given to an event still in the future, i.e., the re-reception of the Civil Law in the territory of the former Panama Canal Zone.[1] For it does seem that, after a strange interlude of seventy years more or less, the Civil Law will be returning to an area from which it was ejected in an unprecedented manner; and if this is not something new under the sun, it is about as close to it as anything in the annals of jurisprudence.

Though the literary allusion to ghosts, with apologies to Dickens, may seem a bit quaint or forced as applicable to juridical reception, it is, in fact, peculiarly apropos. The whole apparatus of United States (Common Law) courts and laws functioning in the Zone is haunted by skeletons in the closet. One skeleton will not stop rattling in the alcove of international law and another in the alcove of domestic or municipal law.

In international law the bedrock question is: Was the Hay/Bunau-Varilla Treaty a binding, valid agreement, or was it void or voidable for fatal defects? If this ap-

---

[1] As this book was going to press, some thought was, at long last, being given to the matter, though not quite in the constructive way that I had in mind. A civil suit had been filed in the United States District Court contending that "President Ford, Secretary of State Henry A. Kissinger and Ambassador Ellsworth Bunker are infringing the constitutional rights of American residents of the Panama Canal Zone by negotiating a new canal treaty with Panama" and asking for a temporary restraining order. District Judge Guthrie F. Crowe had given the officials named 60 days in which to respond. The suit maintained that "extension of Panamanian law to United States residents of the Canal Zone under the proposed new treaty would violate their Fifth Amendment rights 'not to be deprived of property or liberty without due process of law.' "
The *New York Times*, October 2, 1976, p. A-8.

Judge Crowe later rejected the suit, saying that he did not have authority to order named respondents to appear before his court.
The *New York Times*, Dec. 19, 1976, Sec. 1, p. 5.

parition can be gotten past, the next question is: Can the language of the Treaty be interpreted to sanction the creation of a civil government, an exclusively United States Judiciary, and a legal system alien to that of the host country, all of which operate throughout the entire Zone and regulate the activities of all the people thereof, or temporarily therein, even in matters totally unrelated to the "construction, maintenance, operation, sanitation and protection" of the Canal?

In domestic law the question is: Was the Judiciary, and the civil government of which it was and is an appendage, created and perpetuated during the crucial years of the reception in violation of the Constitution of the United States?

I did not invent these skeletons (which I have verbalized in the form of questions), or even deliberately set out to look for them; but there they are. I did set out to examine, analyze, and trace the course of the Common Law reception in the Canal Zone. In the doing thereof I found there was no way to avoid, even had I wished to, dealing with a great deal of both factual and argumentative material relating to these questions. I have tried to present it fairly, letting the chips fall where they may. If most of the chips seem to have fallen in a manner displeasing to advocates of the status quo, it was not by design. Some, in fact, fell the other way, which may be equally displeasing to my Panamanian friends, but that cannot be helped either.

In this book I have not tried to please or displease, nor have I answered the questions. I am not sure that they can be answered. I am sure that they are disturbing enough to be taken seriously, and I am convinced in my own mind, which I see no point in trying to conceal, that the proper course now is to wipe the slate clean and start over with a new treaty regulating the status of the Canal and establishing a viable, realistic relationship between the United States and Panama. That, of course, is the big subject, to which I will address a few more remarks in the Afterword, but which I must not permit to draw me away from the more limited subject of this chapter, the same being simply to stimulate anticipation of and planning for the pragmatic problems which will arise as jurisdiction over persons, property, and causes

of action is transferred from the Canal Zone courts to Panamanian courts.

Although some examples from the way the Common Law reception was carried out will undoubtedly be useful, as I said in the Foreword, it seems almost certain that the time span will be much more compressed as there will be less reason for gradualism. Nor will there be any reason to expect the kind of hiatus which occurred in 1904 when the Panamanian courts abruptly ceased functioning in the Zone before the Zone courts were ready to start. Still less is it possible to imagine that the Canal Zone Code will continue to be applied for thirty years in the territory returned to the jurisdiction of Panama as was the Civil Code of Panama in the Canal Zone from 1904 to 1933. Nevertheless, the courts of Panama will have occasion for many years to come to take into account the effect of the Common Law on transactions occurring during the seventy-year interlude, just as the courts of the Canal Zone took into account the effect of the Civil Law on transactions occurring before 1904 (and to a lesser extent before 1933).

Even on the level of mundane administrative matters many decisions will have to be made and procedures worked out. The Annual Report of the Isthmian Canal Commission for 1908, under the heading "Relations with Panama" (p. 256), mentions cryptically as one of the subjects discussed: "The transfer of old government records from the Zone to Panama; . . ." This must have referred to official Colombian/Panamanian documents of the various municipal courts and other governmental bodies left behind in the territory which became the Canal Zone. Obviously this same need will arise again, with the difference that this time they will be United States Government records, copies of which at least will be needed by the Government of Panama in order to ensure an orderly continuation and proper administration of justice.

Will the Civil Law courts of Panama, in applying a Canal Zone Code provision in effect at the time and place the cause of action occurred, give it a Civil Law interpretation; as the Canal Zone courts increasingly gave a Common Law interpretation to provisions of the Civil Code?

In *"Juicio ejecutivo seguido por Carlos Carbone contra Juan Esquivel"* the *Corte*

Suprema de Justicia de Panamá held (II *Registro Judicial* 61, 1905) that the Judges of Panama had not lost their jurisdiction in cases triable by them prior to the American possession of the Canal Zone (see chap. IV, pp. 41-42). What would happen if the United States courts should take a similar position with respect to cases triable by them in the Zone prior to the dissolution of the Zone?

Will the Panamanian law in the territory of the former Zone make any concessions to the law of the land with which the inhabitants are familiar? Or will demographic conditions change so swiftly that this will not be a significant factor?

If a cautious projection may be made, it seems likely that the new treaty will transfer jurisdiction of the present Zone in two stages, with the first stage leaving a small "Canal Area" or something similar, as provided in the 1967 drafts, which will be under a joint administration. This would seem to offer the possibility of a transition proving ground in which the Common Law would be ascendent in matters directly related to the operation and protection of the waterway and the Civil Law ascendent otherwise. As I have pointed out elsewhere, the two legal families as a whole, consonant with a world-wide trend, are already closer together than they were in 1904. In the "Canal Area" a conscious effort could be made to "edge the law along," as Mr. Justice Holmes put it, and help advance the day when there will no longer be any differences between the two families.

AFTERWORD

When I first started thinking about this book in 1971, with the primary intent of filling a perceived gap in the legal history bibliography of the Canal Zone, I could see already that it would not have much purpose or meaning unless some of the strands of the past were picked up and tied to the living, moving fabric of the present and future. This I have tried to do as unobtrusively as possible and without drawing too much attention away from the primary intent. It has required striking a delicate balance in view of the contemporaneous controversy which has been swirling about the projected new Panama Canal treaty since about 1964, growing increasingly heated as this book neared completion in the presidential election year of 1976, and I can only hope I have succeeded.

In preparation, originally, for some sensible closing lucubration, I studied the provisions of the aborted 1967 draft treaties almost to the point of overkill, reaching the conclusion that, if perfected, the United States would have had a new treaty arrangement, if not "vastly advantageous" (as John Hay said of the Hay/Bunau-Varilla Treaty), at least somewhat advantageous, considering the different times and circumstances. In truth, the advantages to the United States were sufficiently conspicuous that the new treaty package would have had rough sledding in the Panamanian National Assembly, but still might have been maneuvered through if the President of the United States and the Senate had acted quickly and a few incidental enticements had been added. But the sense of the Senate was hostile, the President was hesitant, and that opportunity, if it actually existed, slipped away. Since then Panamanian aspirations, supported by world public opinion, have so increased that no Panamanian Government, not even the present military dictatorship, would be likely to risk incurring the wrath of outraged nationalism by proposing to accept the 1967 terms.

Consequently, any idea of basing the Afterword on the assumption that a new treaty would not differ substantially from the 1967 draft package is no longer tenable. There would seem to be little point, therefore, in making any further reference to it, though the judicial structure provided therein for the "Canal Area" is ingenious and much of it may survive for an interim period as I suggested in chap. VIII. I cannot say that with any assurance, however, as I am not privy to the current state of negotiations which, as of this writing, re-

126

main classified and properly so. It is possible that the new draft will be finished and released to the public by the time, or shortly after, this book appears in print, bringing instant obsolescence to any speculations I might make here. Hence, I will not make any.

Having ruled out recourse to the crystal ball, let us see if there is anything with a sufficiently durable half-life to be said about the current (summer of 76) outpourings in the news media, in periodicals both learned and otherwise, and on the campaign trail. From the relatively stationary position of a book, which, one hopes, will continue to be worth reading for at least a few years, it is not feasible to jump with both feet, as the saying goes, into that kind of a running dialogue. After a period of cautious, and sometimes awe-stricken, observation, however, I believe I can isolate from the sound and fury at least one note which is not too perishable, is intrinsically important, has been sounded repeatedly, is potentially capable of producing catastrophic results, and which offers an opening for some comment of more than transient significance.

I am talking about sovereignty (that inescapable if indefinable word again) and the fact that a candidate who came within a hair of wresting the Republican nomination from an incumbent President of his own party garnered a great deal of his popular support, and delegates, partly on the strength of a blatantly and patently erroneous statement that the United States is "sovereign" in the Canal Zone to the same extent as in Louisiana or Alaska.[1] Though

---

[1] The Republican Convention's platform committee was not ready to go that far, rejecting by a vote of 55 to 43 a plank favored by some conservative supporters of Reagan which said that the United States should never surrender "sovereign rights over control and operation of the Canal Zone." The committee agreed to drop the word "sovereign" in that context, but included in the relevant plank a reference to the "if-it-were-the-sovereign" language of the 1903 treaty. The plank further provided that "the U.S. negotiators should in no way cede, dilute, forfeit, negotiate or transfer any rights, power, authority, jurisdiction, territory, or property that are necessary for the protection and security of the U.S. and the entire western Hemisphere." The fact that the United States is using the Canal Zone as a military base for operations extending over the entire Hemisphere—a use beyond the purpose for which

the contrary has been clearly proved in a number of ways, and it is almost unanimously rejected by reputable international law scholars, the statement is apparently believed by millions of Americans, possibly even a majority. The effect that such a widespread misconception could have on prospects for ratification of the new treaty— the only hope for a peaceful solution in Panama—can only too easily be imagined.[2]

---

rights were granted in the 1903 treaty—has long been one of the sore spots in United States relations with Panama. At the least, it would seem a gratuitous irritation to put a fine point on it. (Though Ford won the nomination, the platform, and especially this plank, was largely the work of Reagan sympathizers.) The corresponding plank in the Democratic platform says simply:

We pledge support for a new Panama Canal treaty, which insures the interest of the U.S. in that waterway, recognizes the principles already agreed upon, takes into account the interest of the canal work force, and which will have wide hemispheric support.

Though one of the "principles already agreed upon" (Kissinger/Tack Joint Statement of February 7, 1974) is that "the Panamanian territory in which the canal is situated shall be returned to the jurisdiction of the Republic of Panama," Democratic presidential candidate Jimmy Carter in the second debate on October 6, 1976 inexplicably declared that the United States under his administration would never give up control of the Canal Zone. One can only hope that he was ill advised on that occasion and that President Carter will, in the end, adopt a more flexible and realistic posture, "which will have wide hemispheric support." He has in the past shown an open-minded and reassuring capacity to learn and to change course in the light of better information.

Shortly after writing the immediately preceding words, with some trepidation at my own effrontery in appearing to be counseling the President, I was heartened to find so wise and experienced a political observer as Marquis Childs expressing much the same idea. In a column headed "Disquiet Over Carter's Intentions" concerning the Panama Canal Zone, he said:

It should not be hard for Carter to ignore the words he spoke in the heat of his exchange with the President. He will have a chance in the interregnum to insure that the negotiations with Panama continue.

The Washington Post, Nov. 16, 1976, p. A-15.

[2] As recently as July 1976 to my certain knowledge (and probably continuing as this book goes to press) Phillip Harman (see chap.

Many well-intentioned efforts have been made by more responsible speakers and

IV, n. 68) was still producing a prolific correspondence addressed to the Supreme Court, the Department of State, members of Congress, and others in an effort to prove that the United States has territorial sovereignty in the Canal Zone, citing as his authority a recent article by Alfred J. Schweppe, an attorney from Seattle, Washington, identified as a former chairman of the American Bar Association's Committee on Peace and Law. Mr. Harman's big guns are:

(a) The decision of the Supreme Court in Wilson v. Shaw, 204 U.S. 24 (1906), in which the Court said

A treaty with [Panama], ceding the Canal Zone, was duly ratified. . . . It is hypercritical to contend that title of the United States is imperfect . . .

and which decision, Mr. Harman emphasizes, has never been overruled;

(b) A decision (not cited, but no matter) of the Fifth Circuit Court of Appeals that the Canal Zone is "unincorporated territory of the United States";

(c) Mr. Schweppe's conclusions that

While an actual instrument of cession or conveyance was not used in 1903, the language is the legal equivalent and gives the United States as good a title as it has to Louisiana, Alaska, Arizona and New Mexico.

Without undertaking a thoroughgoing refutation, which is possible but would be too great a digression, may I offer the following brief reactions, respectively.

(a) As to the ill-considered use of the word "ceding" in Wilson v. Shaw, seized on happily ever since by proponents of a certain point of view, one can only say that "to err is human" and this is neither the first nor the last time that the Supreme Court has had occasion to remind us that it is, after all, only human. It is true that Wilson v. Shaw has never been expressly overruled, but the word "ceding," which was not essential to the decision, has in subsequent cases been conspicuously disregarded, somewhat as an embarrassing gaffe might be in polite society. In any event, being the unilateral interpretation of a treaty, Wilson v. Shaw could hardly make binding international law. Further reasons for the unreliability of Wilson v. Shaw on the question of sovereignty are given in the law article by Weiner (see bibliography).

(b) There is probably no single subject in United States decisional law on which there is more confusion and inconsistency than the question of whether the Canal Zone is a "territory" of the United States. It has been held to be a territory for some purposes and not for others. Plucking one case out of this welter of contradictions does not prove anything.

writers to set the record straight. Unfortunately, the truth, and particularly the whole truth about such a complicated subject, is more difficult to articulate, and requires a little more mental effort to grasp, than an untruthful but simplistic, jingoistic slogan. I happen to have at hand two recent articles from *The Washington Post* which illustrate both (a) the difficulty and (b) the disarray among persons who are on the side of truth and basically in agreement but have varying degrees of knowledgability leading to distracting internecine disputes.

In *The Washington Post* of May 3, 1976, Marilyn Berger weighed in against Ronald Reagan with an article containing the following paragraph:

While the United States has acted as if it were sovereign in the Zone and offended the Panamanian sense of nationhood, the attributes of sovereignty were missing. Take just two examples: An American can remain in the Canal Zone only so long as he or she is employed there. A person born in the Zone of Panamanian parents is not an American citizen [as he or she would be if born in Louisiana or Alaska].

The second example hits the target. It is valid, succinct evidence of a missing attribute of sovereignty.

The first is not quite that simple. While there may be something to it, it is rebuttable and is not, on the whole, a good example for the case to be made. The decision to make employment a condition of residence was, in the first instance, simply an administrative policy adopted unilaterally by the United States Government and resulting in the forced removal of the indigenous population (see chap. V, p. 70) as well as a ban on general immigration. In 1911 the head of the Department of Civil Administration of the

(c) Both the Louisiana Purchase and the Alaska Purchase are unequivocal self-described instruments of cession. If the parties had intended the 1903 treaty to be such an instrument, they could very easily have said so rather than leaving it to lawyers to search for a "legal equivalent." Mr. Schweppe seems to be using the word "title" as if it were the legal equivalent of territorial sovereignty. It is not. Oil-rich Arabs now buying up great tracts of choice real estate in England no doubt are acquiring good title, but territorial sovereignty will remain with the United Kingdom no matter what happens to the real estate titles.

Zone government had advocated throwing open the Zone to settlement by "loyal American citizens" as a kind of buffer to protect the Canal (see chap. V, p. 67) and nobody raised any question about insufficient attributes of sovereignty to support such a policy, which was eventually rejected for other reasons. One author, writing about the "depopulation" policy decision (see chap. V, note 62) said: "It was determined that the Canal Zone should be used for the operation of the canal, rather than for a habitation for such settlers as might choose to go there. . . ." All true, but observe that such determination was made solely by the United States Government, an act indicating exercise of sovereignty rather than any missing attributes thereof.

Now it is also true that what was originally a unilateral policy was made into a bilateral agreement by Article III, #2 of the Treaty of 1936 with Panama (53 Stat. 1807); but it may be questioned whether a commitment made in a treaty to follow a certain policy is evidence that the party lacked the attributes of sovereignty which it must have possessed in order to make the treaty.

In *The Washington Post* of May 15, 1976, an article by John M. Cabot [3] headed "Misleading Canal Debate" complained that the Berger article "should be enlightening but is actually about as misleading as anything I have noted Gov. Reagan as saying." Cabot is more knowledgable, by reason of his experience, about the Canal Zone than is Berger (after all, a journalist, even though a quick study, can't know everything about everything), but the only criticism he has of her first example is that:

Ms. Berger notes that "An American can remain in the Canal Zone only as long as he or she is employed there" but she fails to note that the same is true of Panamanians.

The same is true of Panamanians (or Patagonians for that matter) because of the cited clause in the Treaty of 1936, but Mr. Cabot does not explain any of that (understandably as he has several other points and if he explained all of them his

article would be too long to print) and I am afraid that the average newspaper reader after finishing Mr. Cabot's article is still being misled by the Canal debate.

The confusion is not lessened appreciably by articles such as the one in *U.S. News & World Report*, issue of May 24, 1976, page 29, which uses the following examples to show missing attributes of sovereignty:

(a) Americans are not permitted to own property in the Zone because the land could one day revert to Panama;

(b) Children of Panamanians born in the Canal Zone are Panamanian citizens.

Example (a) is related to Berger's first example and contains the same fallacy. It is simply another facet of the unilateral "depopulation" policy decision, explained in some detail in chap. V, whereby the United States Government bought up all private land titles, thus turning the Zone in effect into one great Government reservation (a partial, belated victory for Senator Morgan —see chap. VI, note 36). While it is true that the land could one day revert to Panama, and probably will, that was not foreseen in 1912 and was not a factor in the decision—which can be easily demonstrated by the simple fact that neither are Panamanians allowed to own property in the Zone. When the United States assumed control of the Zone in 1904, private land titles were not affected by the transfer of jurisdiction.[4] If the Zone should "one day revert to Panama," private land owners— if there were any—would presumably be protected by the same rule of international law.

Example (b) is simply a restatement, in weaker form, of Berger's second example.[5]

---

[3] Identified as "former Chief of Division of Caribbean and Central American Affairs, former Assistant Secretary of State and former ambassador to Colombia" and as "chief U.S. negotiator of what became the treaty of 1955."

[4] On the contrary, they were specifically, though perhaps unnecessarily in international law, protected by Article VI of the Hay/Bunau-Varilla Treaty: "The grants herein contained shall in no manner invalidate the titles or rights of private land holders or owners of private property in the said zone . . . "

[5] Though true, it is misleading by omission, being only a half-truth at best. The 1972 Constitution of Panama defines the national territory as all that space between the border with Colombia and the border with Costa Rica. It further provides that all persons born in the national territory are Panamanians by birth. Hence, Panamanian citizenship is bestowed even on the offspring of an American soldier

There is nothing wrong with the latter, as I have said, but the point might have been made a little clearer, I think, by contrasting the unrestricted application of the American *jus soli* in Louisiana and Alaska, regardless of parentage or any other circumstances, with the total absence of such application in the Canal Zone.

If I were to attempt to debate in the popular media the preposterous proposition advanced by Gov. Reagan, I would go no further than the following additional examples, not because they are by any means exhaustive but because they can be expressed briefly and do not require long supportive explanations:

(1) The very language of the treaty on which the proposition depends, i.e., the grant of authority which the United States would possess "if it were the sovereign. . . ." If language means anything, "if it were" must surely mean it actually is not.

(2) Such power and authority as the United States does exercise in the Zone is dependent upon the use to which the territory is put (viz., for the operation of a canal). If it ceased to be used for such purpose, jurisdiction would automatically revert to Panama. This would certainly not be the case if the United States were sovereign as in Louisiana and Alaska.

(3) If the United States were really sovereign in the Canal Zone, it could cede the territory to a foreign power if it wished to do so. It cannot.[6]

I believe there is little to be gained by any further attempt to clarify the debate over sovereignty, which will doubtless continue to be muddled for the invincible reason that public interest has finally been aroused to the point where every com-

mentator feels impelled to comment whether qualified or not. That is freedom of speech and I would be the last to deny anybody's right to get into the act. Whereupon, admitting again my own lack of knowledge of the specific terms of the new treaty, I will offer my philosophy, if I may use so grand a word, about it in general terms.

Leaving aside sentimentality and nostalgia, what is our real national interest in the Canal for the future? I would answer that it is only to be assured of continued efficient operation, reasonable tolls, uninterrupted access, and that the Canal will never be allowed to fall under the control of a third power. So long as the treaty accomplishes those ends, I fail to see any peril in giving up the Zone or in turning over operation of the canal to the Panamanians after they have demonstrated sufficient technical and administrative competence.[7] Realistically, and the Panama-

---

[6] Allowing the territory to revert to the control and jurisdiction of Panama, as envisioned in the new treaty, would not be ceding the territory to a foreign power. It would merely be relinquishing to the power in which titular sovereignty has always remained certain rights to the exercise of authority which that power had previously granted by treaty.

who happens to be stationed at Ft. Clayton in the Canal Zone at the time of the blessed event. The child is, of course, also an American citizen by birth, but by application of the principle of *jus sanguinis* whereas the Panamanian citizenship is acquired by *jus soli*. *Jus soli* is inseparable from the fact of sovereignty over the territory, while *jus sanguinis* has nothing to do with it.

---

[7] The Canal is run mostly by Panamanians now except in the very top supervisory and the most highly skilled technical positions, for which they could be trained; they are not stupid. I will not go into the military/defense aspects except to observe that (1) the preponderance of opinion in the Pentagon is now ready to go along with the new treaty, if not enthusiastically, (2) external threats would have to be countered in any case by our overall military power applied to defending the approaches at some distance from the Canal itself, (3) the only plausible threat on the Isthmus would be from sabotage, for which the Panamanians would have no motive if the Canal were theirs; the *Guardia Nacional* is quite capable of defending against sabotage from any other source, but would probably welcome assistance from the United States for that purpose if necessary.

With respect to the general principle of giving up the Zone, even William F. Buckley, Jr., arch-conservative columnist who supported Ronald Reagan in the Republican primaries, now adheres to that principle. In mid-October 1976 he made a trip to Panama, visited the Zone, interviewed a few people, and wrote:

My own conclusion? Establish that which is necessary for the defense of the Canal, and require it.

Agree that payments by American shipping will flow into a fund for the generous resettlement of the American community in Panama.

Require that there be no discriminatory pricing of tolls going through the Canal.

nians know this as well as we do, they will be dependent on the support and cooperation of the United States as far into the future as it is possible to see. While I believe that, in spite of everything that has happened to strain it, there is still an immense reservoir of good will toward the United States, I would not be so naive as to depend on that for future observance of treaty obligations. The essence of the treaty must be a real partnership and I would depend for assurance of performance on the manifest self-interest of both parties. In the long run, that is the only reliable assurance for the continued observance of any treaty, regardless of what international law text writers may say.

Some "Zonians" have already been quoted as saying they will pack up and leave the next day after the territory passes to Panamanian jurisdiction. I am at a loss to understand their reasoning (unless it is that they cannot bear the thought of giving up certain comforts and privileges to which they have become accustomed but which they will not find in the United States either). Several thousand Americans have been living in the Republic under Panamanian jurisdiction for many years—I myself did for three years—and if they are suffering any undue hardship by reason of their nationality I never heard of it. There is a large American business community which prospers and will prosper more when the present uncertainty is resolved. The Panamanian economy is very closely tied to the United States—they do not even have a paper currency of their own, using Ameri-

can dollars— [8] and Panama always suffers more than the United States economically whenever outbreaks of violence over the canal upset the equilibrium. Nevertheless, they will continue to occur until some unpleasant truths have been faced and corrected.

The Panama Canal reorganization legislation of 1950, adjusting the law to the socio-political reality, placed the Canal Zone Government on a par with the Panama Canal Company (which actually operates the Canal), tacitly recognizing that what we have is not just a waterway with a supporting administrative apparatus, but an American colony with a waterway running through it. The civil government of this colony, with its own Common Law courts and laws, has in time become, like beauty, almost its own excuse for being, quite independently of the waterway. Unlike beauty, however, we must now realize that it was not destined to be a joy forever but to have a rather more finite life.

As to why this is so, I could not explain better than by quoting from a report submitted in 1900 by Senator John Tyler Morgan of Alabama, that most valiant and persistent fighter in all the Congress for an American interoceanic canal.[9] This report concerned a House bill appropriating money for the acquisition of a right of way through Costa Rica and Nicaragua (the route which Morgan always favored), but that the principle would be equally applicable to Panama is obvious:

This duty enjoined on the President is a distinct recognition of the sovereignty

---

Then get out.

We could stay in. We have a right to stay in. Make that point clear, and then get out —while the initiative is still, clearly, our own. That is the way great nations should act.

The Washington Star, October 18, 1976, p. A-15.

Various indicators suggest that Buckley was more than just an isolated voice from the traditionally more conservative element of American public opinion. For example, the principle was also approved on November 10, 1976 by the Conference of U.S. Catholic bishops. The bishops voted 170 to 61 for the dissolution of "the vestiges of a relationship which more closely resembles the colonial politics of the 19th century than the realities of an interdependent world of sovereign and equal states."

The Washington Post, Nov. 11, 1976, p. A-3.

[8] This fact is apparently not very well known. In the October 1976 issue of *Foreign Affairs*, in an article on Latin America written by the Director of Studies for the Council on Foreign Relations, one finds the following puzzling statement (p. 203):

. . . in Panama, the dollar still circulates as freely as the country's own paper money (sic).

[9] Senator Spooner himself, whose amendment diverted the canal from Nicaragua to Panama, said of Morgan: "Upon whatever route an isthmian canal shall be constructed, the Senator from Alabama will forever stand in the memory of the people as the father of the isthmian canal; for, in season and out of season, in sunshine and in storm, unappalled by obstacles . . . with lofty patriotism and unfaltering purpose, he has, with rare skill, tireless industry, and splendid advocacy, fought for an isthmian canal." Mack, *Land Divided*, pp. 422-23.

of those States and their ownership of the country through which the canal is to be constructed. The President is not empowered or advised to encroach upon the sovereignty of those States.

The acquisition of the sovereign ownership of a tract of country including the line of the canal, would separate Nicaragua into two parts, between which the sovereignty of the United States would be interposed.

An act more fatal to her autonomy cannot be conceived, and if her Government had the power to do this, under her constitution, which forbids any cession of territory to a foreign State, the severance of her territory by such mutilation would destroy its territorial integrity and with it the Republic.

Such an effort is beyond the purpose of the House bill, and is unnecessary to the enjoyment of any privilege or right that relates to the ownership, control, or management of the canal.[10]

---

[10] Senate report 1337, 56th Cong., 2d sess., part 3, p. 2.

AUTHOR'S NOTE

There are numerous quotations in this book, from the shakers and movers themselves, designed to show in context (simply as a matter of objective and corrective truth) that the United States does not have, and was never intended to have, complete territorial sovereignty in the Canal Zone, as in Alaska and Louisiana. I could have used even more but I did not want to suffocate the reader with an avalanche of evidence which would have been superfluous to the primary theme—an examination of the Common Law reception—and would have appeared to overemphasize the secondary theme—the controversy over a new Panama Canal treaty. Any readers who would like further assurance on this point may find additional pertinent quotations in a "Guest Editorial" by Senator Gale McGee which appeared in the October 1976 issue (Vol. 5, No. 4) of *International Law News,* a publication of the American Bar Association.

BIBLIOGRAPHY

I—Primary Sources

A. *Manuscript Collections*

Records of the Panama Canal, Washington National Records Center, Archives Branch, Record Group No. 185.

Herrán Papers. Archives, Georgetown University, Washington, D.C.

William Howard Taft Papers (microfilm), Library of Congress.

Theodore Roosevelt Papers (microfilm), Library of Congress.

Department of State, National Archives (microfilm), 234/18.

General Records of the Department of Justice, Records Group 60, National Archives.

B. *Published Public Documents*

1. United States

U.S. President. "Executive Orders Relating to the Panama Canal (March 8, 1904, to December 31, 1921)," Annotated 1921. Mount Hope, Canal Zone: The Panama Canal Press, 1922.

U.S. President and U.S. Congress. "Treaties and Acts of Congress Relating to The Panama Canal," Annotated 1922. Mount Hope, Canal Zone: The Panama Canal Press, 1922.

U.S. President. "Laws of the Canal Zone, Isthmus of Panama, Enacted by the Isthmian Canal Commission, August 16, 1904 to March 31, 1914." Mount Hope, Canal Zone: The Panama Canal Press, 1922.

U.S. President. "A Compilation of the Acts of the Philippine Commission." Manila, P. I.: Bureau of Printing, 1908.

U.S. President. "Postponing Effective Date Transfer of the District Court of the United States for the Panama Canal Zone to Department of Justice." Executive Order No. 6243 dated August 5, 1933.

U.S. President. "Organization of Executive Agencies." Executive Order No. 6166 dated June 10, 1933.

U.S. Department of State. *Digest of International Law* 5 by Green Hayward Hackworth.

U.S. Department of State. *Foreign Relations of the United States.* 1902 (Hay-Pauncefote Treaty), 1903, 1904 (Hay/Bunau-Varilla Treaty) 1922 (Thomson-Urrutia Treaty), 1923 (vol. 2).

U.S. Department of State. *Treaties and other International Acts of the United States of America,* edited by Hunter Miller, Volume 5. (Treaty of Peace, Amity, Navigation, and Commerce with

New Granada, signed at Bogota December 12, 1946.) (Clayton-Bulwer Treaty.) (Treaty of Peace, Friendship, Limits, and Settlement (with additional and secret article which was not ratified), with Map of the Mexican States and with Plan of the Port of San Diego, signed at Guadalupe Hidalgo February 2, 1848— Treaty of Guadalupe Hidalgo).

U.S. Department of Justice. *Attorneys General Opinions.* vol. 11, 391. vol. 24 (The Panama Canal Title), 37.

U.S. Department of War. *Reports of the Isthmian Canal Commission, 1905-14.*

U.S. Congress. Senate. *Report of the Secretary of State with accompanying correspondence in relation to the proposed interoceanic canal between the Atlantic and Pacific oceans.* S. Ex. Doc. 112, 46th Cong., 2d sess., 1880.

U.S. Congress. Senate. *Interoceanic Canals.* S. Rept. 1337, 56th Cong., 2d sess., 1900-01, pts. 3-6.

U.S. Congress. Senate. *Report of the Isthmian Canal Commission, 1899-1901.* S. Doc. 54, 57th Cong., 1st sess., 1901.

U.S. Congress. Senate. *A Bill to provide for the temporary government of the Panama Canal territory, the protection of the canal works, and for other purposes.* S. 4513, 58th Cong., 2d sess., 1904.

U.S. Congress. Senate. *Constitution of the Republic of Panama.* S. Doc. 208, 58th Cong., 2d sess., 1914.

U.S. Congress. Senate. *A Bill to provide for the temporary government of the Canal Zone at Panama, the protection of the canal works, and for other purposes.* S. 5342, 58th Cong., 2d sess., 1904.

U.S. Congress. Senate. *Hearings before the Committee on Interoceanic Canals of the United States Senate in the Matter of the Senate Resolution Adopted January 9, 1906 Providing for an Investigation of Matters Relating to the Panama Canal, etc.* (Of particular interest, though not specifically referred to in the text, is the *Testimony of William Nelson Cromwell, Esq.* beginning on p. 1041.). S. Doc. 401, 59th Cong., 2d sess., 1906.

U.S. Congress. Senate. *Panama Railroad.* S. Rept. 5179 to Accompany S. 6539, 59th Cong., 2d sess., 1907.

U.S. Congress. Senate. *Diplomatic History of the Panama Canal.* S. Doc. 474, 63d Cong., 2d sess., 1914.

U.S. Congress. Senate. *Revision of Canal Zone Laws—Fixing Status of Offenses.* S. Rept. 941, 72d Cong., 1st sess., 1932.
This report contains much basic material on Canal Zone legal history—not limited to fixing status of offenses.

U.S. Congress. Senate. *Revision of Canal Zone Laws—Prohibit Gambling.* S. Rept. 943 to accompany [numerous House Bills preliminary to the enactment of a complete code of laws for the Canal Zone] 72d Cong., 1st sess., 1932.
This Report contains much basic material on Canal Zone legal history—not limited to gambling.

U.S. Congress. House. *Translation of the Civil Code in Force In Cuba, Porto Rico, and the Philippines.* H. Doc. 1484, 60th Cong., 2d sess., 1909.
This Report, in 4 vols., contains an enormous amount of basic material in addition to translation of the codes.

U.S. Congress. House. *The Story of Panama. Hearings on the Rainey resolution before the Committee on Foreign Affairs of the House of Representatives.* Washington, Govt. Print. Off., 1913.

U.S. Congress. House. *Revision of Canal Zone Laws.* H. Doc. 460, 71st Cong., 2d sess., 1930.

U.S. Congress. House. *Amend the Penal Code of the Canal Zone.* H. Rept. 531, 72d Cong., 1st sess., 1932.
This Report contains much basic material on Canal Zone legal history—not limited to the Penal Code.

U.S. Code (1926), Preface.

U.S. Code (1962), Preface.

Canal Zone Code (1934). Public Law No. 431, 73d Cong. (H.R. 8700), not published in the *Statutes at Large.*

Canal Zone Code (1962). Published in *Statutes at Large* as separate volume 76A.

The Code of Civil Procedure of the Canal Zone. Washington: Government Printing Office, 1907.

The Civil Code of the Republic of Panama and Amendatory Laws Continued in Force in the Canal Zone, Isthmus of Panama, by Executive Order of May 9,

1904. Translated by Frank L. Joannini. Washington, D.C.: 1905.

The Law of Civil Procedure in Force in Panama and the Canal Zone. Translated by Frank L. Joannini. Washington, D.C.: 1905.

An Act Temporarily to provide revenues and a civil government for Porto Rico, and for other purposes (Foraker Act). Statutes at Large, vol. 31 (1900).

An Act To provide for the opening, maintenance, protection, and operation of the Panama Canal, and the sanitation and government of the Canal Zone (Panama Canal Act). Statutes at Large, vol. 37 (1912).

An Act To provide for the construction of a canal connecting the waters of the Atlantic and the Pacific Oceans (Spooner Act). Statutes at Large, vol. 32 (1902).

An Act To provide for the temporary government of the Canal Zone at Panama, the protection of the canal works, and for other purposes. Statutes at Large, vol. 33 (1904).

An Act to amend sections 7, 8, and 9 of the Panama Canal Act, etc. Statutes at Large, vol. 42 (1922).

An Act Relating to the liability of common carriers by railroad to their employees in certain cases. Statutes at Large, vol. 35 (1908).

An Act Granting to certain employees of the United States the right to receive from it compensation for injuries sustained in the course of their employment. Statutes at Large, vol. 35 (1908).

An Act Relating to injured employees on the Isthmian Canal. Statutes at Large, vol. 35 (1909).

An Act to establish a Code of Laws for the Canal Zone, and for other purposes. Statutes at Large, vol. 48 (1934). (Printed in a separate volume entitled, "Canal Zone Code, 1934." Text not printed in Statutes at Large.).

An Act to revise and codify the laws of the Canal Zone. Statutes at Large, vol. 45 (1928).

An Act Making appropriations to supply urgent deficiencies in appropriations for the fiscal year nineteen hundred and fourteen and for prior years, and for other purposes. Statutes at Large, vol.

38 (1914). (See chap. VII, pp. 116-17 of text.)

An Act To authorize and provide for the maintenance and operation of the Panama Canal by the present corporate adjunct of the Panama Canal, as renamed; to reconstitute the agency charged with the civil government of the Canal Zone, and for other purposes. Statutes at Large, vol. 64 (1950).

California. California Statutes (1850).

California. West's Annotated California Codes (1954), vol. 1. "The Development of Law in California" by William J. Palmer and Paul P. Selvin.

California. West's Annotated California Codes (1954), vol. 6. "The California Civil Code" by Arvo Van Alstyne.

2. Panama

REGISTRO JUDICIAL, Organo del Poder Judicial de la República.

Código Civil del Estado del Panamá. Nueva York: Imprenta de Esteban Hallet, No. 107 Calle de Fulton, 1861.

This was substantially the Bello Code (see chap. III, p. 17 of text) accepted by the State of Panama during a period when it was virtually independent of Bogota.

República de Panamá, CODIGO CIVIL, Edición oficial. Barcelona: Talleres de Artes Gráficas de Henrich y Cía., Calle de Córcega, 48, 1917.

This was the first truly Panamanian civil code, breaking from the Colombian which had been used until 1917 (see chap. VII, note 21 of text). It was adopted automatically by the Canal Zone and used there until 1933.

3. Colombia

Código Civil de Colombia. Madrid: Instituto de Cultura Hispánica, 1963.

Ministry of Foreign Affairs. Protest of Colombia against the Treaty between Panama and the United States. London: Wertheimer, Lea & Co., 1904.

C. Newspapers
The Washington Post
The Washington Star
The New York Times
El Colombiano
La Estrella de Panamá

The Canal Record

The Star and Herald (Panama)

The San Francisco Examiner

D. Books and Pamphlets

Arosemena, Pablo. *La Causa Inmediata de la Emancipación de Panamá.* Panamá: Imprenta Nacional, 1933.

Bishop, Joseph Bucklin. *The Panama Gateway.* New York: Charles Schribner's Sons, 1913.

Bunau-Varilla, Philippe. *The Creation, Destruction, and Resurrection.* New York: McBride, Nast and Company, 1914.

Franck, Harry A. *Zone Policeman 88.* New York: The Century Co., 1913.

Sands, William Franklin. *Our Jungle Diplomacy.* Chapel Hill: The University of North Carolina Press, 1944.

Shonts, Theodore P. *Speech of the Hon. Theodore P. Shonts, Chairman of the Isthmian Canal Commission, before the Knife-and-Fork Club, Kansas City, on the evening of January 24, 1907.* Washington, D.C.: Government Printing Office, 1907.

II—Secondary Sources

Alba C., Manuel M. "Cronología de los gobernantes de Panamá, 1510-1932." *Boletín de la Academia Panameña de la Historia,* VIII (1935).

Arias, Harmodio. *The Panama Canal, A Study in International Law and Diplomacy.* London: P. S. King and Son, 1911. (Reprinted in New York by Arno Press in 1970.)

Bailey, Thomas A. *A Diplomatic History of the American People (chap. 33).* New York: Appleton-Century-Crofts, 1969.

Bemis, Samuel Flagg. *A Diplomatic History of the United States* (chap. XIV). New York: Holt, Rinehart and Winston, Inc., 1965.

Bennett, Ira E. *History of the Panama Canal.* Washington, D.C.: Historical Publishing Company, 1915.

Bishop, Wm. W., Jr. "Unconstitutional Treaties." *Minnesota Law Review* 42 (1958).

"A Caribbean policy for the United States"

(unsigned editorial comment), *American Journal of International Law* VIII (1914).

Castillero Pimentel, Ernesto. *Política Exterior de Panamá.* Panamá: Impresora Panamá, S.A., 1961.

Castillero Reyes, Ernesto de Jesus. *La Causa Inmediata de la Emancipación de Panamá.* Panamá: Imprenta Nacional, 1933.

Cervera, Augusto A. *Jurisprudencia de la Corte Suprema de Justicia.* Panamá: Tipografía Moderna, 1921.

David, Rene and Brierly, John E. C. *Major Legal Systems in the World Today.* London: The Free Press, Collier-MacMillan Limited, 1968.

Dennis, Alfred L. P. *Adventures in American Diplomacy.* New York: E. P. Dutton & Co., 1928.

Du Val, Miles P. *Cadiz to Cathay; the story of the long diplomatic struggle for the Panama Canal.* New York: Greenwood Press, 1968. (First published in 1940).

Ealy, Lawrence. "The Development of an Anglo-American System of Law in the Panama Canal Zone." *American Journal of Legal History,* II (1958).

Eder, Phanor James. *Colombia.* London: T. Fisher Unwin, 1913.

Edwards, Albert (pseud.). *Panama.* New York: The MacMillan Company, 1911.

Enciclopedia Jurídica Omeba, XVIII. Buenos Aires: Editorial Bibliográfica Argentina S.R.L., 1964.

III *Encyclopedia of the Social Sciences,* 1930 ed. S.v. "Codification" by Charles Sumner Lobingier.

Fast, Howard. *Goethals and the Panama Canal.* New York: Julian Messner, Inc., 1942.

Feilchenfeld, Ernst H. *Public Debts and State Succession.* New York: The MacMillan Company, 1931.

Foster, John W. *A Century of American Diplomacy.* New York: Houghton Mifflin Co., 1900.

Freehoff, Joseph C. *America and the Canal Title.* (Published by the author) 1916.

Gailbrath, W. O. *Colombia.* London & New York: Royal Institute of International Affairs, 1953.

Goethals, George W. *Government of the Canal Zone*. Princeton: Princeton University Press, 1915.

Hamilton, Peter J. " Germanic and Moorish elements of the Spanish civil law." *Harvard Law Review* XXX (1917).

Hammarskjold Forum, 6th, New York, May 28, 1964. *The Panama Canal; background papers and proceedings*. Richard R. Baxter and Doris Carroll, authors of the working paper. Dobbs Ferry, N.Y.: Oceana Publications, 1965.

Hanrahan, David G. "Legal Aspects of the Panama Canal Zone—in Perspective." *Boston University Law Review* 45 (1965).

Haskin, Frederick J. *The Panama Canal*. New York: Doubleday, Page & Company, 1913.

Hedrick, Basil C. and Hedrick, Anne K. *Historical Dictionary of Panama*. Metuchen, J. J.: Scarecrow Press, 1970.

Howarth, David. *Panama*. New York: McGraw-Hill Book Co., 1966.

9 *International Encyclopedia of the Social Sciences*, 1968 ed., S. v. "Common Law Systems" by Edward McWhinney.

Jackson, William K. "The Administration of Justice in the Canal Zone." *Virginia Law Review* 4 (1916).

Johnson, Willis Fletcher. *Four Centuries of the Panama Canal*. New York: Henry Holt & Co., 1907.

Katz, Wilber Griffith. "Federal Legislative Courts." *Harvard Law Review* 43 (1930).

King, Thelma H. *El Problema de la Soberanía en las Relaciones entre Panamá y los Estados Unidos de América*. Panamá: Ministerio de Educación, 1961.

Lemaitre, Eduardo. *Panamá y Su Separación de Colombia*. Bogotá: Biblioteca Banco Popular, 1971.

McCain, William D. *The United States and the Republic of Panama*. Durham: Duke University Press, 1937.

Mack, Gerstle. *The Land Divided: A History of the Panama Canal and Other Isthmian Canal Projects*. New York: Alfred A. Knopf, 1944. (Reprinted in New York in 1974 by Octagon Books).

Mellander, G. A. "Magoon in Panama." Unpublished Master's thesis, The George Washington University, 1960.

————. *The United States in Panamanian Politics*. Danville, Illinois: The Interstate Printers and Publishers, Inc., 1971.

Miner, Dwight Carroll. *The Fight for the Panama Route*. New York: Columbia University Press, 1940.
The Hay-Herran Treaty—never ratified—is reproduced in Appendix C.

Moore's Federal Practice (1974) 1.

Nadelman, Kurt H. "The Judicial Dissent." *American Journal of Comparative Law*, 8 (1959).

Nichols, Madaline, W. "Las Siete Partidas." *California Law Review*, 20 (1932).

"Note and Comment." *Michigan Law Review*, 4 (1905-06).

"Note and Comment." *Michigan Law Review*, 17 (1918-19).

Padelford, Norman J. *The Panama Canal in Peace and War*. New York: The MacMillan Company, 1942.

Plucknett, Theodore F. T. *A Concise History of the Common Law*. Boston: Little, Brown and Company, 1956.

Pombo, Manuel Antonio and Guerra, José Joaquín. *Constituciones de Colombia*. Bogotá: Biblioteca Popular Cultura Colombiana, 1951.

Rodríguez Ramos, Manuel. "Interaction of Civil Law and Anglo-American Law in the Legal Method in Puerto Rico." *Tulane Law Review* XXIII, No. 1 (1948).

Roosevelt, Theodore. "The Panama Blackmail Treaty." *Metropolitan* 41 (1915).

Schlesinger, Rudolf B. *Comparative Law*. Mineola, New York: The Foundation Press, Inc., 1970.

Schmidt, Gustavus. *Civil Law in Spain and Mexico*. New Orleans: privately printed, 1851.

Schoff, Willard H. *Why the Colombian Treaty is not Justified by Facts* (publisher unknown) 1914.

Sociedad Panamá de Acción Internacional. *Panama-United States Relations*. Panamá: Sociedad Panamá de Acción Internacional, 1934.

Stone, Melville E., Jr. "Theodore Roosevelt—please answer." *Metropolitan* 34 (1911).

Terán, Oscar. *Del Tratado Herrán-Hay al Tratado Hay-Bunau Varilla*. Panamá:

Imprenta de "Motivos Colombianos," 1934.

Thomson, Norman. *Colombia and the United States*. London: N. Thomson & Co., 1914.

Tomes, Robert. *Panama in 1855*. New York: Harper and Brothers, 1855.

Uribe, Antonio José. *Colombia y los Estados Unidos*. Bogotá: (publisher unknown) 1931.

Vance, John Thomas. *The Background of Hispanic-American Law*. New York: Central Book Company, 1943.

La Vigencia de Andrés Bello en Colombia. Bogotá: El Gráfico Editores, Ltda., 1966.

Walton, Clifford Stevens. *The Civil Law in Spain and Spanish-America*. Washington, D.C.: W. H. Lowdermilk and Co., 1900.

Weiner, Richard M. "Sovereignty of the Panama Isthmus." *N. Y. U. Intramural Law Review* 65 (1960).

Woolsey, L. H. "The Sovereignty of the Panama Canal Zone." *American Journal of International Law* XX (1926).

Wyse, Lucien N. B. *Le canal de Panama, l'Isthme américain, explorations; comparaisons des tracés étudiés, negociations; état des travaux*. Paris: Hachette, 1886.

LIST OF CASES CITED

American Insurance Company v. Canter, 1 Pet. 511.

Balzac v. Porto Rico, 258 U.S. 298.

Blankard v. Galdy, 2 Salkeld 411.

Canal Zone v. Houston, 2 Canal Zone Reports 239.

Carbone v. Esquivel, II *Registro Judicial* 61.

Cariño v. Insular Government, 212 U.S. 449.

Coulson, Adolphus, *ex parte* in the Matter of, 212 U.S. 553.

Díaz A., Domingo et al. v. Patterson, 263 U.S. 399.

Dorr v. United States, 195 U.S. 138.

Doyle v. Fleming, 219 F. Supp. 277.

Fitzpatrick v. The Panama Railroad Company, 2 Canal Zone Reports 111.

Freeborn v. Smith, 2 Wall. 160.

Glidden Company v. Zdanok, 370 U.S. 530.

Government of the Canal Zone v. Baldomero Cortéz (no citation).

Gris v. The New Panama Canal Co., II *Registro Judicial* 59.

Jackson v. Smith, Auditor, 3 Canal Zone Reports 59.

Kung Ching Chong v. Wing Chong, 2 Canal Zone Reports 25.

McConaughey v. Morrow, 263 U.S. 39.

McGrath v. Panama R. R. Co., 3 Canal Zone Reports 410.

Meléndez v. Union Oil Company, 1 Canal Zone Reports 106.

O'Donoghue v. United States, 289 U.S. 516.

Oli Nifou, Petitioner, In the Matter of, 198 U.S. 581.

Olivieri v. Biaggi, 17 Puerto Rican Reports 676.

Panama Railroad Co. v. Bosse, 249 U.S. 41.

Panama Railroad Company v. Rock, 266 U.S. 209.

Panama Refining Co. v. Ryan, 293 U.S. 388.

Pérez v. Fernández, 202 U.S. 80.

Perrenoud et al. v. Salas, 1 Canal Zone Reports 24.

Playa de Flor Land and Improvement Co. v. United States, 70 F. Supp. 281.

Schechter Corp. v. United States, 295 U.S. 495.

United States of America v. Andrade, 1 Canal Zone Reports, 64.

Vallarino, Darío, *Registro Judicial* vol. XXII, No. 62

Velasco, Donaldo, *contra por rapto, Registro Judicial*, vol. II, No. 41.

Villalobos et al. v. Foleston et al., United States of America, Intervenor, 2 Canal Zone Reports 34.

Wilson v. Shaw, 204 U.S. 24.

SUBJECT INDEX

Act to provide for the temporary government of the Canal Zone at Panama (April 28, 1904), 55, 79-80, 81. *See also* Kittredge Bill

Act to revise and codify the laws of the Canal Zone, 117

Acts and ordinances of the Isthmian Canal Commission, 55, 56

"The Administration of Justice in the Canal Zone" (Jackson), xx n 7

Alabama claims, 45

Alaric II, 9

Alaska, 43 n. 109, 127, 129, 139

Alaska Purchase, 128 n

Alcalá, Ordenamiento de, 10 n. 11, 12, 13

Alfaro, Ricardo J., 41 n. 102, 42 n. 104

Alfonso VIII, 11

Alfonso X, "the Wise", 11, 12

Alger, Russell A. (Secretary of War), 7

Algeria, 49

Amador Guerrero, Dr. Manuel: sent to negotiate canal treaty with U.S., 37; Panama's first President, 38; mentioned, 34, 35

America and the Canal Title (Freehoff), 48 n. 127

American Insurance Company v. Canter, 73, 74

American Society of International Law, 42, 48 n. 129

Ancon, Canal Zone, 66, 76, 79 n. 32

Angarita (compiler of Civil Law decisions), 101 n. 23

annexation: of Panama to the U.S., 38 n. 91, 74

appeal: proposed methods of, 79-80; to U.S. Supreme Court, 80-81, 88; continued failure of Congress to provide for, 82; to Fifth Circuit Court of Appeals in New Orleans, 88-89, 90

appellate decisions; form and style, 101-103

Appropriations Act: (April 6, 1914), 116-17; (March 3, 1933), 92 n. 75

Arabs, 10, 128

Arango, José Augustín, 34, 36, 37

Arias, Arnulfo, 50, 65 n. 47

Arias, Harmodio, 23 n. 19, 86-87

Arias, Tomás, 36, 38 n. 91

Arosemena, C. C., 34

Arosemena, Pablo, 32, 38, 85 n. 52

Articles of Confederation, 47

Aspinwall, Panama, 24. *See also* Colón

Aspinwall, William Henry, 22

Aspinwall case, 42 n. 104

Attorney General: opinions of, 35; supervision of Canal Zone courts, 92

audiencias (high courts), 14, 34 n. 65

Autonomic Charter of 1897 (of Puerto Rico), xiv, 5

Autos Acordados o Resoluciones de Consejo, 13

Autos acordados, 14

Balboa: Magistrate's Court, 39 n. 94; division of U.S. District Court, 90

Baldwin, Hanson W., 57 n. 18

Balzac v. Porto Rico, 74

Belize, Honduras: Common Law reception, 1; compared to Canal Zone, 80

Bello, Andrés, 16-17

Bello Code (1855 Code of Chile): modified by Law 57 and Law 153, 17; mentioned, 16-17, 46 n. 121, 115, 135

Bennett, Ira E., *History of the Panama Canal,* 63 n. 42

Bentz, Paul A., 117, 120

Berger, Marilyn, 128-29

140

091193